S0-BKA-019

# A LIBRARY, MEDIA, AND ARCHIVAL PRESERVATION GLOSSARY

# A LIBRARY, MEDIA, AND ARCHIVAL PRESERVATION GLOSSARY

John N. DePew
with C. Lee Jones

**ABC-CLIO**
Santa Barbara, California
Denver, Colorado
Oxford, England

Copyright © 1992 by ABC-CLIO, Inc.

All rights reserved. No part of this publication may be reproduced, stored in a retrieval system, or transmitted, in any form or by any means, electronic, mechanical, photocopying, recording, or otherwise, except for the inclusion of brief quotations in a review, without prior permission in writing from the publishers.

ISBN 0-87436-576-7

99 98 97 96 95 94 93 92 10 9 8 7 6 5 4 3 2 1

ABC-CLIO, Inc.
130 Cremona Drive, P.O. Box 1911
Santa Barbara, California 93116-1911

The paper used in this publication meets the minimum requirements of the American National Standard for Information Sciences—Permanence of Paper for Printed Library Materials, ANSI Z39.48—1984.

Manufactured in the United States of America

225.84
D441Li

L. I. F. E  Bible College
LIBRARY
1100 COVINA BLVD
SAN DIMAS, CA 91773

For Joan

039791

# P reface

The purpose of this glossary is to bring together many of the terms that relate to the conservation and preservation of archival, library, and media center materials, many of which are scattered in articles, books, dictionaries, glossaries, and reports throughout the literature of preservation. The terms are drawn not only from the field of library and information science, but from the binding, paper, photographic, and preservation reformatting literature, as well. The glossary also contains building, HVAC, insurance, and statistical terms that are useful in understanding those aspects of the preservation of informational materials. A few acronyms and abbreviations for selected associations and scientific terms are included. An extensive list of organizations and sources of supply and equipment is in *A Library, Media, and Archival Preservation Handbook,* the companion volume to this glossary. The authors attempted to select terms that the nonspecialist in conservation would find helpful. Conservators and those who wish to study preservation in more depth should consult the specialized dictionaries, encyclopedias, and glossaries in the fields of paper, photography, and other media for additional definitions.

Most of the definitions in this work reflect the state of technology during the 1980s and early 1990s. The definitions were, whenever possible, drawn from authoritative sources. Many of the terms, however, do not have precise meanings and have not been standardized, this is particularly true for the sound recording terminology. In such cases, definitions the authors consider to be the most generally acceptable are presented. When a term has more than one definition, each is numbered and the arrangement follows the pattern of entries relating to book and paper first, then audio, then photographic topics. Synonyms are given at the end of the definition.

Sources are in parenthesis at the end of the definitions. For example: the source for *Openability,* (47:181), refers to page 181 in Roberts and Etherington, *Bookbinding and the Conservation of Books; A Dictionary of Descriptive Terminology* in the Sources section of the glossary. When there is more than one definition per term, the source for each is at the end of each inclusive definition. Definitions that do not cite a source were defined by the authors.

For the most part, terms are alphabetized in uninverted form; for example, the definition of *alkaline paper* is under that form, rather than inverted as *paper, alkaline.*

Three types of references are used: "see," "see also," and words spelled out in capital letters. "See" references are usually used to refer the reader to the preferred form of the term. "See also" directs the reader to related terms or other aspects of the subject. The user who does not understand terms used within a definition will frequently find the first use of the term in the definition in capitals and defined elsewhere in the glossary. Occasionally a phrase in capital letters is actually two (or more) combined terms, e.g., *CALCIUM CARBONATE BUFFER*; in such cases each term is defined separately.

The arrangement of the glossary is letter-by-letter, rather than word-by-word. For example, *copyboard* files before *copy print,* and *recorded book* files before *record head.*

The authors are not aware of any other glossary that attempts to cover the entire spectrum of archival and library preservation. It is hoped that this lexicon will be helpful not only to archivists and librarians whose everyday work involves preservation, but also to those whose collateral duties include preservation and/or who are responsible for the administration of preservation activities in their organizations. *A Library, Media, and Archival Preservation Handbook* expands many of the definitions included in this volume.

The authors are indebted to Robert B. Carneal, recently retired Head of the Laboratory Services of the Motion Picture, Broadcasting, and Recorded Sound Division of the Library of Congress, for reviewing, revising, and making suggestions for the disc and magnetic media terms. Robert J. Milevski, Preservation Librarian at Princeton University, revised a number of book and paper terms. Each of his contributions are identified in the list of sources. Sherry Stafford, faculty secretary at the School of Library and Information Studies at Florida State University spent many hours typing the manuscript. Without her efforts and the support of the library school it is doubtful this project could have been completed. And last, but not least, Terry LaTour, a graduate assistant at the school, carefully, patiently, and with unfailing good humor, reviewed various drafts of the manuscript, conducted research, and performed the many menial tasks necessary to bring the work to its final form.

Finally, as noted at the beginning of the preface, this dictionary is not meant to include every term used in the conservation and preservation of library and archival materials, nor is it meant to provide an exhaustive definition for each term, only (in most cases) a brief explanation. The field of preservation is dynamic and continually growing—to include all terms in one work is patently impossible. Nevertheless, the authors accept full responsibility for the inclusion and exclusion of terms and for any errors, inadvertent or otherwise.

# A LIBRARY, MEDIA, AND ARCHIVAL PRESERVATION GLOSSARY

# A

**berration**   Any anomaly in the creation of an optical image such as ASTIGMATISM, CURVATURE OF FIELD, or CHROMATIC ABERRATION.

**Abrasion**   HAIRLINE surface defects on the print or film surface not penetrating to the base of the film. May result from moving contact with another surface. Also visible surface defects from rubbing or friction against the EMULSION.

**Abrasion marks**   See ABRASION.

**Absolute humidity**   The amount of water present in a given volume of air. It is usually expressed in pounds per cubic foot or grams per cubic meter. (36) See also RELATIVE HUMIDITY.

**Accelerated aging**   Methods of speeding up the deterioration of materials, such as paper, ink, film, etc., to estimate their long-term storage and use characteristics. The specimen is usually heated in an oven under specified controlled conditions. It is generally accepted that heating paper for three days in an oven at 100°C is equivalent to AGING it approximately 25 years under normal library storage conditions.

**Accelerator**   In photographic DEVELOPERs, chemical compounds that speed the rate of development.

**Accidental erasure**   The DEMAGNETIZATION of an already recorded magnetic tape through accidental means, causing loss of sonic content. This is usually brought about by mistakenly recording over a tape that had been recorded earlier, sometimes simply because the record switch on the tape machine is activated instead of the play switch. It can also be achieved by bringing an external magnetic field (from a motor, a vacuum cleaner, etc.) into too close contact with stored tapes. (4:267)

**Accordion fold**   See CONCERTINA FOLD.

**Acetate**   See CELLULOSE ACETATE.

**Acetate base**   (1) In magnetic recording, a material consisting of CELLULOSE ACETATE used as a tape base (i.e., the BACKING on which the magnetic oxide is carried). Cellulose acetate tends to break rather than

3

stretch when subjected to excessive stress. Since breaks can be mended easily and cleanly, acetate backings offer some insurance against mishandling, such as stretching. MYLAR™, a POLYESTER, however, has superior qualities as a backing, and acetate is no longer used. **(2)** Photographic SAFETY FILM base composed of cellulose acetate or triacetate. See ACETATE FILM.

**Acetate disc**   An ANALOG DISC with a recording surface of one of the various ACETATE compounds on a metal or glass base. Acetate blank discs were used to make instantaneous or nonprocessed recordings in the 1940s before the introduction of magnetic tape. In the manufacture of LONG-PLAYING AUDIODISCs today, "acetate" is an alternative term for LACQUER DISCs used to cut MASTER DISCs. (52:25) See also LACQUER DISC.

**Acetate film**   Photographic SAFETY FILM with a base composed of CELLULOSE ACETATE or TRIACETATE. Most film in use today has an ACETATE BASE, but all film used for PRESERVATION purposes is POLYESTER-based film. Replaced NITRATE FILM.

**Acetic acid**   Used in photography in stop and fixing baths and in hardener formulas. A colorless acid.

**Achromatic colors**   "Achromatic" literally means without color, but in common usage refers to white, black, and gray; they have no color hue.

**Acicular**   Needle shaped.

**Acid**   A chemical substance that can form hydrogen IONs when dissolved in water. Acids have a pH below 7.0 and are capable of neutralizing ALKALIs. Acids damage paper and other organic substances by weakening the molecular bonds in CELLULOSE. Such damage in paper results in yellowing and brittleness. Acid can be present in paper containing impure GROUNDWOOD PULP, ALUM-ROSIN SIZING, and other materials added during the papermaking process. It can also be introduced from atmospheric pollutants or through migration from materials in contact with each other. See also ACID BOOKS; ACID-FREE; ACID MIGRATION.

**Acid books**   Books manufactured with paper that is acidic (below 7.0 pH) but not yet BRITTLE. Because of this acidity, these books will become brittle in time. See also ACID; ACID-FREE; ACID MIGRATION; PERMANENT PAPER; pH.

**Acid-free**   Paper and other materials that have a pH of 7.0 or higher. Acid-free paper-based materials may be produced from any CELLULOSE fiber source if precautions are taken to eliminate, minimize, or remove ACID from the paper PULP during the manufacturing process. They may also be called acid-neutral. Acid-free is not a synonym for ALKALINE or buffered, however. Acid-free paper-based materials may not contain alkaline buffering agents, i.e., an ALKALINE RESERVE, to protect them from future acid attack. These acids may be produced from residual chemicals in the manufacturing process, e.g., aluminum sulfate (ALUM), chlorine, or atmospheric pollutants, e.g., sulfur dioxide. (36) See also PERMANENT PAPER; NEUTRAL; ALKALINE PAPER; pH.

**Acidic paper**   See ACID BOOKS.

**Acid migration**   This occurs when ACIDs from acidic materials transfer to materials with less or no acids, causing stains or discoloration, weakening, and embrittlement. For example, acids from boards, endpapers, protective tissues, and paper covers may migrate to less acidic paper either through direct physical contact, or by vapor action when in close proximity to each other. (36) Also called acid-transfer.

**Acoustical recording**   "The earliest, commercially practical method of recording by causing sound waves to actuate a stylus attached to a diaphragm. The stylus mechanically engraves a sound track mimicking the sound waves. The method was used before electrical recording replaced it in the 1920s. Acoustical recording is also called mechanical recording. An acoustic recording also refers to the disc or cylinder produced through this method." (4:267)

**Across the grain**   See AGAINST THE GRAIN.

**Acrylic**   A polymethyl methacrylate plastic noted for transparency, light weight, weather resistance, colorfastness, and rigidity. In addition to these qualities, acrylics are important in preservation because of their stability, or resistance to chemical change over time, a characteristic not common to all plastics. Acrylics are available in sheets, films, and RESINOUS ADHESIVES. Acrylic sheeting is often substituted for glass in framing. It is available under various trade names (e.g., Plexiglas™ and Lucite™), is shatterproof, and can be purchased with an ULTRA-VIOLET LIGHT filtering capacity. (28:25)

**Actinic light**   Radiation that causes photochemical reactions in PHOTO-SENSITIVE materials.

**Activator**   **(1)** In photography, a chemical compound used to start or speed up development. **(2)** Also part of a two-part DEVELOPER, the addition of which speeds development action. It is usually dissolved in an acid solution.

**Actual cash value**   Usually the REPLACEMENT COST (new) of the property LOSS less depreciation for wear and tear and obsolescence. (54:51)

**Acuity**   Perceived crispness or SHARPNESS. An ability to show a sharp line between areas of high and low exposure.

**ADC**   See ANALOG-TO-DIGITAL CONVERTER.

**Additive**   Any material added to the COATING of magnetic discs or tape, other than the oxide and the binder resins, to foster specific desired effects such as lessening friction, softening or plasticizing the binder, retarding fungus growth, or making the coating conductive. For examples of additives, or where they may be used, see COATED PAPER SUPPORT; FURNISH; METHYL CELLULOSE; POLYESTER; POLYETHYLENE; SIZE.

**Adhesive**   A substance capable of bonding materials to each other. The adhesives used in ARCHIVAL work must exhibit three properties: (1) they must wet the surfaces to be joined but not so much as to cause the adhered materials to COCKLE; (2) they must have sufficient flexibility so as not to crack when the JOINT is flexed; and (3) they must be strong but not as strong as the material they bond, so that stress to the point of failure of the joint will not damage the archival material but will result only in the failure of the adhesive. (47:5) In LIBRARY BINDING and preservation work, three main groups are used: STARCH PASTEs, ANIMAL GLUEs, and synthetics. One of the most widely used synthetics is POLYVINYL ACETATE (PVA). See also ANIMAL GLUE; COLD-SETTING ADHESIVE; GLUE; HOT-MELT ADHESIVES; METHYL CELLULOSE; POLYVINYL ACETATE (PVA) ADHESIVE; STARCH PASTE.

**Adhesive binding**   A relatively economical form of binding where single book leaves are attached together to form a TEXT BLOCK by applying a flexible GLUE to the SPINE. Adhesive binding generally results in a book that opens easily and lies flat. Adhesive binding, however, is not a satisfactory method of binding coated and similar papers. "Two basic methods are used to secure the leaves in adhesive binding: (1) application of the adhesive to the edges of the collected and clamped leaves, without fanning, which results in little if any penetration of adhesive between the sheets; and (2) fanning the clamped leaves, either in one direction or both (see FAN ADHESIVE BINDING), so that the adhesive is applied a slight distance onto the leaves, thus forming a more secure bond. A HOT-MELT ADHESIVE is usually employed in the first method, whereas a cold RESINOUS ADHESIVE, e.g., POLYVINYL ACETATE, is typical in the latter method. DOUBLE-FAN ADHESIVE BINDING using a slow-drying POLYVINYL ACETATE (PVA) ADHESIVE can be quite durable. However, a hot-melt adhesive is impermanent and forms a rigid spine which rapidly deteriorates." (38:212) Also called PERFECT BINDING. Perfect binding, however, does not employ double fanning the adhesive. See PERFECT BINDING.

**Adjuster**   The insurer's representative who determines the extent of the insurer's LIABILITY for LOSS when a CLAIM is submitted. (25:93)

**AG (average gradient)**   See CONTRAST.

**Against the grain** The direction across or against which the majority of the FIBERs in MACHINE-MADE PAPER or BOARD are oriented, i.e., MACHINE DIRECTION. The GRAIN direction of a well-produced book always runs from HEAD to TAIL. This allows the leaves of the book to open easily and to lie flat (when opened). Paper folded and bound into book form against the grain will neither open as easily nor lie as flat. Synonymous with ACROSS THE GRAIN. (36) See also GRAIN; MACHINE DIRECTION; WITH THE GRAIN.

**Aging** "A general term describing the natural degradation of PAPER, ADHESIVEs, leather, PHOTOGRAPHs, and other archival materials, while in storage. With some textiles, aging denotes OXIDATION by exposure to air. Aging is greatly influenced by the environment in which the materials are stored." (47:7) See also ACCELERATED AGING.

**AIIM** Association for Information and Image Management. Formerly the National Micrographics Association.

**Air bells** More commonly AIR BUBBLES. Caused by air trapped in solution, preventing complete contact of the solution with the film and resulting in poorly developed spots. This failure of contact between film and DEVELOPER is most often caused by poor agitation of the developer solution. (1:5)

**Air bubbles** Empty spaces in OPTICAL glass. See AIR BELLS.

**AKD** Alkyl ketene dimer. A synthetic SIZING used in making ALKALINE PAPER. See ALKYL KETENE DIMER SIZING (AKD).

**Albertype** See COLLOTYPE.

**Album** (1) "For sound recordings [AUDIODISCs], a container for records or a container with one or more records. Prior to the introduction of long-playing (LP) microgroove records in 1948, recordings containing multiple discs—sets—were frequently sold in book-like albums containing SLEEVEs or envelopes for the individual records. Empty albums of different sizes with varying numbers of sleeves were also sold to afford better appearance and protection for individual records which were usually sold in comparatively flimsy paper sleeves. Some (mostly) early long-playing, multiple-record sets were issued in albums, but most such sets have been issued in various types of sleeves inserted in BOXes or SLIPCASEs. Starting about 1950, the term album has increasingly come to be used for single-disc record issues with multiple selections as well as multiple-disc sets." (4:268) See also ALBUM NUMBER; BOX; SLIPCASE. (2) In photography, a multi-page book designed to accept mountings of photographs.

**Albumen emulsion** A medium, often made from egg whites, used for LIGHT-SENSITIVE COATINGs on some photographs, glass slides and glass negatives.

**Album number** "Manufacturer's/producer's issue/catalog/order number for most multiple-disc [AUDIODISC] sets; the term is also used for some post-78-rpm single discs. For multiple-disc sets, the album number is used instead of the individual record issue numbers for ordering purposes in most—but by no means all—cases. Sound archivists need to be aware also that during the 78-rpm era, particularly in Europe, even major manufacturers did not always assign album/set numbers to multiple record sets or issue them with albums." (4:268)

**Alcohol** A colorless, volatile, flammable organic solvent also described as ethyl alcohol or ethanol ($C_2H_5OH$). It is used as an identifier when examining collodion EMULSIONs. Methyl alcohol, or methanol ($CH_3OH$), should not be used in the preservation of paper-based materials. Methanol is used, however, for ULTRASONIC cleaning of LP recordings.

**Alcohol spot-test** A methyl alcohol test used to determine the type of EMULSION on a film. Instructions for the test are contained in Rempel's *The Care of Black and White Photographic Collections: Identification of Processes*. (44:4–6) See also WATER SPOT-TEST.

**Alginate acid** An insoluble, colloidal acid, ($C_6H_8O_6$), found in the cell walls of various kelps and used for SIZING paper.

**Alignment** The correct positioning of the tape heads in tape recorders with reference to the magnetic tape's path, and also adjustment of the recorder's electronics for the best FREQUENCY RESPONSE and lowest distortion products. (4:268)

**Alignment tape** A special tape recording used in aligning and calibrating the playback electronics of tape recorders. The alignment tape contains test tones at specified frequencies. Also known as test tape. (4:268)

**Alkali** Any strong, caustic, water-soluble substance with a pH above 7.0 and capable of neutralizing acids. Alkalies are used in ADHESIVEs and in DEACIDIFYING and buffering paper. The most common buffers are MAGNESIUM CARBONATE and CALCIUM CARBONATE. See also ALKALINE RESERVE.

**Alkaline** A way of designating the acid content of a substance is by using the pH SCALE of 0 to 14. The NEUTRAL point is 7.0. Paper with a pH above 7.0 is alkaline. Alkaline-buffered paper contains an alkaline BUFFER to guard against future acid formation by absorption of air pollutants. See also ALKALINE RESERVE; pH.

**Alkaline-buffered paper** See PERMANENT PAPER.

**Alkaline paper** "Paper produced with ALKALINE-based chemistry is ACID-FREE, having a pH of 7.5 or greater. Under proper storage conditions, such paper will remain strong and supple for hundreds of years. While alkaline, PERMANENT PAPER does not last forever, it will last several hundred years, as compared to several decades for acidic paper. It is sometimes referred to as long-lasting paper." (5) See PERMA-NENT PAPER.

**Alkaline reserve**   A BUFFER or reserve of any stable ALKALINE substance added to paper to counteract the formation of acids in the future. For example, "soaking paper in a solution of CALCIUM BICARBON-ATE or MAGNESIUM BICARBONATE adds a small amount of calcium or magnesium bicarbonate which neutralizes any ACID present and also provides a reserve to counteract acid which may enter the paper at some future time. Papers which are to remain ACID-FREE for long periods of time, e.g., 500 years, should have approximately three percent precipitated carbonate by weight of paper." (47:8) See also BUFFER; DEACIDI-FICATION; PERMANENT PAPER.

**Alkenyl succinic anhydride (ASA)**   A synthetic SIZING material used in making ALKALINE PAPER. Patented in 1963, it is more reactive than AKD, cures more quickly, and works above a pH level of 5. See ALKA-LINE PAPER; ALKYL KETENE DIMER SIZING; SIZE.

**Alkyl ketene dimer sizing (AKD)**   A type of internal SIZE that works in an ALKALINE pH range. Invented in the early 1950s, it made possible for the first time the manufacture of alkaline sized paper under normal commercial conditions. It is typically prepared from a stearic acid and added to the PULP SLURRY in the form of an EMULSION. It does not spread evenly over the FIBER surfaces until it reaches the DRYER section, where it gets "ironed in" to the WEB. AKD is used in all sorts of paper and BOARD, including milk cartons and paper cups, as well as in ARCHIVAL paper. It works in the pH range 6–9. If CALCIUM CAR-BONATE is used as a FILLER, a small amount of ALUM can be used as a retention and drainage aid without significantly affecting the PERMA-NENCE of the paper—but little if any research has been done on this particular issue. (33:19) See also ALKALINE PAPER; AQUAPEL; SIZE.

**All along**   A method of SEWING through the fold one SECTION or SIGNATURE at a time to another to build up the TEXT BLOCK. The thread passes in and out along the entire length of the fold of one section, from KETTLE STITCH to kettle stitch, then travels to the next section where the pattern repeats itself. Synonymous with "one sheet on" and "one on." (36) See also TWO ALONG.

**All risk**   A name given to an insurance policy that covers all risks of LOSS or damage except those that are specifically excluded. (13:25) See also NAMED OR SPECIFIC PERILS CONTRACT.

**Alpha cellulose**   The portion of CELLULOSE that is insoluble under specified conditions. Also known as true cellulose. Alpha cellulose consists principally of cellulose, and its presence in PAPER or BOARD is an indication of the material's stability and PERMANENCE.

**Alum**   Either aluminum sulfate ($Al_2(SO_4)_3 \cdot 14H_2O$), ($Al_2(SO_4)_3 \cdot 18H_2O$), or a mixture of these hydrates is added with ROSIN SIZE to paper PULP or FURNISH while it is in the BEATER to impart a harder and more water resistant surface to the finished SHEET. The alum makes rosin precipitate out of solution while it is in close contact with the fibers of the papermaking slurry. As a result, the fibers are coated and impregnated with a solid and water-resistant mixture of rosin and what is probably a compound of rosin and aluminum oxide. (47:9) Alum/rosin sizing, used in most MACHINE-MADE PAPERs from the 19th century to the present, is a primary source of ACID in paper. Excessive use of alum is considered detrimental to PAPER PERMANENCE, leading to severe paper deterioration. Fortunately, many paper mills are now switching to ALKALINE papermaking processes. (36) See also ROSIN SIZE.

**Aluminum disc**   An instantaneous recording in which the grooves containing the signal are embossed directly into the metal base, which has no COATING. Aluminum discs were extensively used in the recording industry before the development of acetate discs or magnetic tape. Playback was usually accomplished with shaved wood, fiber, or cactus needles. Jeweled pickups specially made for the aluminum disc groove widths are now used extensively for playback.

**Aluminum sulfate ($Al_2(SO_4)_3$)**   See ALUM.

**Amberol cylinder**   "A type of CYLINDER introduced by Edison in 1908 with a recording surface made of Amberol (a patented waxlike metallic soap compound) and a playing time of four minutes, which was double the time of the earlier wax cylinders due to an increase in the number of CUTS PER INCH from 100 to 200. Superseded in 1912 by the acoustically superior BLUE AMBEROL CYLINDER." (52:26) See also BLUE AMBEROL CYLINDER; CELLULOID CYLINDER; WAX CYLINDER.

**Ambient light**   (1) Normal light levels in a given environment. (2) Light surrounding a particular object, exclusive of any light brought to bear for photographic purposes. (1:7)

**American National Standards Institute, Inc. (ANSI)**   See ANSI.

**American Paper Institute**   See API.

**Ammonia process**   A diazo material development process using immersion in an atmosphere of concentrated ammonia. See DIAZO PRINT; DIAZO PROCESSOR/DUPLICATOR.

**Ammonium thiosulfate**   Used in some fixing solutions and known as HYPO.

**Amplitude**   Another term for level or volume of an electrical or an acoustical signal. The intensity is measured from peak to peak on this electrical waveform.

**Amplitude distortion**   See HARMONIC DISTORTION.

**Amplitude/frequency response**   See FREQUENCY RESPONSE.

**Amplitude nonuniformity**   A term used in conjunction with magnetic tape testing that refers to the reproduced peak-to-peak voltage and its variation from the input values.

**Amplitude reference tape**   See STANDARD AMPLITUDE REFERENCE TAPE.

**Analog**   The representation of a smoothly changing physical variable (temperature, for example) by another physical variable (such as the height of a column of mercury).

**Analog disc**   "A conventional AUDIODISC, recorded and played back with a STYLUS, and which stores the audio signal in the form of continuous and varying GROOVE dimensions that are an imitation or 'ANALOG' of the original sound waveforms. The term encompasses the LONG-PLAYING AUDIODISC and the 78 rpm AUDIODISC." (52:26) See also ANALOG RECORDING; COMPACT DISC.

**Analog recording**   A sound recording in which the characteristics of the stored audio signal are continuously varied in a manner analogous (ANALOG) to the varying amplitude of the original input signal. The signals may be in the form of controlled variations in the magnetization of a tape, or in the variable GROOVE dimensions of a conventional AUDIODISC (ANALOG DISC) or a CYLINDER. (52:26) See also DIGITAL SOUND RECORDING.

**Analog-to-digital converter (ADC)**   An electronic device used at the input of digital audio equipment to convert ANALOG signals to digital values whose numbers represent the AMPLITUDE and frequency information, at each calculated time interval sampling.

**Anchorage**   The degree to which the magnetic tape oxide COATING adheres to the base film. (49:149) It can be measured by checking how easily the coating can be lifted from the BACKING with adhesive tape or a specially designed knife. (4:269)

**Animal glue**   An ADHESIVE consisting of a hard protein, chiefly gelatinous substance obtained by boiling animal hides and bones. PLASTICIZERs must be added to animal glue to improve its elasticity and resilience; otherwise, it is too brittle (when dry) for bookbinding purposes. When dissolved in warm water, animal glue is tacky and viscous and forms a strong bond when it dries. Animal glue will deteriorate over time, becoming hard and brittle, losing its ADHESIVE qualities. (36) See also COLD-SETTING ADHESIVE; GLUE; HOT-MELT ADHESIVE; POLYVINYL ACETATE (PVA) ADHESIVE; and STARCH PASTE.

**Animal size**   A glutinous material used to fill the pores of paper during or after the papermaking process. Animal size is prepared by boiling the hides and bones of animals. (36) See also GLUE, GELATIN, and SIZE.

**Anion**   A negatively charged ION.

**Anisotropy**   Directional dependence of magnetic properties leading to the existence of easy, or preferred, directions of magnetization. Shape anisotropy is the dominant form in ACICULAR particles. (49:149)

**ANSI**   An acronym for the American National Standards Institute. ANSI is the coordinator of America's voluntary standards system—a federation of standards writing organizations, commerce and industry, and public and consumer interests—and it represents the U.S. in the development of international technical standards. It also serves as a clearinghouse and information center for American National Standards and international standards. (36) ANSI does not develop standards itself. See also NISO.

**Antibloom agent**   An agent that prevents the magnetic COATING of tape from SHEDDING excess powdery residue. (4:269)

**Anticurl coating**   A coating applied to the opposite side of the base film from the EMULSION to prevent CURL.

**Antifungus agent**   An agent added to rice and wheat STARCH PASTEs to inhibit MOLD growth. Also added to the COATING compositions of discs and tapes to retard the growth of FUNGI. See also ORTHO-PHENYL PHENOL.

**Antihalation**   A strategy for reducing HALATION, or light scattering or reflection within a FILM. Light can be reflected from the base or lower layers of a film and cause SHADOWs or ghosts. A light-absorbing material covering the FILM BASE beneath the EMULSION can be used as an antihalation undercoat. Other approaches include using light-absorbing dyes in the manufacture of the film base itself; adding a light-absorbing coating to the back of the film base; and using a light-absorbing dye in the emulsion itself. (1:9)

**Antihalation dyes**   Dyes used in or on the film support, or in the EMULSION itself, to prevent HALATION during exposure. Eliminating halation helps retain the IMAGE clarity available in the camera system used to expose the film.

**Antihalation undercoat**   See ANTIHALATION.

**Antique**   The roughest surface of uncoated paper normally used in publishing, consequently the bulkiest paper per inch.

**Antistatic element**   An electrical conductor, usually CARBON BLACK, used to make the coating of a disc or tape recording (blank, MASTER, or pressed) conductive, in order to prevent the buildup of electrical charges due to friction, which lead to STATIC (distortion in playback). (4:270)

**Aperture**   **(1)** An opening through which light passes, often known as a LENS OPENING or lens stop. **(2)** The opening in a card designed to hold microfilm FRAMEs.

**Aperture card**    A card specially designed to hold individual FRAMEs or strips of frames of MICROFILM for use.

**Aperture disk**    A disk used in some DENSITOMETERs with holes ranging from 1 to 3 mm to vary the size of the sensing area of the instrument.

**API**    An acronym for the American Paper Institute, the trade association of pulp paper and paperboard manufacturers in the United States.

**Apparent density**    The apparent weight per unit volume of a SHEET of paper. It is calculated by dividing the BASIS WEIGHT of the paper by its caliper (THICKNESS). The numerical value depends upon the definition of a REAM, i.e., whether 480, 500, 516, etc. sheets. Consistent numerical values can be obtained by using in every case the basis weight in metric units ($g/m^2$) and the thickness in millimeters. (47:11; 15:16) See also BASIS WEIGHT; DENSITY; POINTS PER POUND; SPECIFIC GRAVITY.

**Apparent specific volume**    The volume per unit mass of paper, i.e., the reciprocal of APPARENT DENSITY.

**Appraisal**    The monetary evaluation of BOOKs, MANUSCRIPTs, documents, and other items of value for INSURANCE, tax, gift, or other purposes.

**Aquapel**    Trade name of the first AKD put on the market. It was used in 1959 in the PERMANENT/DURABLE text paper developed by William J. Barrow. (33:20) See ALKYL KETENE DIMER SIZING (AKD).

**Aqueous solvent**    "Water or watery substance used to dissolve chemicals." (55:107)

**Archival**    "A non-technical term suggesting that a material or product is PERMANENT, DURABLE or CHEMICALLY STABLE and thus suitable for PRESERVATION purposes. There are no standards describing how long an archival or archivally sound material will last." (22:14)

**Archival film**    A photographic FILM that is suitable for the preservation of records having permanent value when the film is properly processed and stored under ARCHIVAL STORAGE CONDITIONS, provided the original images are of suitable quality. Archival microfilms will retain their original information-bearing characteristics indefinitely if they conform to the specifications in ANSI IT9.1, *Imaging Media (Film)—Silver Gelatin Type—Specifications for Stability,* and are stored under the conditions specified in ANSI PH1.43, *Photography (Film)—Processed Safety Film—Storage,* and ANSI IT9.2, *Imaging Media—Photographic Processed Films, Plates, and Papers—Filing Enclosures and Storage Containers.* (48:18, 25–26) See also ARCHIVAL; ARCHIVAL QUALITY; LONG-TERM FILM; MEDIUM-TERM FILM; SHORT-TERM FILM; and PRESERVATION MASTER NEGATIVE.

**Archival quality** **(1)** A frequently misused term applied to materials, often supplies, when characteristics of PERMANENCE and high quality are trying to be conveyed. Descriptions employing this phrase in vendors' catalogs, etc., should define it in with precise chemical and physical specifications. **(2)** Descriptive of PROCESSED FILM or PRINTs that are capable of retaining their original characteristics without loss of quality over an indefinite period of storage under controlled conditions. (23:28) Also, the ability to resist deterioration. (42:188)

**Archival standards** The standards that must be met by a given type of recording material or process for this material to retain specified characteristics. See also ARCHIVAL QUALITY. (42:188)

**Archival storage conditions** Conditions suitable for the PRESERVATION of paper, photographic PRINTs or film, or other media having permanent value. For example, ANSI PH1.43, *Photography (Film)— Processed Safety Film—Storage*, and ANSI IT9.2, *Imaging Media—Photographic Processed Films, Plates, and Papers—Filing Enclosures and Storage Containers*, contain storage specifications for processed films.

**Archival value** The determination in appraisal that records are worthy of indefinite or permanent preservation by an archival agency. Sometimes referred to as historical, continuing, or enduring value.

**Archive master** See PRESERVATION MASTER NEGATIVE.

**Archives** The organized body of noncurrent records made or received in connection with the transaction of its affairs by a government or a government agency, an institution, organization, or other corporate body, and the personal papers of a family or individual, that are preserved because of their continuing value. Also used to refer to the agency responsible for selecting, preserving, and making available such material, as well as the repository itself. (42:188)

**Archives box/container** A storage ENCLOSURE of pressed cardboard, frequently lined with ACID-FREE paper, designed for archives or MANUSCRIPTs, and available in letter or legal size, with a normal capacity of about one-third cubic foot. See also DOCUMENT CASE; RECORDS CENTER CONTAINER/CARTON. (16:417–418)

**ARL** Association of Research Libraries. An organization consisting of the major research libraries in the United States and Canada.

**Artifact (photographic)** The product of light on a LIGHT-SENSITIVE EMULSION producing an IMAGE. It does not include photomechanically produced images. (44:29)

**Artifactual value** A volume that has artifactual value is important as a physical object, in addition to any value it may have for the information it contains. For example, an ordinary edition of the Bible may have artifactual value because of its unique binding; an herbal because it contains hand-colored illustrations; a novel because it was signed by, or belonged to, a major author or a historically significant person. (26:13)

**Artotype**　See COLLOTYPE.

**ASA**　See ALKENYL SUCCINIC ANHYDRIDE.

**As-built drawings**　Drawings created after the construction of a building, depicting the building and its systems as they actually are, which may be different from the building as represented in the design drawings. (30:75)

**ASCII (non-image) text storage**　Use of the American Standard Code for Information Interchange (ASCII) computer code to produce a computer-readable version of text. ASCII is sometimes promoted as a means of preserving books and documents. It has an advantage over DIGITAL IMAGERY because it is possible to search (on a computer) for names, terms, phrases, or by subject. It is also possible to index and compare texts. See also DIGITAL IMAGERY.

**ASHRAE**　American Society of Heating, Refrigerating and Air Conditioning Engineers, the primary professional society for HVAC engineers.

**Aspect ratio**　The width-to-height ratio of an IMAGE, document, etc.

**Asperities**　Small projecting or rough imperfections on the surface of the magnetic tape COATING that limit and cause variations in HEAD-TO-TAPE CONTACT.

**Asperity noise**　Literally, roughness NOISE. Hiss, caused by ASPERITIES in the surface of recording tape.

**Astigmatism**　A LENS fault causing unequal light ray convergence and producing "fuzzy" images.

**ASTM**　An acronym for the American Society for Testing and Materials, a scientific and technical organization formed for the development of standards of characteristics and performance of materials, products, systems, and services, and the promotion of related knowledge.

**Audiocassette**　See CASSETTE.

**Audiodisc**　A SOUND RECORDING on a thin, flat disc, usually of VINYL, which is impressed with a continuous fine spiral groove carrying recorded sounds. A stylus on the playback device follows the groove as the disc revolves. The changes in form of the sides of the groove causes the stylus to vibrate and produce electric impulses that are converted to sound. The most common speed of audiodiscs is 33 1/3 rpm, other speeds are 78, 45, and 16 2/3 rpm. The production of audiodiscs has dropped significantly because of the popularity of the AUDIOCASSETTE and COMPACT DISC in the entertainment world. Synonymous with phonodisc, phonograph record, and disc. (1:14) See also COMPACT DISC.

**Audioreel**   An open REEL holding recorded audiotape that is to be played REEL-TO-REEL. Synonymous with audiotape reel and sound tape reel. (1:14)

**Audio spectrum**   The range of the electromagnetic spectrum audible to humans that ranges approximately from 15 Hz to 20,000 Hz.

**Audiotape**   See CASSETTE; CARTRIDGE; MAGNETIC TAPE.

**Autocatalytic**   A self-sustaining decomposition of a chemical compound, often accompanied by a very rapid release of energy. (55:107)

**Automatic exposure**   EXPOSURE control by photoelectric means for maintaining substantially constant exposure in the FOCAL PLANE for a range of field LUMINANCE. (42:189)

**Automatic threading**   A system in which film is threaded through a mechanical system, reader, duplicator, etc., with the only intervention being activation of a start signal.

**A-wind**   See WIND.

**Azimuth alignment**   Alignment of the recording and reproducing gaps so that their center lines lie parallel with one another. The angle of these gaps is at right angles to the direction of tape travel. This is done to obtain optimum high-FREQUENCY RESPONSE. Misalignment of the gaps causes loss in OUTPUT at short WAVELENGTHs.

**Azo dye**   A chemical compound formed in the development of DIAZO materials, the result of reactions between DIAZONIUM SALTS and any of several coupling agents. The coupling agent controls the resulting color of the IMAGE, ranging from blue to black with several intermediate shades. (1:18)

# B<sub>ack</sub>   See SPINE.

**Backboard**   The part of a MAT, made from a solid piece of MATBOARD, that functions as a protective support for the artwork. (28:25)

**Backcoating**   A layer of light-absorbing material on the back of a FILM BASE.

**Backed**   "A book that has had its SPINE shaped to create SHOULDERs to receive the BOARDs. See BACKING." (47:14) See also SHOULDER.

**Back edge**   The left edge of a RECTO, corresponding to the right edge of a VERSO. It is the BINDING EDGE in the ordinary bound book. (1:18)

**Background**   The area of a PAGE, FRAME, or printed sheet upon which no information is recorded. The MARGIN.

**Background density** The OPACITY of the noninformation area of micro-form. Also known as *D*Max or MAXIMUM DENSITY. See also DENSITY (D). (42:190)

**Backing** **(1)** "In BOOKBINDING, the process of shaping a ridge or SHOULDER on each side of the SPINE of a TEXT BLOCK after ROUND-ING it, and prior to LINING it. Backing accommodates the thickness of the BOARDs, and provides a HINGE along which they swing. The sewn sections of a book, after gluing, are placed securely between backing boards after rounding, and hammered to splay them outwards from the center of the book. The dimension of the shoulders is determined by the thickness of the boards to be used, which, in turn, is determined by the size and bulk of the book. In addition to accommodating the boards, backing also: allows for the SWELL of the spine caused by the thread used in SEWING, or by excessive GUARDING; helps to prevent the spine of the text block from collapsing into a concave shape over time; helps impart more flexibility to the book by creating a slight crease in each LEAF near the spine; and makes a better JOINT for the COVER, one which opens easier and is stronger, since the point of strain during opening is spread over a strip of the covering material, e.g., a FRENCH JOINT." (47:15) See also ROUNDING; SHOULDER. **(2)** In magnetic tape recording, the backing is the base carrying the magnetic oxide COAT-ING. The backing or base gives strength and permits flexibility, and is thick enough to hinder PRINT THROUGH. Common materials are acetate, POLYESTER, and POLYVINYL CHLORIDE. Less common is stainless steel; paper was used in the early days of tape. Thicker backing produces higher quality sound, but less playing time; thinner backing permits longer playing time. **(3)** The base of a LAMINATED DISC, also known as the CORE. See also CORE. (4:270) **(4)** "In photography, a dark layer affixed to a FILM BASE in order to reduce HALATION or to improve DAYLIGHT LOADING characteristics of the film. Synony-mous with backcoat." (1:19) See also BASE STOCK.

**Back lining** **(1)** The fabric (CRASH, CANTON FLANNEL) and/or paper strip glued to the back of a volume in order to strengthen it. **(2)** Also a draft paper with either creped or flat FINISH that is glued to the backbone of sewed books to bind the SIGNATURE and to keep the backbone of the book free from the backbone of the cover. If sewn books require the strongest possible construction, they are made TIGHT BACKed, whereby the book back liner is glued to the CASE back liner. See also LINING.

**Backstrip** In bound books, the portion of covering material over the SPINE extending from JOINT to joint. (1:19) See also SPINE and back, which are sometimes used synonymously, and INLAY.

**Bakelite** "A synthetic resin developed in the early part of this century and widely used as a substitute for hard rubber or celluloid. It was used in the production of some phonograph records, and is almost identical to the 'Condensite' used by Edison in the coating of his 'Diamond Discs.' " (4:270)

**Balancing**   The measurement and adjustment of the actual flows of air, water, etc., in ducts or pipes against the intended design flows in an HVAC distribution system.

**Band**   A section of one side of a conventional AUDIODISC that is separated from other sections by a visible strip of lowered GROOVE intensity. Also called a "cut." (52:27) See also TRACK.

**Bands**   "The CORDS or thongs on which the SECTIONs of books are sewn." (47:16) See also CORDS; TAPES.

**Band width**   The distinct annotated range or frequencies within the performance range of a recorder with respect to some other characteristics such as NOISE levels, saturation, or upper or lower frequency extremes.

**Bar code**   A set of coded rectangular marks.

**Barking**   "The operation of removing bark from PULPWOOD prior to chipping, screening, etc. This is carried out by means of a knife (disk), drum, abrasion, hydraulic barker, or by chemical means." (15:31)

**Barrow process**   A process of document repair and RESTORATION named after William J. Barrow (1904–1967) that involves DEACIDIFICATION, the use of tissue to increase the strength of the original, and THERMO-PLASTIC LAMINATION. The lamination process is not easily reversible and has largely been replaced by ENCAPSULATION. (1:20) Barrow developed two methods of deacidification suitable for use on single-sheet items. They both neutralize the ACID in paper, wash out the polyglycuronic acids and stain from the CELLULOSE oxidation, and deposit buffering salts in the fibers to inhibit further acid contamination. The first process is to immerse ACIDIC PAPER in a saturated solution of CALCIUM HYDROXIDE. Then the paper is immersed in a dilute solution of CALCIUM BICARBONATE (carbon dioxide bubbled through calcium carbonate in water) to remove excess calcium hydroxide. The second process is to soak the acidic paper in a solution of MAGNESIUM BICARBONATE (carbon dioxide bubbled through MAGNESIUM CARBONATE in water). (47:18) See also DEACIDIFICATION.

**Base**   The transparent plastic material that is coated with a photographic emulsion or other substance. BASE STOCK is usually made of CELLULOSE TRIACETATE or POLYESTER. See BASE STOCK; FILM BASE.

**Base color**   Hue or tint of the base material.

**Base density**   The transmission DENSITY of the base film stock excluding all other layers.

**Base plus fog**   The transmission DENSITY of the base and the processed but unexposed EMULSION of a FILM. Includes the inherent density of the FILM BASE and the density effect of development processes on the emulsion.

**Base stock**   A transparent plastic material, usually of CELLULOSE TRI-ACETATE or POLYESTER, upon which a photographic EMULSION and/or other materials may be coated. Other common BASE SUPPORT materials include paper, plastic, and glass, although any material capable of maintaining an IMAGE can be utilized. Also called base support.

**Base support**   See BASE STOCK.

**Basic size**   The size of paper SHEETs, used for calculating the BASIS WEIGHT of paper. A few of the specifications for basic sizes in use in the United States are:

| Type of Paper | Size (in inches) |
| --- | --- |
| Bible | 25 x 38 |
| Book | 25 x 38 |
| Cover | 20 x 26 |
| Manuscript | 18 x 31 |
| Newsprint | 24 x 36 |
| Writing | 17 x 22 |

**Basis weight**   The basis weight indicates the actual weight of a REAM (500 SHEETs) of paper measuring 38 inches by 25 inches. The more dense and thick each sheet of paper in the ream, the heavier the ream. The standard, or basic, size ream varies with different grades of paper. (47:19) For example, 500 80 lb. coated 25x38 inch sheets weigh eighty pounds.

**Bast fibers**   "FIBERs obtained from the inner bark or phloem of a woody plant. Examples of bast fiber plants harvested annually and used in papermaking are FLAX, hemp, jute, KOZO and MITSUMATA." (15:34)

**Bath**   Any PROCESSING solution for photographic material. See also RINSE.

**Battery operated psychrometer**   A PSYCHROMETER that includes a built-in battery-operated fan and motor. It works on the same principle as the SLING PSYCHROMETER, except that a small electric motor–driven fan produces the required airflow across the two bulbs. It is more accurate than the manually operated SLING PSYCHROMETER.

**Beater**   "A machine used in papermaking. It consists of a tank or tub, usually with a partition or mid-feather, that contains a heavy roll designed to revolve against a bedplate. Both roll and bedplate may have horizontal metal bars set on edge. The PULP in a water SLURRY circulates between the roll and bedplate and is rubbed, cut, macerated, and separated into FIBER. Sometimes FILLERs, LOADING, dyes, etc., are added to the STOCK in the beater. Some authorities contend that the beater, introduced in 1670, was partially responsible for the decline in quality of paper, as minuscule iron particles, breaking away from the sides or working parts of the machine, entered the paper and caused it to deteriorate." (47:20) See also HOLLANDER.

**Beater-sized**   "A paper which has been SIZEd by means of materials added to the BEATER, or if not the beater, to the PULP before SHEET formation, as contrasted to paper that has been SURFACE SIZED, or TUB SIZED." (47:20) It usually refers to the use of ROSIN SIZE and ALUM, but other sizing agents may be used. See also ENGINE SIZING; SIZING.

**Bench sewing**   In hand binding, the use of a SEWING FRAME set on a bench when joining SECTIONs together by HAND SEWING them through the fold onto CORDS or TAPES.

**Betamax**   Half-inch videocassette format manufactured by Sony and aimed mainly at the domestic market. Largely overtaken by the VHS format.

**Bibliographic target**   In PRESERVATION MICROFILMING, an image of the catalog card or printout of the bibliographic record from a machine-readable database. See TARGET.

**Binaural**   See STEREOPHONIC.

**Binder**   "(1) One who binds a book. (2) A looseleaf binder or notebook. (3) A material used to cause other materials to bond, or adhere, or, in papermaking, to cause FIBERs to bond, COATINGs to adhere, etc. (4) An adhesive substance, usually of liquid or molten form, used to create adhesion between aggregates, globules, etc. It is distinguished from an ADHESIVE in that it performs an internal adhesive function rather than a surface adhesive function." (47:20–21) (5) "In magnetic tape recording, a compound consisting of organic resins used to bond the oxide particles to the base material. The actual composition of the binder is considered proprietary information by each magnetic tape manufacturer. The binder is required to be flexible and still maintain the ability to resist flaking or shredding binder material during extended wear passes." (49:149)

**Binder's board**   "A high quality single-ply, thick, machine-made PAPER-BOARD produced especially for bookbinding and consisting of layers of PULP pressed into flat, smooth sheets. [Binder's board] has a definite GRAIN direction. It is made to full thickness in one operation and is hard, flat, and nonwarping. It ranges in thickness from 30 to 300 POINTs (0.30 to 0.300 of an inch). Important properties are smoothness, uniformity, high density, stiffness, and strength." (15:38) See also BOARD.

**Binder's title**   "The title lettered on the COVER of a volume by a binder, as distinguished from the title on the publisher's original cover (the cover title)." (1:23)

**Bindery record**   See BINDING RECORD.

**Bind in**   To fasten supplementary material securely into a bound volume.

**Binding** **(1)** The methods by which leaves, SECTIONs, SHEETs, SIGNATUREs, etc., are held together in a BOOK. The process of book-binding may be grouped into three operations: LEAF ATTACHMENT, FORWARDING, and finishing. Synonymous with bookbinding. **(2)** The COVER of a volume. (1:23)

**Binding cloth**   See BOOK CLOTH.

**Binding edge**   In binding, the edge at which the leaves are affixed to one another.

**Binding record**   "A record of library materials sent to a bindery; usually includes information on title, style of binding, etc. Synonymous with bindery record." (1:24)

**Binding slip**   "A card, slip, sheet, or other form of written [or printed] instructions sent to the bindery with each volume, or set of volumes, specifying the binding requirements for that volume or set. The typical binding slip generally specifies the author (if any), title (sometimes abbreviated), classification number, other bibliographical information, binding style (unless previously agreed upon), color of covering mate-rial, as well as any peculiarities of the book that should be brought to the attention of the binder, such as margins, condition of the paper, FOLDOUTs, loose material (for pockets), etc. A multiple form provides identical copies for the binder, as well as the library, and serves as verification for the work specified." (47:24)

**Binding specifications**   Specifications of materials and methods of manu-facture of LIBRARY BINDING. The most commonly used specifications in libraries is the *Library Binding Institute Standard for Library Binding, 8th Edition* (1986). It includes specifications for binding unbound materials, rebinding worn volumes, and binding new books.

**Bit**   As applied in magnetic recording, it represents one recorded informa-tion cell. (49:149)

**Bit density**   See PACKING DENSITY.

**Bit error rate**   This term, used in high-density digital recordings or high-density recording, refers to the number of errors a specific digital recording may contain, and is expressed in errors per data bits, such as 1 in $10^6$, or one error in one million data bits. (49:149)

**Black body**   A body that absorbs all light falling upon it.

**Black disc**   See LONG-PLAYING AUDIODISC.

**Black liquor**   An ALKALINE spent liquid obtained from the pulp-wash-ing system. Its makeup varies considerably depending on the mill and method of cooking. It has an intense black color and, depending upon its characteristics, is often used on dirt roads to control dust. Other by-products using black liquor include a food source for commercial yeast production. (15:40)

**Blade coater**   See BLADE COATING.

**Blade coating**   "A method of COATING paper during papermaking. A flexible blade is set at an adjustable angle against a WEB of paper or board supported by a soft, usually rubber-coated baking roll." (15:41)

**Blanket insurance policy**   "An insurance contract that covers several classes of property at a single location or at multiple locations." (25:93)

**Bleaching**   In photography, the conversion of metallic silver into SILVER HALIDEs preparatory for other processes such as TONING, intensifying, reducing, or removal in reversal processing.

**Bleed**   An illustration that runs off the edge of the page. (1:25)

**Bleed line**   See BLEED.

**Bleed-through**   Printing or images that show through from one side of a page to the other side of the source document being filmed, copied, or printed. (1:25)

**Blemish**   Microscopically small reddish or yellowish spots that may occur on SILVER GELATIN FILM during storage. REDOX (oxidation-reduction) blemishes are caused by local OXIDATION of image silver, resulting in the formation of minute deposits of colored colloidal silver. Under extreme conditions, information loss may occur. The oxidation is caused by oxidizing gasses from environmental sources, including the deterioration of film containers.

**Blind tooling**   The tooling of a design on a book cover without putting on gold leaf. (1:25)

**Blip**   See SENSING MARK.

**Blister**   A photographic film anomaly characterized by separation of EMULSION from base.

**Blocked up**   Areas in a NEGATIVE that appear solid without detail discrimination. Normally caused by overdevelopment or overexposure.

**Blocking**   (1) Occurs when wetted coated leaves in a TEXT BLOCK adhere to one another as they dry. (2) The tendency for adjacent layers of tape on a REEL to stick together, usually due to long-term storage under high tension and high humidity and temperature conditions. (4:271) (3) An undesirable condition in which a dry adhesive film is reactivated by heat, pressure, moisture, etc., and adheres to a material in contact with it. (47:26) Can occur in adjacent layers of other materials in rolls or sheets.

**Blotting paper**   A soft, unsized paper sheet or board used to absorb moisture. It is often made from high-grade rag or COTTON LINTERS, CHEMICAL or MECHANICAL WOOD PULPs, or their mixtures. Blotting paper is porous, bulky, has a low FINISH, and little strength. (47:27)

**Blowback**   OPTICAL ENLARGEMENT of a microfilm image.

**Blow up**   Any ENLARGEMENT of an IMAGE.

**Blue Amberol cylinder**   A type of CYLINDER introduced by Edison in 1912 with a plaster of Paris core and a blue celluloid recording surface, and a playing time of four minutes or more at 160 rpm. (51:27) See also AMBEROL CYLINDER; CELLULOID CYLINDER; WAX CYLINDER.

**Blue Wool lightfastness standards**   Specially dyed textiles are made in such a way that the more sensitive standard textile will achieve just "appreciable fading" in half the time needed for the next most sensitive standard to do so, and so on. The Blue Wool standards have been adopted as an ISO (International Organization for Standardization) standard. Eight specially prepared blue dyed wool samples are supplied on a card. They are chosen so that standard number 2 takes roughly twice as long to be perceptibly faded as standard 1, standard 3 roughly twice as long as standard 2, and so on through to standard 8. The measurement cannot give a good idea of how much exposure to light the item to be tested will stand in any given situation. (51:183) See also LIGHT DAMAGE SLIDE RULE.

**Board**   A generic term for a stiff and thick paper often used for book covers. The distinction between board and paper is that board is usually heavier in BASIS WEIGHT, thicker, and stiffer than paper. Most sheets 0.012 or more inches in thickness are considered to be boards, while nearly all less than 0.006 inch are termed paper; most of those in between these dimensions are also classed as paper. (47:27) See also BINDER'S BOARD; FIBERBOARD; PRESSBOARD; SOLID BOARD.

**Board cutter**   "A lever type of cutter mounted on a flat bed and used for cutting BINDER'S BOARD, and similar materials. The bed is equipped with a movable gauge against which the stock is placed for accurate cutting, and a foot-operated clamp which secures the material for cutting. The blade usually has one or more counterweights at the end opposite the handle to help prevent the knife from falling accidentally, and also to reduce the effort required to raise the blade." (47:27)

**Bolt**   **(1)** A length of woven cloth as it comes off the loom (with two finished edges, the SELVAGE). (38:212) **(2)** The folded edge at the HEAD, TAIL, or FORE EDGE of a SECTION of an unopened book.

**Bond**   "A contract binding one party financially for the performance by another of an agreed-upon obligation." (25:93)

**Bone (the action of boning)**   "To remove air bubbles, smooth, flatten, and ensure adhesion between two materials by rubbing with a flat tool made of bone or plastic, which is called a BONE FOLDER or folder." (38:213)

**Bone folder**   A flat piece of bone or plastic, six to nine inches long, about one inch wide and 1/8 inch thick, with rounded corners and edges; used to rub along the fold of a sheet of paper to bend it squarely into position.

**Book**   **(1)** A group of sheets of paper bound along one edge and enclosed within protective covers to form a volume, whether written, printed, or

blank. **(2)** UNESCO defines a book as "a non-periodical printed publication of at least forty-nine pages, exclusive of cover pages." **(3)** To qualify
for the U.S. Postal Service special fourth-class postal rate (book rate), a
book must consist of at least 8 printed pages, consisting wholly of
biography or reading matter with incidental blank spaces for notations
and containing no advertising matter other than incidental announce-
ments of books. **(4)** A collection of MANUSCRIPT or printed leaves
fastened together to form a volume or volumes, forming a bibliographical unit, distinct from periodicals and from other forms of material, such
as films, prints, maps, etc. See also PAMPHLET.

**Bookbinding**  See BINDING.

**Bookboard**  See BINDER'S BOARD.

**Book cloth**  A generic term for the woven fabrics used in covering books.
They are usually woven cotton fabrics, which may be bleached or
mercerized, dyed, FILLED with pigment colors, gelatinized, starched,
coated or impregnated, CALENDERED, and embossed (grained). They
are divided into classes according to type and quality. Specifications for
the fabrics used for book cloths are:

BOOK CLOTHS
(starch-filled and impregnated)

| Group | Weight |
|-------|--------|
| A     | Light  |
| B     | Medium |
| C     | Heavy  |
| C-1   | Heavy  |

BUCKRAMS
(starch-filled and impregnated)

| Group | Weight |
|-------|--------|
| D     | Light  |
| E     | Medium |
| F     | Heavy  |

"PYROXYLIN-treated" means either pyroxylin-coated or pyroxylin-
impregnated cotton fabrics.

**Book cover**  See COVER.

**Book cradle**  A rack or stand, constructed of wood and/or metal with
Plexiglas™ or glass plates, that supports bound volumes for microfilming in a position so pages are open flat and parallel to the FOCAL PLANE
of the camera. Some models press the pages up against the filming plate
(focal plane fixed), while others require constant adjustment of the
filming plate down onto the opened pages (focal plane variable).

**Book endpaper**  See ENDPAPERS.

**Book jacket**  See DUST JACKET.

**Book return (or drop)**  "A box or chute provided so that readers can return books when a library is closed or where drive-in facilities are available." (23:77)

**Bookworm**  "The larvae of various insects that injure books by boring small holes in the binding and leaves." (1:29)

**BOT**  Marker indicating the beginning of a magnetic tape.

**Bound book**  "Originally, a hand-bound book with BOARDs attached to the handsewn SECTIONs before gluing or pasting the covering material to the boards. The term as now generally used includes CASEd books." (1:30)

**Box**  A container for maps, bundles of loose sheets, samples of material, disintegrating books, reels of microfilm, sheets of microfiche, etc., that may be open at one end or completely closed.

**bpi**  Bits per inch.

**B position**  See COMIC MODE.

**Brayer**  A small roller used for applying pressure to an ENCAPSULATED document in order to expel the entrapped air and bind the tape securely to the top and bottom POLYESTER sheets.

**Breaking length**  The length of a strip of paper, cut either in the MACHINE or CROSS DIRECTION, or a strip of cloth, cut either in the WARP or FILLING direction, which would break of its own weight when suspended vertically. It is a value calculated from the TENSILE STRENGTH of the material. Under normal circumstances paper will have a greater breaking length in the machine direction than in the cross direction, and cloth a greater breaking length in the warp direction than in the FILLING. (47:38)

**Breaking strength**  (1) See BURSTING STRENGTH. (2) The breaking load or force, expressed in pounds per inch, required to rupture a material, such as cloth, film, or paper. See TENSILE STRENGTH. (47:38)

**Breast roll**  "A large-diameter roll around which the WIRE passes at the machine HEADBOX just at or behind the point where the STOCK is admitted to the wire by the stock inlet." (15:56)

**Brightness**  Obvious differences in light intensity or IMAGE clarity.

**Bristol**  A lightweight, thin PAPERBOARD with a smooth surface; used for LINING the SPINE of a book COVER or CASE and for book POCKET or small PORTFOLIO construction. (38:213)

**Brittle**  (1) A condition of paper indicating a very low FOLDING ENDURANCE prior to breaking. Brittleness is usually attributed to acidity in the paper from manufacture or storage, causing a chemical deterioration of the CELLULOSE FIBERs. See ACIDIC PAPER. **(2)** A basic characteristic of acetate films as they age.

**Brittle books**   Books the pages of which have become so fragile that they cannot be circulated. More generally, any book, PAMPHLET, newspaper, or document printed on ACID-bearing paper. (55:107)

**Broke**   "Paper that has been discarded anywhere in the process of manufacture. 'Wet broke' is paper taken off the WET PRESS of a paper machine; 'dry broke' is made when paper is spoiled in going over the DRIERS or through the CALENDERs, TRIMMED off in the rewinding of the rolls, trimmed from sheets being prepared for shipping, or discarded for manufacturing defects. It is usually returned to a repulping unit for reprocessing." (15:58)

**Broken back**   The back of a book broken open from HEAD to TAIL. Also called broken binding. (23:95)

**Broker**   See INSURANCE BROKER.

**Bromide film**   Photographic FILM that is SENSITIZED with an EMULSION of silver bromide suspended in GELATIN. (1:32)

**Bromide paper**   PHOTOGRAPHIC PAPER that is SENSITIZED with an EMULSION of silver bromide suspended in GELATIN. (1:32)

**Bronzing**   The change to a purple-brown (bronze) tone sometimes undergone by the blacks of bromide prints due to inappropriate PROCESSING or faulty paper. Also known as plumming. (8:154)

**Brown stain**   In magnetic recording, a discoloration of the head top surface, usually a chemical reaction between the head surface materials and either the tape binder, tape lubricant, or head bonding materials. Its origin is not well understood, but it is known to occur in the presence of low HUMIDITY. (49:150)

**Brush-finish coating**   A paper COATING that is given an especially high polish by running the dried or partially dried coated paper over a revolving drum provided with six or more rapidly revolving cylinder brushes that contact the coated surface of the sheet. (15:60)

**Bubble**   Commonly used defect term for AUDIODISC recordings. It is most often the result of faulty PRESSING. (4:272)

**Buckle**   **(1)** A curvature of film due to shrinkage of the edges while the film is rolled, usually caused by storage at improper HUMIDITY in combination with overly tight winding. Temporary buckle results from loss of moisture from the edges of the film when stored under dry air conditions. Permanent buckle is caused by loss of solvent from the edges of the film when stored under moist conditions. **(2)** Piling up of film in a camera, CASSETTE, jacket or MAGAZINE due to a film-transport malfunction. (17:169) **(3)** In magnetic tape, the deformation of the circular form of a tape PACK that may be caused by a combination of improper winding tension, adverse storage conditions, and/or poor REEL HUB configuration. (49:150)

**Buckling**   See BUCKLE.

**Buckram**   "A strong, coarse woven cotton (sometimes LINEN) cloth that has been dyed and filled with STARCH under heat and pressure. Buckrams are frequently coated with PYROXYLIN or ACRYLIC and used for commercial LIBRARY BINDING." (38:213)

**Buffer**   In the context of ALKALINE papermaking, an ACID absorber or ALKALINE RESERVE, such as a CALCIUM CARBONATE FILLER, which maintains the pH in the NEUTRAL or ALKALINE range by reacting with acidic gases from the environment or from the deterioration of the paper itself. (33:20) See also NEUTRALIZATION; PERMANENT PAPER.

**Building envelope**   "Generally, the exterior walls, windows and roof of a building; 'weather envelope' is the outside of the building envelope which resists weather." (30:75)

**Building-in**   Fixing the COVER to a book. Newly cased-in TEXT BLOCKs are placed between smooth or brass-edged boards. The boards and books are then placed in a STANDING PRESS or BUILDING-IN MACHINE until the paste used to attach the CASE to the text block dries so that the boards will not WARP.

**Building-in machine**   A hydraulic machine used to duplicate the action of a hand book press. The cased-in TEXT BLOCK is placed between the platens of the machine, which then close and exert great pressure. Heated jaws simultaneously compress the CASE along its HINGEs to form tight front and back JOINTs and dry the books in seconds. (26:13)

**Buildup**   A term referring to the accumulation of debris and magnetic particles deposited by magnetic tape on the heads of a tape recorder, which causes head-tape separation and an increase in friction. Solvent cleaning of the tape recorder heads will usually remove such buildup. (4:272)

**Bulk eraser**   Also known as a degausser, a machine that removes all traces of previously recorded signals from the magnetic emulsion of a tape and leaves it in a completely demagnetized state. Important in order to minimize both NOISE and distortion when reusing tape. ERASUREs made using a bulk eraser generally result in a greater SIGNAL-TO-NOISE ratio than those erased on a tape recorder through the ERASE HEAD. (4:272) See also DEMAGNETIZATION.

**Bump**   Commonly used defect term for AUDIODISC recordings, implying a raised surface on a portion of the playing area of the disc that could cause sonic distortion or groove jumping by the stylus. (4:272)

**Burn-in**   A photographic technique for exposing only parts of an IMAGE to additional light while protecting the remainder.

**Burst binding**   "An ADHESIVE BINDING method in which slits are cut through the folds of each SECTION and ADHESIVEs applied to the SPINE of the TEXT BLOCK in such a way that the adhesive is forced through the slits, attaching all leaves together. Many new bindings may appear to be SMYTH-SEWN when they are actually ADHESIVE BOUND." (38:213)

**Burst factor**   "The BURSTING STRENGTH of paper in grams per square centimeter divided by the BASIS WEIGHT of the paper in grams per square meter, which also gives the burst factor as a numerical value." See also BURST RATIO. (47:42–43)

**Bursting strength**   "A measure of the ability of a sheet to resist rupture when pressure is applied to one of its sides by a specified instrument, under specified conditions. Testing for the bursting strength of paper is a very common procedure, although its value in determining the potential PERMANENCE or DURABILITY of paper is suspect." (47:43) See also BURST FACTOR; MULLEN; POINTS PER POUND.

**Burst ratio**   "The BURSTING STRENGTH of a material in POINTS PER POUND." (47:43) See also BURST FACTOR.

**Butt splice**   See SPLICE.

**Butt weld**   See SPLICE.

# C

**-1 (book cloth)**   See BOOK CLOTH.

**Calcium bicarbonate (CaC$_4$)**   The second step in Barrow's two-step DE-ACIDIFICATION process. See BARROW PROCESS; CALCIUM CARBONATE.

**Calcium carbonate (CaCO$_3$)**   An ALKALINE chemical used as a BUFFER in papers and boards. Also used to make bicarbonates by bubbling through dilute solutions. CaCO$_3$ is one of the most stable, common, and widely dispersed materials in nature. It can be precipitated by reaction of calcium chloride and sodium carbonate in water solution, or by passing carbon dioxide through a suspension of hydrated lime (Ca(OH)$_2$) in water. See BARROW PROCESS.

**Calcium hydroxide (Ca(OH)$_2$)**   The first step in Barrow's two-step DE-ACIDIFICATION process. See BARROW PROCESS.

**Calender**   A series of horizontal cast iron rollers (similar in appearance to the rollers in old domestic washing machines equipped with clothes wringers) with hardened, chilled surfaces resting one on another in a vertical bank at the DRY END of the papermaking machine. The newly made, dried paper WEB is passed between the calender rolls to increase the smoothness and GLOSS of its surface. (47:44)

**Calendered**   "A paper or cloth that has been given a smooth surface by passing it through a CALENDER one or more times." (47:44)

**Calender sizing**   SIZE is applied to paper or PAPERBOARD at the CALENDER. See also SIZING; SURFACE-SIZED; TUB-SIZED.

**Calibrate**   To adjust equipment—for example, microfilm cameras, DENSITOMETERs, SENSITOMETERs, consoles, and tape recorders—to a standard so that their measurements are similar and complementary.

**Caliper**   See THICKNESS.

**Cambric**   "A fine, closely woven white LINEN fabric, used in LIBRARY BINDINGs for HINGEs, SPINE LININGs, extensions, etc." (47:45)

**Camera**   An OPTICAL device for exposure of LIGHT-SENSITIVE materials.

**Camera base**   The table-like structure or bed used to support the LIGHT ARMS and CAMERA HEAD in PLANETARY CAMERAs.

**Camera head**   That part of a camera system incorporating film housing, film transport, and LENS.

**Camera master**   The raw film stock that, when exposed and processed, becomes the first-generation microfilm. See also FIRST-GENERATION FILM; MASTER FILM; PRESERVATION MASTER NEGATIVE.

**Camera negative**   See CAMERA MASTER.

**Camera-processor**   A device incorporating the functions of both camera and film processor. Not acceptable for PRESERVATION MICROFILMING.

**Cancel**   "(1) A replacement LEAF or leaves, printed because of a mistake in the original printing, an imperfect page, etc., that is to replace the corresponding faulty SECTION before the book is actually published. (2) In bookbinding, in a broad sense, all leaves that are not to be bound in. This applies specifically to the waste sheets." (47:46)

**Candela**   Equal to $1/60$ of the luminous intensity per square centimeter of a black body radiator operating at the temperature of freezing platinum. Formerly candle. (31:7) See also LUMEN.

**Candle**   See CANDELA.

**Canton flannel**   Cotton cloth fleeced on one side. Often used as a BACK LINING to provide additional strength.

**Caoutchouc binding**   A method of binding that was introduced about 1840. The spine folds of the SIGNATUREs were cut off and the separate leaves attached to each other and to a BACKSTRIP by a coating of flexible rubber solution and CASEd. The rubber solution eventually disintegrated and the leaves fell out. Probably the first form of ADHESIVE BINDING. The process was abandoned about 1870, the method being revived in the late 1940s when the so-called PERFECT BINDING method was developed. Also called gutta-percha binding.

**Capstan**   The spindle connected to the motor of a tape recorder that moves the tape at constant speed across the heads. (4:273)

**Carbon black**   An inert filler used to protect the basic resin in a record compound from the action of light by absorbing RADIANT ENERGY. It is also used as an anti-static element in magnetic tape. (4:273)

**Card-to-card printer**   A film duplicator that holds a card, JACKET, or MICROFICHE in contact with unexposed film in order to create a copy IMAGE when controlled amounts of light flow through the MASTER onto the raw film. The raw film may be in sheet form or be cut from a roll into sheets after exposure.

**Card-to-roll printer**   A film duplicator in which individual fiche, cards, or JACKETs are placed in contact with unexposed film in order to create a copy IMAGE when controlled amounts of light flow through the MASTER onto the raw film. The raw film, initially in roll form, may be processed either in sheets or as a roll.

**Carriage**   The part of a microfilm READER that holds and transports the microfilm.

**Cartridge**   **(1)** A single CORE container enclosing processed microforms, for insertion into readers, reader-printers, and retrieval devices, requiring no threading or REWINDING. **(2)** A small case in the tone arm of a conventional record player containing the stylus and the mechanism that converts its motion into electrical impulses. (52:27) **(3)** An endless loop of magnetic tape on a single core sealed in a plastic container for use in tape players and recorders. Eight track tape cartridges were popular for a short period of time until being successfully overtaken commercially by audiotape CASSETTEs, which, in turn, are being challenged by audio COMPACT DISCs. See also CASSETTE.

**Case**   **(1)** "The finished COVER of a CASE-BOUND book. The case consists of two BOARDs, an INLAY, and covering material. It is made separately from the TEXT BLOCK and is later attached to it in a step called CASING-IN." (26:13) **(2)** "In statistics, the unit on which VARIABLEs are measured. Examples: if the number of volumes in branch libraries are measured, the cases would be branch libraries; if the level of acidity in a group of volumes is measured, the cases would be volumes." (7:107)

**Case binding**   See CASE-BOUND.

**Case-bound** "A binding method where the TEXT BLOCK and COVER are made separately and attached in an operation called CASING-IN. Case binding differs from traditional hand bookbinding where the text block and cover are constructed as a single unit." (38:213)

**Casing-in** "The process of attaching the TEXT BLOCK to its COVER, usually by gluing or pasting the SUPER and endsheets, placing the cover around the text block, and pressing until dry." (38:213)

**Cassette** (1) A compact tape-recording system that utilizes a length of recording tape (audio or video) and two HUBs inside a sealed plastic shell. The best known versions are the compact cassette introduced in 1964, and, today, the most frequently used form of tape for home recording and playback, and the VIDEOCASSETTE for recording and playback over television. The tape used in the compact cassette is narrower and thinner and runs at a slower speed than the normal tape used in reel-to-reel tape recording. (4:273) (2) A double-CORE container enclosing processed ROLL MICROFILM for insertion into readers, microprinters, and retrieval devices. See also CARTRIDGE.

**Cassette tape**   See CASSETTE; VIDEOCASSETTE.

**Cation**   A positively charged ION.

**CD**   Abbreviation for COMPACT DISC.

**CD-ROM**   COMPACT DISC–read only memory. CD-ROM is a computer peripheral that employs compact disc technology to store large amounts of data for later retrieval. The data is placed on the disc at the time of manufacture. The capacity of a CD-ROM disc is about 550 megabytes, the equivalent of 250,000 typewritten pages. (20:51) See also COMPACT DISC; LASER DISC.

**Cellophane tape**   See PRESSURE-SENSITIVE TAPE.

**Celluloid cylinder**   A CYLINDER, usually of four minutes' duration, with a recording surface of celluloid. First issued for public sale in 1900 by the Lambert Record Company of Chicago, celluloid cylinders proved much more durable than either AMBEROL or WAX CYLINDERs. (52:27) See also BLUE AMBEROL CYLINDER.

**Cellulose**   The basic FILLER in paper. It is a complex polymeric carbohydrate $(C_6H_{10}O_5)_n$ having the same percentage composition as STARCH, i.e., 44.4 percent carbon, 6.2 percent hydrogen, and 49.4 percent oxygen. (47:49) It is the chief component of the cell walls of plants, wood, etc. These FIBERs have the unique property of adhering together to form a mat, i.e., paper, from a water suspension.

**Cellulose acetate**   A clear, hard, and glossy acetate salt of CELLULOSE. It is a transparent plastic produced by the action of ACETIC ACID on cellulose. Used in heat-sealing LAMINATION, as a SAFETY FILM

BASE, and also as a magnetic tape base. It is the most fungal resistant of the cellulosics, and was the best instantaneous audio recording medium for many years until magnetic tape was produced on a POLYESTER base. However, it is an unstable medium with a limited storage life. See also ACETATE BASE; CELLULOSE NITRATE; CELLULOSE TRIAC-ETATE; LACQUER DISC; SAFETY FILM.

**Cellulose ester**   A FILM BASE composed mainly of CELLULOSE esters of acetic, propionic, or butyric acids or mixtures thereof. (42:189)

**Cellulose nitrate**   A material produced by the action of nitric acid on CELLULOSE; used extensively as a FILM BASE until 1951. Because it is highly unstable, subject to OXIDATION and denitration, and is extremely flammable, cellulose nitrate has been largely replaced by CELLULOSE ACETATE and CELLULOSE TRIACETATE.

**Cellulose triacetate**   A transparent plastic more dimensionally stable than CELLULOSE ACETATE, widely used as a FILM BASE for SAFETY FILM because of its transparency and relative nonflammability. For PRESERVATION purposes, largely replaced by POLYESTER-base safety films. (1:38) Also used as a MAGNETIC TAPE BASE. See also SAFETY FILM.

**Center start disc**   This is a disc recording (usually vertically cut) that requires the pickup and stylus to move from the center of the disc outward (having the beginning of its modulated groove at the outer edge of the inside margin). It is commonly abbreviated as C/S. (4:274)

**Certification**   (1) In microfilming, a statement indicating that the IMAGEs are complete and accurate reproductions of the ORIGINALs. (2) Validation of the accuracy of measuring equipment or use of required standards.

**Certified bindery**   A LIBRARY BINDERY that adheres to the binding specifications of the LIBRARY BINDING INSTITUTE.

**Certified tape**   Tape that is electrically tested on a specified number of tracks and is certified by the supplier to have less than a certain total number of permanent errors. (49:150)

**Certifier**   Equipment that evaluates the ability of magnetic tape to record and reproduce. The equipment normally counts and charts each error on the tape, including the level and duration of DROPOUTs. In the certify mode, the equipment stops the tape at an error to allow for visual inspection of the tape to see if the cause of the error is correctable or permanent. (49:150) See also EVALUATOR.

**cfm**   Cubic feet per minute, a common measure of airflow quantity.

**Chain lines**   The widely spaced parallel WATERMARK lines about one inch apart caused by the chain wires on a paper MOLD. The lines are created by the impression in the PULP of very thin wires or threads, which are used to sew the numerous, narrowly spaced LAID WIRES to the supporting ribs of the mold. (29:114) The chain wires are slightly thicker than the laid wires, which run perpendicular and are attached to them for support. Chain lines are visible when held up to the light, and generally run parallel with the GRAIN direction. They are often simulated on MACHINE-MADE PAPER. Chain lines can be produced on machine-made paper, in which case grain direction of the paper is usually parallel to the chain lines. (38:213)

**Chain stitch**   See KETTLE STITCH.

**Channel**   A single path for recording or reproducing sound. For stereo sound, for instance, a separate left and right channel of information must be supplied. (4:274)

**Channel separation**   The degree to which sound signals on one CHANNEL are not picked up by an adjacent channel.

**Chase**   A vertical compartment or space in a building for ducts, pipes, and wiring.

**Chatter**   An erratic spotted pattern in record grooves with short alternate light and dark strips. It is caused by a poor cutting stylus or one set at a wrong angle. Too deep a cut in thin disc coating may also produce a similar effect, which is most likely to occur close to the center of the record. (4:274)

**Chemical fog**   In photography, "a chemically initiated BACKGROUND DENSITY occurring either previous to or during development." (21:5) See also FOG.

**Chemical pulp**   See CHEMICAL WOOD PULP.

**Chemical stability**   "Not easily decomposed or otherwise modified chemically. This is a desirable characteristic for materials used in PRESERVATION, since it suggests an ability to resist chemical degradation (such as embrittlement of paper) over time and/or upon exposure to various conditions during use or storage. Other terms used loosely as synonyms: inert, stable, chemically inert." (22:14)

**Chemical wood pulp**   "Paper PULP made by cooking wood chips with sulfate, sulfite, or soda to remove LIGNIN. After cooking, the pulp is washed to remove the processing chemicals and other impurities. PERMANENT PAPERs and boards can be made from chemical wood pulp." (45:87) See also SULFATE PULP; SULFITE PULP.

**Chilled water**   "Water at around 42 to 55°F, circulated in a building to provide cooling. Chilled water must usually be at 42 to 44°F to provide effective dehumidification." (30:75)

**Chiller**   "A piece of equipment which usually chills water, which is then used to cool the inside of a building; heat is rejected by either an exterior CONDENSER, or through the use of CONDENSER WATER. Most chillers, such as reciprocating, centrifugal and screw chillers, create their cooling effect through vapor compression (see COMPRESSOR); some are absorption chillers, which create a cooling effect through the use of a heat source, such as steam, hot water or hot gas." (30:75)

**Chip**   Commonly used defect term for AUDIODISC or CYLINDER recordings. It usually refers to a small missing piece from the edge or RIM of the recording, while dig or GOUGE refers to a PIT or small break in the horizontal surface further in from the rim. (4:275) See also GOUGE.

**Chloride film**   Photographic materials SENSITIZEd with an EMULSION of silver chloride, used mainly for CONTACT COPYing. (1:42)

**Chromatic aberration**   Light of different wavelengths focusing at different planes, usually because of a lens anomaly.

**Chrome tape**   See CHROMIUM DIOXIDE.

**Chromium dioxide (CrO$_2$)**   A compound of magnetic particle oxide used as a COATING on some magnetic tape, especially CASSETTE tape. Chromium dioxide tape has a much better SIGNAL-TO-NOISE RATIO and response to short WAVELENGTHs at lower speeds than non-chromium coated tapes. It is also used in video recording and computer tapes. (4:275)

**Cinching**   Pulling film or tape too tight when wound on a HUB. This can cause fluted edges on either the film roll or the tape roll.  If carried to extremes, it will cause film or tape breakage or permanent deformation and may result in straight longitudinal scratches called cinch marks.

**Cinch marks**   See CINCHING.

**Cinefilm**   Synonymous with motion picture film.

**Cine mode**   **(1)** The arrangement of IMAGEs on roll film in which the lines of print or writing are perpendicular to the length of the film for horizontal script and parallel for vertical script. **(2)** The arrangement of images on a MICROFICHE in which the first microimage is in the top left-hand corner of the GRID PATTERN and succeeding microimages appear in sequence from top to bottom and in COLUMNs from left to right. (17:179–180) Technically referred to as Position A orientation in the ANSI USA Standard Specifications for 16mm and 35mm Silver Gelatin Microfilms for Reel Applications. Synonymous with motion picture orientation. See also COMIC MODE.

**Claim**   "A formal, written demand by the insured for payment for a LOSS coming under the terms of the insurance contract." (25:93)

**Class A binding**   Obsolete term used to describe a superseded LIBRARY BINDING INSTITUTE library binding standard.

**Cleaner**   See WINDER/CLEANER.

**Clear base**   A material without color used to carry photographic EMULSIONs. DENSITY measure of these bases is normally 0.06 density points or less.

**Clearing** (1) In SILVER FILM processing, the removal of SILVER HALIDEs in the FIXING BATH, though up to 5 percent actually still remain. (2) In VESICULAR FILM processing, exposure of developed film to ULTRA-VIOLET radiation to reduce any remaining DIAZONIUM SALTS.

**Cleat** See KERFS.

**Cleat sewing/lacing** "A machine method of ADHESIVE BINDING developed to use less INNER MARGIN than OVERSEWING. Thread covered with glue is laced around large notches cut out of the SPINE." (38:213) See also KERFS; SAW-KERF BINDING; SMYTH-CLEAT SEWING.

**Closed joint** A JOINT that is formed when the covering boards are laced on right up to the BACKING SHOULDERs. Also called a tight joint. See also FRENCH JOINT; JOINT; LACING-IN. (47:56)

**Cloth** A term applied to any binding, with or without BOARDs, that is fully covered in cloth. (1:47) See BOOK CLOTH. See also CLOTHBOUND.

**Clothbound** A book bound in full CLOTH over stiff BOARDs.

**Cloth joint** A piece of CLOTH is used to reinforce the ENDPAPER folds at the JOINTs on the inside of very heavy or large books. The sewing to the TEXT BLOCK should be through the cloth.

**Cloth sides** A book COVER that has cloth sides, but a SPINE of other material. (1:47)

**cm/s** Abbreviation for centimeters per second, the rate of speed at which magnetic tape travels past the recording or playback heads of a tape recorder or player.

**Course groove** See STANDARD GROOVE.

**Coat or coated** See COATING.

**Coated paper** A slick, glossy paper to whose surface a COATING of adhesives, clay, CALCIUM CARBONATE, or other mineral pigments or mixture of pigments has been added to provide a smoother base for printing. (9:14) Coated paper is difficult to successfully ADHESIVE BIND because adhesives do not readily penetrate the coating to adhere to the paper fibers. (38:214) The term is used to distinguish it from LOADED papers, in which the clay is mixed with the pulp during manufacture. See also DULL; GLOSS; MATTE.

**Coated paper support** "In photography, a base support of paper which has had its surface texture altered from the natural rough texture by the addition of another layer. A common additive is barium sulphate in GELATIN to provide a smooth, nonporous surface for the EMULSION layers." (44:29)

**Coating** (1) The term applied to the layer of adhesive mixture, clay, CALCIUM CARBONATE, pigment, or mixture of pigments applied to the surface of paper to provide a smoother base for printing. (2) A term applied to the film of substances, usually clear, used as a barrier or other functional covering on the surface of paper or paperboard. (9:14; 15:98) See SURFACE-SIZED, FILM-COATED. **(3)** The magnetic layer of a magnetic tape, consisting of oxide particles held in a binder, that is applied to the base film. (49:150) The coating carries the magnetically recorded signal. **(4)** The outer layer on a LAMINATED DISC or CYLIN-DER in which the grooves are cut. (4:276) **(5)** Any one of several layers applied to the FILM BASE, the outer layer often providing modest protection against mechanical damage.

**Coating, anticurl**   See ANTICURL COATING.

**Coating, protective**   See PROTECTIVE COATING.

**Coating resistance**   "The electrical resistance of the COATING measured between two parallel electrodes spaced a known distance apart along the length of tape. On the specification sheets this is called resistivity." (49:150)

**Coating thickness**   The thickness of the magnetic COATING applied to the base film. (49:150) In general, thin coatings on magnetic tape have excellent RESOLUTION at the expense of reduced OUTPUT at long WAVELENGTHs. Thick coatings give high output at long wavelengths at the expense of resolution. (4:276) Thickness of tape is inversely proportional to PRINT THROUGH.

**Coating-to-backing adhesion**   See ANCHORAGE.

**Coating transfer**   Refers to the sticking of the oxide of one layer of magnetic tape to the BACKING (base material) of the adjacent layer of magnetic tape. Coating transfer occurs during storage when tape tension, temperature, and humidity are incorrect, causing multiple problems in playback of the tape.

**Cobalt thiocyanate**   "A cobalt salt used to roughly measure RELATIVE HUMIDITY (RH). Paper that has been impregnated with the salt will turn from blue to pink, depending on the RH. The color can be compared to standard colors to indicate the approximate RH. This method is not particularly accurate—the RH can not be measured to better than five percent—and it does not lend itself to measurements in large rooms. It is inexpensive, however, and can be used in exhibit cases." (32:11) See also HAIR HYGROMETER; HYGROMETER; PSYCHROMETER; RE-CORDING HYGROTHERMOGRAPH; RELATIVE HUMIDITY; and SLING PSYCHROMETER;

**Cockle**   The wrinkling or puckering caused when paper (or any sheet) dries unevenly.

**Codex**   An ancient book composed of leaves of writing material fastened together so as to open like a modern book, as distinct from a SCROLL or VOLUMEN, which it superseded. It was introduced originally in the

First Century A.D. The English word derives from the Latin *caudex* or *codex*, meaning a tree trunk or stem stripped of bark. Originally, the name was applied to two or more tablets of wood, metal, or ivory, hinged together with rings, the inner sides of which were covered with wax that could be inscribed with a stylus. Later on the term was applied to books of this format made of PAPYRUS, VELLUM, or PARCHMENT.

**Coefficient of friction**   The tangential force required to maintain (DYNAMIC COEFFICIENT) or initiate (static coefficient) motion between two surfaces divided by the normal force pressing the two surfaces together. (49:150)

**Coherent radiation**   Radiant waves in phase both temporally and spatially, such as a laser beam.

**Coil binding**   See SPIRAL BINDING.

**Co-insurance clause**   A provision in a property policy that requires that the policyholder carry insurance equal to a specified percentage of the property's value. (25:93)

**Cold-setting adhesive**   An ADHESIVE that sets at a temperature below 20°C (68°F). Most adhesives used by library binders are cold-setting.

**Collate**   See COLLATION.

**Collation**   Checking that a book is complete before binding, REBINDING, or reformatting. This is done by examining the SIGNATUREs, leaves, and illustrations to determine that they are complete and perfect.

**Collection development**   A term that encompasses a number of activities related to the development of the library collection, including the determination and coordination of selection policy, assessment of needs of users and potential users, collection use studies, collection evaluation, identification of collection needs, selection and acquisition of materials, planning for resource sharing, COLLECTION MAINTENANCE, and weeding. (1:49)

**Collection maintenance**   A term covering all of the activities carried out by a library to preserve the materials in its collections, including binding, MENDING, REPAIRING, materials conversion, etc. One aspect of COLLECTION DEVELOPMENT. (1:49)

**Collimate**   To arrange in parallel to a certain line or direction; to render parallel, such as light rays. "To adjust the line of sight or lens axis of an optical instrument so that it is in its proper position relative to other parts of the instrument." (21:5)

**Collodion emulsion**   One layer of a film structure in which the medium for the LIGHT-SENSITIVE material is CELLULOSE NITRATE (PYROXYLIN) in ether and alcohol. (44:29)

**Colloid**   A gelatinous material that when in a liquid form will not diffuse easily through vegetable or animal membranes. (43:290)

**Colloid emulsion**   One layer of the film structure in which the medium for the light-sensitive material is a COLLOID. Photographic organic colloids include ALBUMEN, GELATIN, GLUE, GUM ARABIC, and STARCH. (44:29)

**Collotype**   A photomechanical image made directly from a hardened EMULSION of bichromated GELATIN on glass. A kind of photogravure, it provides a CONTINUOUS-TONE IMAGE. The process was developed in 1852 by William Henry Fox Talbot. Alphonse Louis Poitevin was the first to use collotype for printing plate production in 1855. Phototype, Albertype, Artotype, Heliotype, and Lichtdruck are forms of collotype. Also called a gelatin print. (23:146)

**Color film**   Any of a variety of films (silver dye–based or dye-based) capable of reproducing color images with relative fidelity with respect to the original.

**Column**   (1) The vertical mast that supports the CAMERA HEAD on a PLANETARY CAMERA. (2) The vertically arranged set of IMAGEs on a MICROFICHE.

**Column stop**   A device to position the head of a PLANETARY CAMERA at either its upper limit or other arbitrarily assigned positions.

**COM**   See COMPUTER-OUTPUT MICROFORM.

**Comic mode**   (1) IMAGEs on MICROFILM arranged so that the vertical axis of the image is perpendicular to the edge of the film, similar to comic strips in newspapers. (2) In the MICROFICHE format, images are arrayed from left to right from the upper left corner across the sheet continuing on each succeeding row. (17:173) In the ANSI USA Standard Specifications for 16mm and 35mm Silver Gelatin Microfilms for Reel Applications, comic mode is called the "B" position. See also CINE MODE.

**Commission on Preservation and Access**   A not-for-profit organization charged with long-range planning for PRESERVATION on a national scale.

**Compact disc**   A recording medium, introduced commercially in 1983, consisting of a 12 cm (4.72 inch) disc, made principally of plastic, coated with a reflective layer of microthin aluminum and a protective layer of lacquer. Also called a digital audiodisc (DAD) or a laser disc. The compact disc is 4 3/4 inches (12 cm.) in diameter, is recorded and played on one side only, and can yield up to 72 minutes of playing time per side. The sonic content consists of digitally encoded sets of numbers translated into minute pits that are etched into the reflective layer of the disc. The pits are read from the inside to the outside of the disc by a low-power laser light beam as the disc revolves at constant linear velocity at angular speeds ranging from 500 to 200 rpm. Best known as a recording medium for ultra high fidelity music. Often abbreviated as CD. (4:276; 20:51) See also CD-ROM; DIGITAL OPTICAL RECORDING; LASER DISC.

**Compatible** Indicates that a chemical or process has no adverse reaction with the various materials or chemicals found in books (e.g., the paper's CELLULOSE, SIZING, FILLERs, pigments, inks, glues, labels, covers, etc., are compatible). (55:107)

**Compressor** "(1) The part of the cooling system which compresses the REFRIGERANT to allow it to move heat from the EVAPORATOR to the CONDENSER; (2) The part of the pneumatic control system for HVAC systems which provides the compressed air for pneumatic operation." (30:76)

**Computer-output microform (COM)** MICROFORMs containing information produced by a projection/exposure device from computer readable data, either ANALOG or digital. (42:189) See also MICROFICHE.

**Concealed joint** See INVISIBLE JOINT.

**Concertina fold** A method of folding paper, first to the right and then to the left, so that it opens and closes in the manner of a concertina. Also called accordion or zigzag fold.

**Condensate** Vapor condensing to a liquid either as the result of steam giving up its heat (such as in a radiator or heating coil) or humid air blowing past a cooling coil causing some of the air's moisture to condense on the coil. (30:76)

**Condensate drain** "Piping which allows cooling coil CONDENSATE (the result of dehumidification) to safely drain to sanitary or storm drains, or to simply be discharged to the outside." (30:76)

**Condensate return** "Piping which returns steam CONDENSATE to the boiler for reheating back to steam." (30:76)

**Condenser** "The part of a cooling system which rejects heat, usually to the outside." (30:76)

**Condenser water** "Water which is used to reject heat from a cooling system; it is usually pumped to a cooling tower where it is cooled." (30:76)

**Condensing lens** A LENS or lens system capable of gathering light and focusing it on the APERTURE of a microfilm READER.

**Condensite** See BAKELITE.

**Conditioning** Placing a material in a special environment in order to put it in a proper state for work or use; for example, when bringing a book from cold storage into a normal working temperature.

**Conductive coatings**   In magnetic tape recording, COATINGs that are specially treated to reduce the COATING RESISTANCE and thus prevent the accumulation of static electrical charge. (49:150)

**Confidence coefficient**   In statistics, the probability level associated with the INTERVAL, generally .95, which indicates that if the sampling process were repeated an infinite number of times, the POPULATION would be expected to fall within the interval 95 percent of the time, and 95 percent of the time the SAMPLE MEAN would be expected to fall within the interval constructed. (7:107) See CONFIDENCE INTERVAL.

**Confidence interval**   In statistics, a RANGE of values that it is expected will contain the value of a quantitative characteristic of a POPULATION or PARAMETER. (1:55) That is, a point above and a point below the SAMPLE MEAN. In setting the limits, it is expected that repeated sample means will fall within them. The usual CONFIDENCE COEFFICIENT is .95, by which it is assumed that if the sampling were repeated an extremely large number of times, 95 times out of 100 the means would be expected to fall within the limits. (7:59) See also CONFIDENCE COEFFICIENT; CONFIDENCE LIMITS.

**Confidence limits**   The outer values of the CONFIDENCE INTERVAL. (7:108) See CONFIDENCE INTERVAL.

**Conifer**   A cone-bearing evergreen tree or shrub, such as a pine or fir. The wood is also termed softwood. See also DECIDUOUS.

**Conjugate leaves**   "The leaves of a SECTION which form one continuous piece of paper, i.e., leaves which are said to belong to one another. The form in which the sheet is imposed and folded determines which leaves are conjugate. In a sixteen-page section, for example, the first and sixteenth, second and fifteenth, etc. leaves will be conjugate." (47:64)

**Conservation**   "The treatment of library or ARCHIVAL materials, works of art, or museum objects to stabilize them chemically or strengthen them physically, sustaining their survival as long as possible in their original form." (22:14) See also PRESERVATION.

**Conservator**   "A specialist with advanced training in the arts and sciences related to the theoretical and practical aspects of CONSERVATION, who is able to prescribe and undertake various physical and chemical procedures and techniques in order to ensure the PRESERVATION of books, manuscripts, records, and other documents, and who adheres to ethical standards established by the profession. Book conservators have traditionally come from bookbinding backgrounds; but formal training in both book conservation and the more general paper conservation is now available." (1:56)

**Constant torque winding/spooling**   Winding on a REEL that has its tension controlled by the diameter of the tape being wound on the receiving reel. As the diameter increases, the tension on the next wrap decreases. This prevents the buildup of tension on the outer layers, especially of large reel-to-reel equipment. The difference between constant torque winding and constant tension winding is minimized on small reels but becomes much more important when using 10-inch or larger reels.

**Constant volume reheat system**    An HVAC system in which all environmental control zones are served by a single common cool air duct from a central air handling system. Each zone in the system is tempered by variable heating of the air as it is delivered to each zone. A hot water, steam, or electric "reheat box" is required for each zone. (30:76)

**Contact copy**    A dimensionally exact copy produced by exposure of raw film stock in contact with a NEGATIVE or POSITIVE MASTER or intermediate. Certain original material may also be contact printed. (1:57) See also CONTACT PRINT.

**Contact paper**    A relatively slow speed developing paper producing a reverse POLARITY image (a NEGATIVE from a POSITIVE and vice versa). (44:29)

**Contact print**    A dimensionally exact duplicate made by exposing raw film stock or photographic paper in direct contact with a NEGATIVE or POSITIVE. (46:153)

**Contamination**    (1) In magnetic tape recording, a thin, tacky (viscous) deposit on the head top surface. This deposit causes a large increase in the effective head-to-tape COEFFICIENT OF FRICTION and may not be removable by solvent cleaning. (49:150) See also TAPE-TO-HEAD SEPARATION CHANGES. (2) In photography, the in-advertent mixing of FIXER and DEVELOPER, causing a strong am-monia odor and adversely affecting film processed in the resulting solutions.

**Continuous-flow camera**    See ROTARY CAMERA.

**Continuous-tone image**    Any image with an uninterrupted range of tonal values; in monochrome film values from black to white. (44:29)

**Contrast**    The range of tonal values between the high and low BRIGHT-NESS areas of a subject or between the high and low DENSITY values of a photographic IMAGE. (42:189) See also DENSITY.

**Control strip**    Pieces of stable film exposed in a carefully calibrated sensitometric device. Processed control strips are used to monitor PRO-CESSOR performance in order to achieve predictable, repeatable results.

**Convectors**    "HVAC terminal equipment which heats a space by inducing convective air flows around its heating elements." (30:76)

**Conventional processing**    (1) For silver gelatin films conventional processing consists of developing, fixing, washing, and drying the exposed film. (2) Dry-silver films are processed with heat. (3) DIAZO FILMs are processed in ammonia, an alkaline environment. **(4)** VESICULAR FILMs are processed by heat. (21:6)

**Coordinate data**   In MICROFICHE, the horizontal and vertical positioning identifiers used to locate individual images.

**Copyboard**   A surface upon which materials to be filmed are placed. (42:190)

**Copy film**   Film used for making duplicates of photographic materials. FINE-GRAIN, CONTINUOUS-TONE film is acceptable for most duplication, but there are a variety of duplicating films to meet specific requirements. Film data sheets available from film manufacturers can assist in selection of alternatives to meet special needs. (46:153)

**Copy negative**   Frequently a second-generation NEGATIVE made for duplicating and/or enlargement purposes. (46:153) It is an exact DUPLICATE of a negative made via an optical system or CONTACT PRINTing using direct duplicating negative film or the INTERPOSITIVE method. See also INTERPOSITIVE.

**Copy print**   A print, either film or paper, made from a COPY NEGATIVE. (46:153)

**Cords**   "Pieces of hemp or LINEN twine around which SECTIONs are sewn. The ends of the cords are laced into the COVER BOARDS. Cords appear as the RAISED BANDS on the SPINE of a hand-bound book. Fake cords were frequently built into 19th century CASES." (38:214) See also TAPES.

**Core**   **(1)** The center portion of a REEL, spool, CARTRIDGE, MAGAZINE, or CASSETTE. **(2)** A cylinder without flanges around which film or paper is wound. (1:61) **(3)** The basic support or central layer of material in a LAMINATED DISC or CYLINDER. In ACETATE or LACQUER DISCs, for example, it can be metal, glass, or fiber. (4:277)

**Core-set**   The tendency for film, tape, etc., to remain curled after unwinding from a REEL or other cylindrical holder. (1:61)

**Corner rounder**   A device for rounding the corners of both paper and POLYESTER sheets. Used to remove the corner points of polyester used in ENCAPSULATION in order to avoid damage to materials during storage.

**Corner(s)**   The juncture of the two edges of a book cover at the FORE EDGE and HEAD and TAIL. (47:65)

**Corrugations**   Wrinkles across the middle of sheets of handmade paper caused by the paper being wetted during printing and not drying evenly thereafter.

**Cotton linters**   The short fibers adhering to cottonseed after the operation of ginning (seed removal and cleaning). Linters are used in the manufacture of cotton FIBER content paper and CELLULOSE derivatives, but the relative shortness of the fibers makes a paper less strong than that made from rag fiber.

**Couch** "(1) The operation of transferring or laying sheets of HAND-MADE PAPER from the MOLD to the FELTs for pressing. (2) To press the newly made sheets of paper on the felts. (3) To press a sheet on the wire of a CYLINDER papermaking machine and transfer it onto the felt for pressing and drying. (4) To press water from a sheet on a COUCH ROLL of a FOURDRINIER MACHINE, or extract water by means of a suction couch preparatory to transferring it to a felt." (47:67)

**Coucher** In hand papermaking, the person who lifts the newly formed sheets of HANDMADE PAPER from the MOLD in which they are formed and stacks them on the couch board. (47:67)

**Couch roll** A roll or cylinder on a papermaking machine that presses the newly formed WEB of paper from the WIRE, de-watering or COUCHing it as the paper transfers to the WET PRESS for further de-watering. (47:67)

**Counter** A device used to record specific occurrences; in a camera to record the number of exposures; in a reader to count the number of frames; etc.

**Coupler** A chemical compound used in DIAZO FILMs to combine with the unradiated DIAZONIUM SALTS to form the image.

**Cover** "The outer protective covering of the TEXT BLOCK. In a HARD COVER book, the cover extends past the edges of the pages. See also SQUARE. The cover of a PAPERBACK or PAMPHLET is usually made of heavier paper stock than the text block and is CUT FLUSH. (38:214) In EDITION and LIBRARY BINDING, the cover is called the CASE." (47:67) See also CASE.

**Coverage** (1) Often refers to INSURANCE or protection, but it can also mean a category of protection in an insurance policy. (54:51) "The guarantee against specific LOSSes provided under the terms of a policy of insurance." (13:118) (2) That portion of an original that can be imaged by a camera system at a given REDUCTION RATIO.

**Cover boards** "Rectangular pieces of MATBOARD, PRESSBOARD, or bookboard used in the construction of a COVER for a book or the outer cover of a PORTFOLIO or BOX." (38:214) See also BOARD.

**Covering material** Paper, leather, BOOK CLOTH, BUCKRAM, or synthetic book cloth used as an outer surface for hard cover books or protective boxes. (38:214) See also BOOK CLOTH; BUCKRAM; LEATHER.

**Cover paper** (1) Any of a wide variety of fairly heavy plain or embellished papers that are converted into COVERs for BOOKs, catalogs, brochures, PAMPHLETs, and the like. (2) A specific coated or uncoated grade made from CHEMICAL WOOD PULPs and/or cotton pulps in BASIS

WEIGHTs ranging from 40 to 130 pounds (20 x 26 x 500) and used as in (1) above. This grade is characterized by good folding qualities, printability, and durability. (15:118)

**Crack** **(1)** Commonly used defect term for AUDIODISC and CYLINDER recordings. It usually refers to a complete fissure through the entire recording visible on both sides and will cause noticeable distortion or faulty tracking in playback. A patina crack is a smaller fissure that does not penetrate through the recording but probably causes a break in the modulated groove. (4:277) **(2)** In magnetic tape recording, a narrow, deep break in the head surface material.

**Crackle** The distorted sound created usually because of a buildup of ELECTROSTATIC CHARGE on the surface of an AUDIODISC, but also because of dust or foreign material permanently embedded in the grooves on a disc, or on the surface of a tape. (4:277)

**Crash** **(1)** A coarse, open weave, heavily SIZED cotton material, sometimes napped on one side, and used in EDITION BINDING for LINING the SPINEs of books. It is not used in library and hand binding because it is too lightweight and flimsy. Also called gauze, MULL, and SUPER. See also MULL; SPINE LINING FABRIC; and SUPER. (47:68) **(2)** Failure, while performing read or write operations, of either a floppy DISK or hard drive; catastrophic for computer-controlled cameras.

**Crawford UV Monitor Type 760** A light monitor that measures the proportion of ULTRAVIOLET radiation to VISIBLE LIGHT coming from a light source. See UV MONITOR.

**Crazing** **(1)** The deformation of a LAMINATED DISC coating layer through cracking. Can be caused by loss of PLASTICIZERs, by excess heat and/or HUMIDITY, etc. (4:278) **(2)** When seen on film, identified as RETICULATION.

**Creep** **(1)** The physical deformation of AUDIODISC recordings due to continuous load pressure either from improper storage or from the force of gravity. It results in both SURFACE IMPRINT from packaging materials, which can impair fidelity by the deformation of the groove walls, and disc warpage. **(2)** In magnetic tape, time-dependent strain (such as curling or LONGITUDINAL CURVATURE) at constant stress causing tape deformation. Creep remains even after removal of tension. Caused by improper winding and storage. (4:278)

**Critical focus** The FOCUS point at which the RESOLUTION of a given lens is at its best (sharpest).

**CrO$_2$** See CHROMIUM DIOXIDE.

**Cropped** **(1)** A book so severely TRIMMED that the text has been cut into. See also SHAVED. (1:63) **(2)** A photographic image deliberately trimmed to create a second image that is only a portion of the original.

**Cropping**   The process of identifying a part of a NEGATIVE or photograph for duplication and/or enlargement while not altering the original image. Cropping marks and instructions are often written directly on prints; thus, original photographs or negatives should not be used for this purpose. (46:153)

**Cross direction**   The direction across (right angles to) the direction a MACHINE-MADE PAPER travels through a papermaking machine. The cross direction of paper usually has less strength and FOLDING ENDURANCE than the MACHINE DIRECTION. See also MACHINE DIRECTION. (47:69)

**Cross linking**   As used in the recording industry, the binding together of adjacent chain molecules in POLYVINYL CHLORIDE (VINYL) by primary valence bonds, which is manifested by embrittlement, warping, and cracking. Usually caused by exposure to ULTRAVIOLET LIGHT or to heat. (4:278)

**Crosstalk**   Magnetic or electrical coupling of signal from one track to another track in the read/write heads on a tape recorder.

**C/S**   See CENTER START DISC.

**Cupping**   See CURL.

**Curl**   Occurs when the outside edge of a magnetic tape or reel of film is longer than the center line. This condition usually develops because of high tension due to storage under poor temperature and HUMIDITY. These conditions can cause improper contact between the tape and the playback heads of the tape recorder leading to signal loss. It can also cause cracking or flaking of the COATING. Microfilm will be difficult to focus on a reader and difficult to duplicate or print. See also EDGE FLUTING.

**Curvature of field**   An ABERRATION of all lenses that causes the plane of the focus to be curved rather than flat. Therefore focus at the corner of an image will be slightly different from that at the center in a properly focused lens system.

**Cut**   (1) A BAND on an ANALOG RECORDING. (2) A GROOVE on a CYLINDER or analog recording. (52:28) See also LATERAL CUT; TRACK; VERTICAL CUT.

**Cut corner pamphlet file**   A free-standing type of BOX, the upper rear corners of which are cut away to half its height, leaving the upper half of the back and top open. It is generally used to house PAMPHLETs, unbound serials, and other such materials in the book stack. See also PRINCETON FILE. (47:71)

**Cut edges**   In binding, the three unbound edges of a book that have been smoothly trimmed with a GUILLOTINE. (1:65)

**Cut film**   Raw film stock cut to specified sizes. Often 105mm film is cut into sheets for use in sheetfed MICROFICHE cameras.

**Cut flush**   A book that has its COVER cut even with the edges of the TEXT BLOCK, so it has no SQUARES. Often described as having flush boards.

**Cut mark**   A mark, usually on roll MICROFICHE film (105mm), used to help guide cutting of the film into individual fiche.

**Cuts per inch**   The number of GROOVEs per inch on a CYLINDER or ANALOG RECORDING. The more cuts per inch, the longer the playing time. (52:28)

**Cutter**   A machine for cutting a WEB of paper into sheets of desired length. It is also called cross cutter or square cutter. (15:126) See GUILLOTINE. See also BOARD CUTTER.

**Cylinder**   (1) On a printing press, a roller carrying the printing plate or the paper. (2) In sound recording, the recording format invented and patented by Thomas Edison. Originally made of a sheet of tin foil wrapped around grooved brass (the signal was embossed into the foil), then wax, and later celluloid. Hollow, tube-shaped, with vertically modulated grooves containing recorded material on the outside surface. Playing time lasted from two to four minutes depending on the playback speed and threads or grooves per inch. See also AMBEROL CYLINDER; BLUE AMBEROL CYLINDER; CELLULOID CYLINDER; WAX CYLINDER. (3) In some reel-to-reel duplicators, the hollow glass tube through which exposure light passes and over which the film passes in order to be exposed.

**Cylinder machine**   (1) A papermaking machine commonly used for the production of fine MOLD-MADE PAPER. The cylinder machine was invented at the beginning of the 19th century. A partially suspended woven metal cylinder mold rotates in a VAT of PULP. A vacuum inside the cylinder hugs the pulp to the screen while sucking out the water, and on the downturn of the cylinder, it transfers the mat of FIBERs to a continuous FELT. (29:114) (2) A machine for playing audio CYLINDERs. See CYLINDER.

**Cylinder record; cylinder recording**   See CYLINDER.

# D

**AC**   See DIGITAL-TO-ANALOG CONVERTER.

**DAD**   Abbreviation for digital audiodisc. See COMPACT DISC.

**Daguerreotype**   The first practical photographic method, in which a photographic image is produced on a copper plate coated with a LIGHT-SENSITIVE layer of silver. The process was invented in 1833 by Louis Jacques Mande Daguerre (1789–1851). The earliest daguerreotypes were unique in that they could not be copied, but the process was superseded in the 1850s by a negative positive process by which an unlimited number of copies may be made.

**Dandy roll**   A cylinder of wire gauze that presses upon the wet PULP just before it leaves the WIRE cloth of the papermaking machine for the rollers. The weaving pattern of the wire of the dandy roll leaves an impression on the moist paper. If the impression is that of fine, even gauze, it is called WOVE PAPER; if the impression is that of parallel lines, it is called LAID PAPER. WATERMARKs are produced by working devices or monograms into the fine wire of the roll. See also WATERMARK.

**Darkroom**   A room in which all forms of light can be controlled in order to handle LIGHT-SENSITIVE materials.

**Darkroom filter**   A filter used to control the WAVELENGTHs of light transmitted by any ILLUMINATION that may be used.

**Darkroom loading**   Loading LIGHT-SENSITIVE materials into a CASSETTE or camera under darkroom conditions in order not to inadvertently expose or FOG the film.

**Dark stability**   A measure of the ability of a COLOR FILM to retain its color values when stored in dark conditions.

**DAT**   See DIGITAL AUDIOTAPE.

**Data density (bpi)**   The number of data characters stored per unit length of tape. (49:151)

**Daylight loading**   Descriptive of some slow-SPEED films that tolerate brief exposure to light without adverse effect. Most MICROFILMs are daylight-loading films.

**dB**   Abbreviation for DECIBEL. Also db. See DECIBEL.

**DBX**   A trademark noise-reduction system designed to eliminate hiss, a noise inherent in the analog tape recording process. (4:279)

**Deacidification (neutralization)**   The removal of ACID (or ALKALI) from a material, such as paper, which causes its pH to approach 7 (neutrality).

**Decibel**   The measuring unit of sound pressure and hence loudness (abbreviated as dB). The decibel is actually a numerical ratio between the sound pressure of a given sound and the sound pressure of a reference sound. Common decibel levels encountered vary from the rustling of grass (15 dB), to conversation (50 dB), to live rock groups (110 dB), to jet plane engines at close range (130 dB). (4:279)

**Deciduous**   A term applied to a tree that loses its leaves annually. Except for tamarack (or larch) and cypress, these are usually broadleaf or

HARDWOOD trees. Opposite of evergreen. (15:130) See also CONIFER; HARDWOOD.

**Deckle**  "In handmade papermaking, the removable, rectangular wooden frame that forms the raised edge to the WIRE cloth of the MOLD and holds the STOCK suspension on the wire. The frame that fits over the mold to prevent the PULP from running off during the dipping and sheet-forming process. The deckle edge is the uneven, feathered edge caused by the deckle frame in the production of HANDMADE PAPER. Originally, this edge was TRIMMED off, but now it is considered a sign of quality and is desirable." (29:114–115) "The deckle edge appears irregular and somewhat feathery; it is often produced artificially in MACHINE-MADE PAPER. On a paper machine, the deckle is the rubber apron or restraint that confines the pulp as it flows on the moving screen." (45:87)

**Deckle edge**  See DECKLE.

**Deductible**  In insurance, a specified initial dollar amount of coverage that the insured agrees to absorb. The insurance company agrees to be liable for any excess over that amount up to the insured amount.

**Defect**  In magnetic tape, an imperfection in the tape leading to a variation in OUTPUT or a DROPOUT. The most common defects take the form of surface projections consisting of oxide agglomerates, embedded foreign matter, and redeposited WEAR PRODUCTs. (49:151)

**Definition**  Overall clarity or crispness of IMAGE produced by lens and film. Distinctness of detail in a photo image, microform image, or enlargement. (17:170) See also RESOLUTION.

**Degauss**  To neutralize the magnetic field of a material (such as electrical equipment or magnetic tape, etc.) by means of electric coils that create a magnetic field cancelling that of the material.

**Degausser**  See BULK ERASER.

**Degaussing**  See DEMAGNETIZATION.

**Deionized water**  A substitute for distilled water in photographic processes. Conditioned with an ION exchange unit that removes both ANIONs (such as chlorine and sulfate) and CATIONs (such as calcium and magnesium).

**Deionizer**  Device using resins in an ION exchange process to remove impurities from water.

**Delamination**  **(1)** The loss of adhesion between layers of a laminated cylinder, disc, or tape, caused by poor fabrication, exposure to fungal attack, or extremes of temperature and humidity; e.g., the PEELING of the acetate layer on a LACQUER DISC. (4:280) **(2)** In photographic films, the separation of one or more layers of the film structure.

**Delta density**  The difference between the Dmin (MINIMUM DENSITY) and Dmax (MAXIMUM DENSITY) of a photographic image.

**Demagnetization**   "The erasure of magnetic tapes by neutralizing the oxide particles in the tape coating, achieved through a high frequency current passing through an ERASE HEAD over which the tape passes, or through the use of a BULK ERASER. Accidental demagnetization can occur when stray, external magnetic fields come into contact with the tape." (4:280)

**Dense**   A subjective evaluation of relative OPACITY, generally applied to film images or areas that are darker than normal. (17:170)

**Densitometer**   An instrument used to measure the optical DENSITY, or degree of blackness, of an image or FILM BASE by measuring the amount of light reflected or transmitted. (42:190) A microdensitometer is used to measure the density of very small areas of a photographic image. (23:402) A TRANSMISSION DENSITOMETER is used for PROCESSED FILM and a REFLECTANCE DENSITOMETER for paper materials. A reflectance densitometer is used to measure the density of an OPAQUE surface (print) before setting the camera and screen for halftone exposure. See also DENSITY (D).

**Densitometric method (silver)**   A procedure used to test for the presence of residual thiosulfate or other potentially harmful residual chemicals in PROCESSED FILMs. The hue of the yellow stain produced determines the relative concentration of thiosulfate remaining. (42:190)

**Density (D)**   **(1)** The ratio of the weight of a material to its volume, or the mass of the material per unit volume. Density is not a measure of POROSITY. (47:75) See also APPARENT DENSITY; POINTS PER POUND. **(2)** Measure of the ability of a photographic NEGATIVE or POSITIVE to transmit light (or of a photograph to reflect light); determined by the density of the silver grains. The dark areas in a photograph are densest; thus dark areas in a negative will transmit less light and the black areas in a print reflect less light. Density is the result of EXPOSURE of raw film stock to light and is usually expressed as the logarithm of OPACITY. (23:191; 46:154) See also CONTRAST; DENSITOMETER.

**Density, background**   See BACKGROUND DENSITY.

**Density change**   The amount of loss or gain in DENSITY as the result of a photographic process (duplication, PROCESSING, TONING, etc.) as measured with a DENSITOMETER, SPECTROPHOTOMETER or similar device. (8:153)

**Density identification area**   A recording at the beginning of the TAPE MARK to identify the method and density of recording. (49:151). See also MAGNETIC TAPE.

**Density, line**   See LINE DENSITY.

**Density, maximum**   See MAXIMUM DENSITY (*DMAX*).

**Density, minimum**   See MINIMUM DENSITY (*DMIN*).

**Density range**   See DELTA DENSITY.

**Depth of field**   The distance between the closest and farthest points from the LENS that remain in acceptable FOCUS at particular focus and APERTURE values.

**Depth of focus**   The optimum distance between lens and film that will produce a sharp image at a given APERTURE value.

**Desiccant**   A nonvolatile chemical compound that attracts and holds moisture from the air. It also releases moisture in the presence of dryer air. SILICA GEL is often used as a desiccant to control atmospheric moisture when documents, photographs, and other materials are in exhibit cases. The application of heat regenerates the moisture-absorbing quality of silica gel.

**Destratification**   "Reducing the natural tendency of air in a tall space to stratify into hot and cold layers, with hot at the top." (30:77)

**Destructive testing**   Any testing procedure that destroys that which is being tested.

**Developer**   Reagents that make LATENT IMAGEs visible. See also DEVELOPING.

**Developer streaks**   Regions of higher or lower than normal DENSITY caused by uneven exposure to DEVELOPER. Often caused by inadequate agitation.

**Developing**   The initial process of making LATENT IMAGEs on exposed PHOTOSENSITIVE materials visible. Developers are composed of a variety of substances, including chemical reagents, dry powders, water, and gas. Liquid DEVELOPERs, such as PQ developer, contain chemical agents for reducing the DENSITY of images on materials SENSITIZED with SILVER GELATIN. (1:72)

**Developing-out-paper (DOP)**   A SENSITIZED CONTACT PRINTing or ENLARGING PAPER that uses a chemical developing stage for producing the image. (44:29)

**Dew point**   The surface temperature at which moisture begins to condense on a surface, i.e., becomes liquid. Specifically, the temperature at which water vapor in the air at a given moisture content and pressure will reach saturation (100 percent relative humidity) and condense. The more humid the air, the higher the dew-point temperature. See also RELATIVE HUMIDITY.

**Diameters**   In photography, the number of times an arbitrary linear element of an image is reduced or enlarged. See also REDUCTION RATIO.

**Diaphragm**   A camera element that limits the APERTURE of a lens, or the field covered by the lens, or both, depending on its location in the camera system.

**Diazo film**    A print film or paper with layers of DIAZONIUM SALTS that, when exposed to a light that is strong in the blue to ultraviolet spectrum, forms an AZO DYE image. Diazo film maintains the POLARITY of the original film (i.e., a POSITIVE original image will be duplicated as a positive image and vice versa). (34:50) Some diazo films have MEDIUM-TERM STABILITY and have a usable life expectancy of at least ten years. Others, which conform to the ANSI IT9.5 *Imaging Media (Film)—Ammonia Processed Diazo Films—Specifications for Stability*, may last for at least 100 years when stored under the conditions specified in ANSI PH1.43 *Photography (Film)—Processed Safety Film—Storage*. (48:23)

**Diazonium salts**    Compounds that are LIGHT-SENSITIVE to the blue to ultraviolet spectrum. In the presence of a color COUPLER (e.g., blue or black) and an ammonia vapor or alkaline solution, they yield a visible image. (34:50) See also DIAZO FILM.

**Diazo print**    A diazo duplicate made on paper, cloth, or plastic base material.

**Diazo processor/duplicator**    A machine that exposes and processes diazo-sensitized materials through immersion in an atmosphere of concentrated ammonia. The procedure alkalizes (neutralizes) the acidic stabilizers in the diazo material.

**Diethyl zinc (DEZ)**    A volatile organometallic compound $(Zn(C_2H_5)_2)$ used to both neutralize and BUFFER paper by adding zinc oxide deposits. The Library of Congress developed a mass DEACIDIFICATION process using DEZ vapor to permeate books and react with all acids in the paper converting them to zinc salts. DEZ neutralizes the acid in the paper while forming zinc sulfate and reacts with the humidity of the paper to form zinc oxide as a base buffer substance. Ethane gas forms as a by-product. The treatment leaves paper with a pH of 7.0 to 7.5 and an ALKALINE RESERVE of 1.5 to 2.0 percent. It does not appear to have any adverse effect on books. DEZ is PYROPHORIC, meaning it will spontaneously ignite if it comes in contact with air. Therefore, the book treatment process must take place in an air-free environment within a vacuum chamber. In fact, the handling of DEZ is problematic because of its high instability and volatility. It not only ignites spontaneously in air, but reacts extremely violently with water, and decomposes at temperatures above 120°C. The mass deacidification process using DEZ basically consists of three steps (with approximately seventeen individual substeps): dehydration, permeation, and rehydration. Dehydration reduces the amount of water in the books to some predetermined amount based on the amount of zinc oxide that is desired. The books are dried in a vacuum chamber to a desired residual humidity content of approximately 0.5 percent of their weight, for a period of between twenty to thirty hours. Permeation exposes the books to gaseous DEZ over a period of six to eight hours. Rehydration soaks the books in water vapor to restore moisture to them. The process is marketed by the current license holder, Akzo Chemicals, Inc. (10:437; 53:5)

**Diffusers**   HVAC terminal equipment that introduces air into a space by mixing and spreading it without blowing it directly on people or objects. (30:77)

**Diffusion**   The scattering of light so that it appears to come from all directions rather than a single point. Overwhelming diffusion will preclude sharp images.

**Diffusion transfer process**   A process in which image-forming materials, such as silver salt or dye, move from one surface to another through a thin layer. A transfer process in which the NEGATIVE and POSITIVE images are formed at approximately the same time is termed a diffusion transfer reversal process. (1:73)

**Diffusion transfer reversal process**   See DIFFUSION TRANSFER PROCESS.

**Dig**   See GOUGE.

**Digester**   A cylindrical or spherical vessel in which PULPWOOD, straw, ESPARTO, rags, or other cellulosic materials are treated under elevated pressure with chemicals and heat to produce the PULP used in the manufacture of paper.

**Digital audiodisc**   See COMPACT DISC.

**Digital audiotape (DAT)**   A magnetic tape developed for digital recording and exhibiting high recording density. See DIGITAL SOUND RECORDING.

**Digital imagery**   Digitally encoding for computer storage and retrieval, through an optical scanning device, page images of books, documents, or other printed matter. Digitally stored information is retrievable at the page (image) level but not the character level; consequently, reformatting and quotation extraction, for example, are not possible at less than the page (or image) level. See also ASCII (NON-IMAGE) TEXT STORAGE.

**Digital optical recording (DOR)**   The digital recording process whereby digital data is stored on a disc surface as a series of tiny pits that can be detected by a focused laser beam for playback purposes. A digital optical recording is capable of storing both audio and visual material. Both DIGITAL AUDIOTAPE and digital optical discs employ similar encode/decode techniques. Their differences are in the manner and density of data storage and playback technology. See also COMPACT DISC; DIGITAL SOUND RECORDING; LASER DISC. (4:281)

**Digital sound recording.**   A sound recording made by the digital recording process whereby the signal corresponding to the original sound waves is stored in digital form, i.e., the intensity of the signal is sampled at close intervals of time and encoded as a sequence of binary pulses on the recording medium. Each measured sample is converted into a binary number, and the binary number stream is stored—most commonly on magnetic tape, although other digital storage devices may be used. For dissemination purposes, the number stream must be reconverted into analog sound. (4:281) See also COMPACT DISC; LASER DISC.

**Digital-to-analog converter (DAC)**   An electronic device used at the OUTPUT of digital audio equipment to convert digital numbers representing level and frequency information back to a continuously varying ANALOG electrical signal for playback. (4:281)

**Dimensional stability**   The ability of photographic materials to maintain their size and shape throughout PROCESSING and beyond in a variety of temperature and HUMIDITY conditions.

**DIN**   Deutsche Industrie Norm. A European FILM SPEED measurement in a logarithmic scale.

**Direct image film**   A duplicating film that, with conventional processing, retains the same POLARITY as the original or the previous film GENERATION, i.e., a NEGATIVE is generated from a negative and a POSITIVE from a positive. Sometimes called non-reversing film or direct duplicating film. See also IMAGE REVERSING FILM. (1:74)

**Direct positive**   (1) Unique photograph for which there is no NEGATIVE; image is laterally reversed but TONAL RANGE correctly approximates object photographed. A tintype is an example of a direct positive image. (46:154) (2) In microfilm, also called print film, the image is not laterally reversed, and the EMULSION side of the film image will   change with succeeding GENERATIONs. See also LATERAL REVERSAL.

**Direct recording**   A phrase used to mean recording live artists directly to disc without going through a magnetic tape recording process first. Recording of a live event directly onto a medium that will be used by the consumer.

**Direct-reversal film**   See REVERSAL FILM.

**Disc**   See AUDIODISC; CD-ROM; COMPACT DISC; VIDEODISC.

**Disc master**   See MATRIX.

**Disc number**   The publisher's number that appears on the label of AUDIODISCs. See also ALBUM NUMBER.

**Disk**   A flat round magnetic device for storing information and programs accessible by computer. A disk can be either a rigid platter (hard disk) or a sheet of flexible plastic (floppy disk). The disk base is coated with a magnetizable material on which data can be recorded and stored along concentric tracks as small magnetic areas forming patterns of binary digits or bits. Information is written onto the disk, and read from it in a disk drive, by read/write heads mounted on arms that move rapidly across the disk. Disks are available in several sizes, the most popular being the 3.5 inch and the 5.25 inch.

**Diskette**   See DISK.

**Dispersion**   **(1)** Distribution of the oxide particles within the BINDER of a magnetic tape. (49:151) **(2)** Distribution of SILVER HALIDE grains in the GELATIN layer of film.

**Dissolution of the emulsion**   See ALCOHOL SPOT-TEST.

**Distortion**   **(1)** Any difference in copying the original. **(2)** A lens ABERRA-TION that causes straight lines to appear curved, especially at the edge of an image. See also HARMONIC DISTORTION.

**Distribution copy**   See SERVICE COPY.

**Distributive control system (DCS)**   A computer system that monitors and helps to operate chemical processes. (55:107) Also known as a process control system.

**Divergence**   Light rays bent away from each other by use of a concave lens or convex mirror.

**Dmax**   See MAXIMUM DENSITY (*DMAX*).

**Dmin**   See MINIMUM DENSITY (*DMIN*).

**Doctor**   A cleaning scraper of wood, metal, or other stiff material installed along the entire length of a roll or cylinder in a papermaking machine to keep it free from paper, PULP, SIZE, etc. (15:142)

**Document case**   A container, commonly 15 x 10 x 3 inches but available in a variety of other sizes, for the flat filing of archives or manuscripts. See also ARCHIVES BOX/CONTAINER. (16:421)

**Dolby**   "Trademark for a noise reduction system used in some tape recordings in which passages in a higher frequency range with low volume are boosted in volume during recording, and reduced in volume during playback on specially equalized equipment, resulting in a reduction in tape hiss." (52:29)

**DOP**   See DEVELOPING-OUT-PAPER.

**DOR**   See DIGITAL OPTICAL RECORDING.

**Dot matrix**   An arrangement of points (ink or light) to form characters. Often used to form characters for header information on MICROFICHE.

**Double-coated tape**   "Tape that has adhesive on both sides. Because of its very good aging properties, Scotch Brand double-coated tape No. 415 is recommended for use in ENCAPSULATION." (28:25)

**Double decomposition**   "A chemical reaction that takes place between two compounds, in which the first and second parts of one compound unite with the second and first parts, respectively, of the other compound. One of the compounds is usually insoluble. The principle of double decomposition has been used in deacidifying paper, as, for example, when a soluble calcium or magnesium salt is dissolved in water and the paper is immersed in it. After the paper has been dried it is then impregnated with a soluble carbonate, such as that of ammonium or sodium. Sodium carbonate and calcium chloride, for example, react to form insoluble CALCIUM CARBONATE and soluble sodium chloride: $CaCl_2 + Na_2CO_3 \rightarrow CaCO_3 \downarrow + 2NaCl$; or, using calcium chloride and ammonium carbonate: $CaCl_2 + (NH_4)_2CO_3 \rightarrow CaCO_3 \downarrow + 2NH_4Cl$. The soluble sodium or ammonium chloride is removed by washing the paper with water, and it is important that the chloride be removed as completely as possible, as its presence in the paper is potentially harmful. The advantage of the double decomposition method is its simplicity, plus the fact that a much greater ALKALINE RESERVE can be deposited in the paper than is generally possible with most other methods." (47:79) See also DEACIDIFICATION.

**Double exposure**   An image created by two instances of RADIANT ENERGY striking SENSITIZED material.

**Double-fan adhesive binding**   ADHESIVE is applied to each side of the BINDING EDGE of a LEAF in an approximately 1/64 inch wide strip. During double fanning, the FORE EDGE of the TEXT BLOCK is clamped so the binding edge is free to fan leaf by leaf against a glue roller. When the text block is fanned in the opposite direction against the glue roller, adhesive is applied to the opposite side of the binding edge of each leaf. Thus each leaf of a double-fan adhesive bound volume may be opened to its innermost edges, facilitating easy reading and photocopying, unlike oversewn or side-sewn volumes. See also FAN ADHESIVE BINDING.

**Double fold**   See DOUBLE LEAF.

**Double leaf**   A double-size LEAF folded at the FORE EDGE or at the top edge of the book. The inner pages are not printed. Synonymous with double fold. (1:79)

**Downtime**   Any period during which equipment scheduled to operate does not do so.

**Drag**   **(1)** In magnetic tape recording, drag occurs when the tape contacts some element in the tape path (such as the head, tape guides, tape bearings, or column walls), causing a tension differential across the contact area. The differential is created by friction and forces on the edges of the tape. (49:151) **(2)** Similar conditions can occur in reel film duplicators and is called SLIPPAGE.

**Driers**   In a papermaking machine, a series of steam-heated metal cylinders or rollers, 30 to 60 inches in diameter, varying in number up to 130 or more, and arranged in two or more tiers. The wet paper or board dries as it passes over and under successive cylinders. (15:147) See also

FOURDRINIER MACHINE. **(2)** In film processors, the final section of the processor through which film passes and is exposed to a hot, dry air environment in order to remove the last traces of surface water prior to being wound onto the take-up REEL.

**Dropout**   Momentary loss of signal. Any tape-caused phenomenon that results in temporary or permanent loss or reduction of signal (sound) for a specified length of time. The most prominent cause of dropouts is surface CONTAMINATION, where a piece of OXIDE SHED or foreign particle adheres to the surface of the tape, causing the tape to lose contact with the tape head. (4:283) Can also occur on AUDIODISCs due to manufacturing and recording defects.

**Dropout count**   The number of DROPOUTs detected in a given length of magnetic tape. (49:151)

**Dry broke**   See BROKE.

**Dry-bulb temperature**   The temperature measured by a typical thermometer, as opposed to wet-bulb. See also WET-BULB TEMPERATURE.

**Dry end**   The drying section at the end of a papermaking machine consisting mainly of steam-heated DRIERS (cylinders), calenders, reels, and slitters, where the damp WEB of paper (containing about 70 percent of water) passes over the drum before it reaches the CALENDER rolls. (23:210)

**Dry mounting**   See MOUNTING.

**Dry-process diazo**   A process during which the diazo development takes place in the presence of a gas rather than a liquid or by action of chemical compounds carried in the film itself. See also DIAZO PRINT.

**Dry-process silver film**   SILVER FILM developed using heat and without GELATIN as the carrier for the silver. Used principally in laser-based COM recorders and available as a camera film only. Under average storage conditions, dry silver microfilms have a life expectancy of at least 25 years, but they do not have archival potential. (48:22)

**Dry silver microfilm**   See DRY-PROCESS SILVER FILM.

**Dual-duct system**   An HVAC system in which a central air handling system provides a set of common hot and cold ducts to serve the environmental control zones. Each zone is tempered by introducing a variable mixture of warm and cool air from the ducts through a "mixing box" for each zone. (30:77)

**Dual-track**   See HALF-TRACK.

**Dub; dubbing**   **(1)** A copy of a sound recording, e.g., a transfer of sound from a disc recording to magnetic tape. **(2)** Adding additional sound to an already recorded source and melding both into a single sound recording.

**Dull** "COATED PAPER whose surface has been left unpolished or has been otherwise treated to provide a non-reflective appearance for better readability or contrast with gloss inks." (9:14)

**Duplex** A microfilming process for recording the front and back of a document in side-by-side images in CINE MODE.

**Duplicate** (1) A copy of a MICROFORM made by CONTACT PRINTing or by optical means. (2) To make multiple copies of a document or microfilm, usually with the aid of a MASTER or intermediate. (42:190)

**Duplicate archive master** See PRESERVATION DUPLICATE.

**Duplicate negative** Exact replica of a NEGATIVE made via an optical system or CONTACT PRINTing using direct duplication negative film or the INTERPOSITIVE method. See COPY NEGATIVE; INTERPOSITIVE.

**Duplicate positive** A positive film copy made via an optical system or CONTACT PRINTing using print film.

**Duplicator** Any machine capable of producing copies of photographic material.

**Durable paper** See DURABILITY (OF PAPER).

**Durability (of magnetic tape)** Usually expressed as the number of passes that can be made before a significant degradation of OUTPUT occurs divided by the corresponding number that can be made using a REFERENCE TAPE. (49:151)

**Durability (of paper)** Durable paper is paper that has a high initial strength and resists wear and tear and is carefully produced from cotton fibers, rags, or a high-grade CHEMICAL WOOD PULP, as opposed to paper produced from a combination of chemical and MECHANICAL WOOD PULPs, which has relatively little initial strength. (22:14; 42:83) FOLDING ENDURANCE and TEARING RESISTANCE are not directly related to paper permanence—that is, its CHEMICAL STABILITY. They are included in the standard *Permanence of Paper for Printed Library Materials* (uncoated) ANSI Z.39.48-1984 (New York: American National Standards Institute, 1985) to ensure reasonable durability of the finished paper. (5) See also ELMENDORF TEST; PERMANENCE; PERMANENT PAPER; TEARING RESISTANCE.

**Dust bug** A well-known AUDIODISC cleaning product manufactured by Cecil Watts, Ltd., of England. It consists of a podium, a carrying arm, and two brushes (rolling and stationary) that track the disc during playback ahead of the stylus. (4:284)

**Dust jacket** A paper jacket folded around books for protective and advertising purposes. Also called book jacket, dust wrapper, jacket, jacket cover.

**Dust spot**   A film anomaly caused by dust between the film and the material being filmed.

**Dust wrapper**   See DUST JACKET.

**DX**   " 'Direct Expansion' cooling system, similar to a residential air conditioner, in which refrigerant is used to cool the air, and then reject the heat directly to the outside air; an intervening liquid is not used for cooling." (30:77)

**Dye back film**   Film having a light-absorbing coating in order to improve daylight loading and/or for ANTIHALATION purposes. See ANTIHALATION.

**Dye stability**   The ability of a COLOR FILM to retain its color values, whether in light or dark storage conditions. (8:153)

**Dynamic coefficient of friction ($U_d$)**   In magnetic tape recording, when the tape is loaded against a body by a normal force $f_N$ and is moving at a speed of over five inches per second, a force of $f_d$ is required to move the tape at steady speed; $u_d = f_d/f_N$. (49:151)

**Dynamic range**   The BANDWIDTH within which a satisfactory SIGNAL-TO-NOISE RATIO is obtained. See also RESOLUTION. (49:151)

**Dynamic skew**   In magnetic tape recording, the change in skew caused by tape motion. (49:151)

**Dynamic tape skew**   See TAPE SKEW.

# E

**cho (pre and post)**   An "echo" of a particular sound signal that, on an AUDIODISC, may appear in the groove before or after that which carries the playing signal. This is due to the gradual relaxation of molecular tensions that occurs after the record has been pressed, and causes plastic deformation of the groove walls. On tape it occurs one turn of the tape before or after normal signal, and is caused by PRINT THROUGH. See also PRINT THROUGH.

**Economy binding**   An inexpensive method for binding library materials. (1:82)

**EDAC**   Error detection and correction of recorded data using simultaneously recorded correction data either added to the data stream or recorded separately on an auxiliary track. (49:151)

**Edge flake**   Commonly used defect term for AUDIODISC or CYLINDER recordings. Refers to the PEELING or flaking of COATING material from the vertical edge of a disc or cylinder. Edge flake can occur more easily than surface flake and causes no damage to the sonic content of the recording. However, it is a signal that the remainder of the coating layer is in danger of deterioration. It is commonly abbreviated as EF. See also FLAKING. (4:284)

**Edge fluting**   (1) A rippling deformation along the edges of magnetic tape brought about because the edges of the tape are exposed to the environment while the center is not. It is similar to CURLing and can be created by heat or HUMIDITY, or by the tape rubbing unevenly against the containing REEL FLANGEs (sides) during playing, winding, or recording. (4:284) See also CURL. (2) In microfilm a rippling deformation caused by similar environmental exposure of the film edges that can lead to separation of the EMULSION from the FILM BASE.

**Edge fog**   Inadvertent exposure of the edges of an unprocessed reel of raw film stock. It may occur at any point from the time the original raw film container is opened until the film has passed through the DEVELOPER section of the PROCESSOR.

**Edgewave**   A phenomenon encountered in photographic materials when the edges have been exposed to and absorbed more moisture then the rest of the material.

**Edition binding**   Identical books bound in quantity, usually for a publisher or distributor, as opposed to binding done for an individual and LIBRARY BINDING. Edition binding usually involves the production of a type of binding known as CASE binding, generally in hard covers. PAPERBACK books and other books with flexible and semi-flexible covers are produced by adhesive binderies, although ADHESIVE BINDING is sometimes used in edition binding. See also CASE-BOUND; LIBRARY BINDING.

**EF**   See EDGE FLAKE.

**Effluent**   (1) Outflow of water from a PULP or paper mill. U.S. Government regulations restrict the impact of effluents on the receiving waters with respect to solids, oxygen demand, toxicity, and color. Mills control these factors by reusing or recycling water used for the various processes and by treating it in their own plants before discharge. (33:20) (2) In film processing, the spent liquids, some of which may pass through SILVER RECOVERY SYSTEMs and sometimes water purification units prior to discharge.

**Eight-track**   Division of a magnetic tape into eight recording CHANNELs along its length. See also FULL-TRACK; HALF-TRACK; QUARTER-TRACK.

**Electrical recording**   A sound recording method introduced in 1925 whereby sound vibrations are transformed into electrical impulses. The impulses activate a STYLUS that cuts the vibration patterns into a GROOVE on an ANALOG RECORDING. Also called electromechanical recording. (52:30) See also ACOUSTICAL RECORDING.

**Electromechanical recording**   See ELECTRICAL RECORDING.

**Electron**   A negatively charged subatomic particle capable of exposing photographic materials.

**Electronic hygrometer**   See HUMI-CHEK.

**Electronically reprocessed stereo**   "Sound recordings made from MONO-PHONIC MASTER TAPEs that have been electronically manipulated to simulate STEREOPHONIC (two-channel) sound. Also called electronic stereo, electronically enhanced for stereo, electronically rechanneled, simulated stereo." (52:30)

**Electrophotographic film**   A FILM BASE coated with a LIGHT-SENSI-TIVE photoconductor that maintains its sensitivity through repeated exposures and that, through electrostatic processing, permits the updating of MICROFILM and MICROFICHE by the addition of new micro-images and the overprinting of superseded images. (42:190) These characteristics preclude consideration of this film for archival purposes.

**Electrostatic charge**   **(1)** The buildup on tape or disc surfaces of electrical charges through friction, or the combination of heat and dryness, which results in STATIC distortion in playback. It also causes dust to be attracted to the disc surface, and if severe enough, can seriously interfere with the performance of the cartridge/pickup. (4:285) **(2)** Very common in high-speed film duplication. If not properly grounded, the built-up charge can arc, creating tree-like images on the processed film.

**Elmendorf test**   A standard test for measuring the internal resistance of paper to tearing action, named after its inventor, Armin Elmendorf. A piece of paper (or several thin pieces) is fixed between two clamps close together, one being fixed and the other attached to the lower end of a pendulum device. The specimen is slit so that only a known distance must still be torn to separate the piece into two. When the pendulum is released, the paper is torn between the fixed and the moveable clamp. The greater the resistance to tearing of the paper, the more the swing of the pendulum is impeded and brought to a standstill, which is indicated by a friction pointer. The pointer indicates a number on a scale, which is the measure of the TEARING RESISTANCE. The higher the number indicates the greater the paper's resistance to tearing. (29:47) See also TEAR FACTOR; TEARING RESISTANCE; TEAR RATIO.

**Emulsion**   Initially a liquid throughout which finely divided grains of a LIGHT-SENSITIVE material (such as SILVER HALIDEs) are dispersed and remain suspended without dissolving. For both PRINTs and NEGATIVEs, liquids commonly used as emulsions have been GELA-TIN, COLLODION, and ALBUMEN because of the ease with which these substances move between liquid and solid states in the presence or absence of water. (46:154) See also GELATIN EMULSION. (44:29)

**Emulsion layer** The coated layer of photographic materials that contains the image-forming LIGHT-SENSITIVE substances or photoconductors. (42:190)

**Emulsion numbers** Code numbers used by manufacturers to identify the production runs during which the film is made. Regardless of tight process control standards and control systems, every EMULSION is slightly different than any previous emulsion.

**Emulsion side** The side of a photographic material upon which the EMULSION is carried as opposed to the BASE side. In microfilm, the emulsion side is the dull side of the film.

**Emulsion speed** A quantitative value indicating how quickly the EMUL-SION will react to RADIANT ENERGY; a value used to establish proper EXPOSURE values.

**Encapsulation** "A form of PROTECTIVE ENCLOSURE for papers and other flat objects. It involves placing the item between two sheets of transparent POLYESTER film that are subsequently sealed around two, three or all edges. The object is thus physically supported and protected from the atmosphere and during handling. The object may continue to deteriorate, however, in the capsule. Because the object is not affixed to the polyester, it can be removed by cutting one or more edges of the polyester." (22:14–15) See also POLYESTER.

**Enclosure** Various types of protective containers constructed for temporary or permanent storage of fragile, valuable library materials and for photographic formats, fiche, REEL FILM, APERTURE CARDs, etc. See BOX; ENCAPSULATION; PHASED BOX; PORTFOLIO; SOLANDER BOX.

**Endleaf** See ENDPAPERS.

**Endpapers** "Blank leaves in the front and back of a book between its COVERs and TEXT BLOCK. In hand binding the basic purpose of the endpapers is to take up the strain of opening the covers of the book. In LIBRARY and EDITION BINDING, particularly the latter, the endpapers perform the crucial function of holding the text block in its covers, or CASE. Those which swing freely are known as flyleaves and those which are affixed to the inside of the boards are known as a PASTEDOWN or board sheets. Often, only the endpapers hold the book and case together. In library binding, the SPINE LINING material helps do this because it is much more substantial than that used in edition binding. The GRAIN or MACHINE DIRECTION of the endpapers should be parallel to the binding margin of the book; otherwise difficulty will be experienced in CASING-IN. When the grain of the paper is at right angles to the binding margin, the expansion of the paper is lengthwise, and, because one edge is secured to the text block (either sewn or tipped to it), that edge cannot expand; consequently the paper will buckle along it. If the book is cased and then pressed, these buckled areas will cause unsightly wrinkles on the board papers." (47:89–92)

**Endsheets**  See ENDPAPERS.

**Engine sizing**  "Hardening paper by adding a moisture-resistant substance such as casein, STARCH or resin to the PULP before the STUFF flows on the machine WIRE. This is the usual method of SIZING the cheaper papers and produces a weaker paper than TUB-SIZING." See also BEATER-SIZED; SIZING. (23:222)

**Enlargement**  A print that is larger than the NEGATIVE; made by projecting an image through a lens onto a light-sensitive photographic material (paper, film, glass, etc.). (46:154)

**Enlarging paper**  A fast-speed DEVELOPING paper giving a reverse POLARITY image (usually POSITIVE) when printed through an optical enlarger from a film image (usually NEGATIVE). (44:29)

**Enthalpy**  Total heat content of air; the sum of sensible and latent heat.

**Envelope**  A folded piece of chemically inert (and for preservation purposes also photographically inert) paper for holding MICROFICHE. See also BUILDING ENVELOPE.

**Environmental control zone**  "The space or group of spaces within a building with separate capabilities for tempering humidity control, which are served by the HVAC system; usually each zone has its own thermostat and humidistat." (30:81)

**Environmentally benign (safe)**  Process that does not release into the environment chemicals that have been shown to, or are suspected to, harm the environment. (53:4)

**EOT**  End-of-tape marker.

**EP**  Abbreviation for EXTENDED PLAY.

**Equalization**  In audio recording, modifying the amplitude/frequency response to produce flat overall characteristics, minimize noise, or give an "artistic effect." This is done by boosting the volume of treble tones and weakening the volume of bass tones; when played back on equipment with the proper regularization, the treble is reduced (and with it a certain amount of surface noise), and the bass is restored by electronic means. (4:285; 52:30) See also NAB.

**Erase head**  A device on a tape recorder used to obliterate any previous recording or magnetic field on the tape. It is activated when the tape recorder is in the record mode. (4:285) See also READ/WRITE ERASE HEAD; RECORD HEAD.

**Erasure**   A process by which a signal recorded on a tape is removed and the tape made ready for rerecording. Erasure may be accomplished in two ways: in AC erasure the tape is demagnetized by an alternating magnetic field that is reduced in AMPLITUDE from an initially high value; in DC erasure, the tape is saturated by applying a primarily unidirectional field. AC erasure may be accomplished by passing tape over an ERASE HEAD fed with high frequency AC or by placing the whole roll of tape in a decreasing AC field (BULK ERASURE). DC erasure may be accomplished by passing the tape over a head fed with DC or over a permanent magnet. Additional stages may be included in DC erasure to leave the tape in a more nearly unmagnetized condition. (49:151–152) See also BULK ERASER; DEMAGNETIZATION.

**Esparto**   "A coarse grass grown chiefly in Southern Spain and Northern Africa, containing short fibers which are usually extracted by alkaline PULPING processes. Esparto pulp is most often used in the production of book papers. Esparto is also known as alfa, esparto grass and Spanish grass." (44:165)

**Etching**   See FUNGAL ETCHING.

**Ethanol**   See Alcohol.

**Ethylene oxide**   "One of the most effective MOLD fumigants for library materials. It has been used as a fumigant in libraries, archives and museums since the early 1930s. It is, however, extremely toxic and carcinogenic; its use is regulated by the Occupational Safety and Health Administration (OSHA). It is seldom recommended or used any more for mold FUMIGATION in libraries and museums." (40:11)

**Evaluator**   Equipment, usually provided as an adjunct to a winder/ cleaner, that evaluates physical and magnetic quality of tape. In contrast to a CERTIFIER, an evaluator does not stop when it detects an error. (49:152)

**Evaporator**   "The part of a cooling system which absorbs heat and provides cooling; usually a coil which has air blown across it." (30:77)

**Even illumination**   Consistent light or radiation levels over the entire image area.

**Exclusions**   Defined exposures or perils designated as not covered under a specific insurance policy.

**Exhaustion**   An inactive state reached by processing solutions due to age or use.

**Expediting expense**   "Expense incurred in order to hasten repair or replacement of property to reduce the amount of LOSS. Expediting expenses generally are covered by a property INSURANCE policy if they do reduce the amount of the loss the insurer would otherwise have to pay." (13:170)

**Expiration date** The date assigned by a photographic material manufacturer beyond which its warranty for performance becomes invalid.

**Expose in sections** Making multiple images in order to capture the entire content of a document that is larger than the image area of the current camera setup. Often done to maintain a given REDUCTION RATIO or to capture documents larger than those allowed by the capability of the camera being used. (42:190)

**Exposure** **(1)** Allowing controlled RADIANT ENERGY to strike sensitive recording material. **(2)** The amount of time radiant energy is allowed to strike the recording material. **(3)** The image resulting from radiant energy on sensitized recording material. (42:191) **(4)** In insurance or RISK MANAGEMENT, the state of being subject to a loss from hazards or perils. (54:51)

**Exposure index** A value indicating the SPEED of a film. When used with a LIGHT METER, the proper exposure settings can be calculated. See also DIN.

**Exposure setting** Shutter speed and/or light value settings that will control the amount of RADIANT ENERGY reaching the film in order to achieve an optimum image.

**Extended play (EP)** A 45 rpm AUDIODISC with a playing time longer than the usual 5 1/3 minutes per side. (52:30)

**Extraneous light** "Uncontrolled illumination such as sunlight that affects the uniformity of illumination of the copy being photographed or the legibility of images in a microform reader." (21:11)

**Exudation** The process, or the product of the process, in which material is emitted or oozes from an object—usually applied to the decomposition (and its products) of disc or tape material. (4:286)

**Eye legible** In microfilming, a characteristic of those TARGETs that can be read without the aid of optical enlargement.

# F

**(book cloth)** See BOOK CLOTH.

**Fabric** See BOOK CLOTH.

**Facsimile** (1) A copy of an original, reproducing its exact form and style. (2) Electronically generated images (text or graphics) transmitted over telephone lines. Commonly referred to as FAX.

**Fade** A subjective characterization of the degree of loss of REFLEC-TANCE of a document, usually through degradation of the paper upon which it is printed.

**Fadeometer** "An ACCELERATED AGING device which exposes samples of colored materials or COATINGs to a carbon arc to determine their resistance to fading. The arc emits an intense ACTINIC LIGHT which in a matter of hours approximates the destructive effect of a much longer period of ordinary daylight. Although it does not exactly duplicate the effect of prolonged exposure to natural light, it is an effective indicator of the light stability that can be expected of the tested material, and of the comparative resistance to fading of a number of samples." (47:96) See also ACCELERATED AGING.

**Fading** A dimming or disappearance (i.e., loss in DENSITY) of the image of a PHOTOGRAPH or NEGATIVE. (44:29)

**Fair market value** "The price of similar pieces presently available; used to establish value in some property insurance policies." (25:94)

**Fan adhesive binding** A method of ADHESIVE BINDING. After TRIM-MING, the back edges of the leaves in a book are fanned to allow the application of a thin strip of ADHESIVE to the back margin. When the back edges are fanned first on one side and then the other for the application of adhesive, the method is called DOUBLE-FAN ADHESIVE BINDING. Each LEAF is joined to the ones on either side of it. This method should not be confused with PERFECT BINDING, in which adhesive is applied to the back edge rather than the back margin. (1:91) See also DOUBLE-FAN ADHESIVE BINDING.

**Fan-coil unit** An HVAC terminal device, usually part of a "two-pipe" or "four-pipe" HVAC system, which circulates the zone air over one or two water coils that can provide heating or cooling. The water is heated or cooled by a central boiler or chiller. In this type of system, each environmental control zone has a fan coil unit. (30:77)

**Fast** (1) High photographic SPEED. (2) Resistance to deterioration or change from external agents.

**Fast film** Films with a very high sensitivity to light.

**Fast wind** (1) The winding of magnetic tape at high speed, usually done to remove a partially played tape from a playback machine in faster time than simply letting it play out at a constant playback speed. This creates a tension in the tape that may cause deformation (i.e., stretching) that could be permanent if the tape is stored in this condition. (4:286) (2) In motorized microfilm readers, a faster wind or rewind speed, often allowing an overrun condition, allows the film surface to drag over glass FLATS, the film itself, or other reader parts, resulting in scratches on the film.

**FAX**   See FACSIMILE.

**fc**   See FOOTCANDLE.

**Feather edge**   See DECKLE EDGE.

**Feathering**   Spreading or bleeding of lines and photographic images.

**Feed spool**   The cylinder holding raw film stock in a camera.

**Felt**   **(1)** "A continuous belt on a papermaking machine, generally made of wool, but also as a combination of wool, cotton, asbestos, and synthetic fibers. Felts perform the function of mechanical conveyors or transmission belts, provide a cushion between the press rolls, and serve as a medium for the removal of water from the wet WEB." (47:99) **(2)** An absorbent material used in some FILM CLEANING machines to apply liquid film cleaner solutions. Can accumulate dust and particles of dirt from the cleaned film and produce film SCRATCHes.

**Felt side**   The top or smooth side of the sheet that has not been in contact with the WIRE during manufacture. The opposite of WIRE SIDE.

**Ferric oxide**   A form of iron oxide (rust) whose chemical formula is $FE_2O_3$. Also known as magnetite. The magnetic particles in most open REEL recording tapes are composed of finely ground and graded ferric oxide. (4:286)

**Ferrotype**   See FERROTYPING.

**Ferrotype plate**   A highly polished plate, often chromium plate on copper, used to produce GLOSSY PRINTs. (1:92)

**Ferrotyping**   **(1)** A change of surface characteristics of a photograph resulting in increased GLOSS. A glossy surface is produced on prints by pressure contact with a heated metal drum or an enameled steel plate. (8:153) **(2)** Glazing, or the appearance of shiny patches on the GELATIN surface of photographs. Brought about by contact with smooth surfaces, particularly plastic ENCLOSUREs or the cover glass in framed pictures, under conditions of high RELATIVE HUMIDITY. If photographs are stored in plastic enclosures under pressure (i.e., in a stack), ferrotyping can occur at moderate levels of relative humidity. (46:154)

**Fiber**   A thread-like body or filament many times longer than its diameter. Elongated, hollow cells comprising the structural units of woody plants. Paper PULPs are composed of fibers, usually of vegetable origin, but sometimes animal, mineral, or synthetic, for special types of papers. The fibers from coniferous trees are ribbon-like and have thin walls. The term "fiber," however, is botanically applicable to HARDWOODs only, while in softwoods such cells are properly called tracheids. (15:172, 455)

**Fiber board**   "PAPERBOARD made of laminated sheets of heavily pressed FIBER." (22:15) See also BOARD.

**Fiber content**   "A statement of the types and percentages of FIBERs used in the manufacture of a PAPER, BOARD, or CLOTH. Important because the quality of the fiber significantly affects both the DURABILITY and CHEMICAL STABILITY of the material." (22:15)

**Fibrillation**   During the beating process in pulp REFINING, the FIBER walls are bruised and roughened in order to create more surfaces for fiber-to-fiber bonding during sheet formation. (29:115) Also called brushing out or beating.

**Fiche**   See MICROFICHE.

**Field**   (1) The effective IMAGE AREA of the OPTICAL system of a camera. (2) A unit of data within a bibliographic record. (42:191)

**Field recording**   "A recording made 'in the field,' i.e., not in a studio, and usually on portable equipment. Common in ethnomusicological documentation and oral history." (52:30)

**File**   (1) A collection of records; an organized collection of information directed toward some purpose. (2) Data stored for later processing by a computer or computer-output microfilmer. (42:191)

**Filler**   A material, typically clay or CALCIUM CARBONATE, added to the FURNISH of paper mainly to increase the smoothness of the paper surface and make it a better printing surface. (33:20)

**Filler boards**   Additional layers of BOARD built into a MAT between the BACKBOARD and WINDOW BOARD that surround the artwork. These filler boards are equivalent in thickness to the artwork's highest point. (28:25)

**Filling (in papermaking)**   See LOADING.

**Filling (in production of book cloth)**   See WEFT.

**Film**   Sheets or REELs of transparent plastic base coated with a LIGHT-SENSITIVE EMULSION. See also DIAZO; POLYESTER; VESICULAR FILM. (42:191)

**Film advance**   (1) Movement of camera film through the exposing area in regular increments for each FRAME. (2) The amount of film so moved.

**Film backing**   See ANTIHALATION.

**Film base**   The material upon which photographic EMULSION is coated along with other COATINGs. It consists of a plastic material, such as CELLULOSE ACETATE or POLYESTER. (1:93)

**Film base density**   The degree of opacity contributed by a FILM BASE material. The measure does not include DENSITY produced by other layers such as the EMULSION, SUBBING, or protective layers added to prevent scratching. (1:93)

**Film channel**    A slot in a FILM JACKET designed to receive strips of film.

**Film cleaning**    A process to remove oils, dust, and foreign particles from photographic materials.

**Film coated**    "In papermaking, having a coating lighter in weight than that on conventional COATED PAPERs. An example is the application of a lightly pigmented STARCH at the SIZE press or CALENDER stack." (15:175)

**Film gate**    A camera design element that precisely positions film in the exposing position and prevents external light sources from reaching the raw film.

**Film insert**    A strip of film cut to fit into the FILM CHANNEL of a JACKET.

**Film jacket**    A transparent plastic sleeve into which individual FRAMEs or strips of microfilm may be inserted. Film that has been prepared in this manner is referred to as jacketed film. (1:94)

**Film plane**    See FOCAL PLANE.

**Film size**    Film width, generally expressed in millimeters, e.g., 16mm, 35mm, or 105mm.

**Film speed**    A relative indication of the sensitivity of a film to light.

**Film unit**    That part of a camera in which the film is accommodated.

**Filter**    Transparent material often placed between the object being filmed and the unexposed film to change the character of the light reaching the film and so enhance the resulting images. See also UV FILTER.

**Finder light**    A camera design element that projects on the COPYBOARD the exact imaging area of the camera.

**Fine grain**    Descriptive of films in which the silver grains are of small size thus allowing recording of small details with low granularity.

**Fine papers**    Paper used for printing, writing, and cultural purposes. (19:9) Sometimes defined as wood-free, white, uncoated printing and writing grades that contain no more than 25 percent MECHANICAL WOOD PULP in the FURNISH. (33:20) Not to be confused with PERMANENT PAPER.

**Fingerprint**    An anomaly in photographs that reproduce fingerprints created by improper handling of the film.

**Finish**    (1) The degree of brilliance, pliability, and working qualities of cloth, leather, or paper. (2) The visual surface properties of paper as determined by its surface contour, gloss, and general appearance. Uncoated printing papers have five major MACHINE FINISHes in order of decreasing degree of smoothness: English, MACHINE, VELLUM, eggshell, and ANTIQUE. (47:101–102)

**First-generation film** Synonymous with CAMERA MASTER, MASTER FILM, PRESERVATION MASTER NEGATIVE, and ORIGINAL FILM. See PRESERVATION MASTER NEGATIVE.

**First-generation image** The print or first reproduction of an object or document, a CAMERA MASTER. A copy made from the first-generation image is termed a second-generation image, etc. The term usually refers to images reproduced on film. (1:95)

**First lining** "The piece of MULL which is glued with a flexible glue to a book after it is sewn and NIPped; it extends to within $1/4$ inch from the HEAD and TAIL of the book and projects $1^1/4$ inch on either side for affixing to the ENDPAPERS to give strength and firmness to the book. A strip of brown paper, the full size of the SPINE, is then stuck over it; this is known as the SECOND LINING. The purpose of this lining is to give strength and firmness to the back of the book." (23:247) See also LINING.

**Fixed focus** Cameras in which the LENS OPENING and film plane are established in the manufacturing process and not alterable by the operator.

**Fixer** Also known as HYPO. Used in film processing to cause photographic materials to lose their sensitivity to light by dissolving the unexposed SILVER HALIDEs. The image will continue to darken if not properly fixed. (46:154) A commonly used fixer is SODIUM THIOSULFATE. See also RESIDUAL HYPO TEST.

**Fixing** The removal of undeveloped SILVER HALIDE crystals in the GELATIN layer from the film or photographic paper. Through the use of a FIXER solution, LIGHT-SENSITIVE crystals are dissolved in water and washed out of the GELATIN layer. This permanently fixes the image on the film NEGATIVE, POSITIVE, or PRINT and prevents further reaction with light. (42:191)

**Flaking** **(1)** In photography, the chipping or fracturing of the EMULSION from the support, particularly along the edges, leaving voids in the image. (44:30) **(2)** The loss of bonding or adhesion between the base and COATING of LAMINATED DISCs or magnetic tape, resulting in pieces of the coating breaking loose from the base. It is essentially the same as PEELING but more localized in effect. (4:287)

**Flange** See REEL FLANGE.

**Flare** Undesirable extraneous light that reaches photographic film during EXPOSURE. It does not form an image but lowers the CONTRAST of the desired image by fogging the film. Flare can be caused by reflection of light from dirty or scratched lenses, defective equipment, or light-colored clothing worn by a microfilm camera operator. (1:96)

**Flashing** Pieces of sheet metal or similar material used to cover and protect the joints or angles where a roof comes in contact with a wall or chimney.

**Flash target**   A visually distinctive TARGET that helps index the material on the film.

**Flat back**   "A TEXT BLOCK that has not been rounded and BACKED. Sometimes referred to as a square back." (26:14)

**Flat back binding**   A binding without the characteristic curved SPINE produced when the TEXT BLOCK is ROUNDED and BACKED. A flat spine encourages the text block to sag away from its cover. Also called square back. See also BACKING; ROUND BACK; ROUNDING.

**Flat bed camera**   See PLANETARY CAMERA.

**Flat finish**   A nonglossy photographic finish free of glare.

**Flat image**   An image that does not swell when spot-tested with water and that does not show relief between SHADOWs and HIGHLIGHTS. The opposite of a RELIEF IMAGE. See WATER SPOT-TEST.

**Flatness of image**   The nature of images produced by a camera lens that produces equal SHARPNESS over the entire IMAGE AREA.

**Flats**   A pair of matched pieces of glass that hold film flat in cameras, projectors, duplicators, readers, etc. (42:191)

**Flax**   "The BAST FIBER of the flax plant which has been the source of LINEN for several millennia. Linen rags, cuttings, threads, etc., have long been used in papermaking." (15:179)

**Flexible binding**   "A binding that allows the book to lie flat when open. This is largely achieved by using a FLEXIBLE SEWING and flexible glue." (23:250)

**Flexible sewing**   "Sewing a book on RAISED BANDS or CORDS, passing the thread entirely round all the bands which are then laced through the BOARDs. It is the strongest form of sewing. A style of binding which allows the book to lie flat when open." (23:250)

**Float**   An artwork so secured in a MAT that all the edges of the item can be seen through the WINDOW OPENING.

**Flotation**   A way of COATING photographic paper with either a sensitizing or EMULSION liquid by floating the piece of paper on the surface of the coating liquid. (8:153)

**Flow camera**   See ROTARY CAMERA.

**Flush binding**   A binding in which the COVERs do not project beyond the TEXT BLOCK. See also TRIMMING.

**Flush boards**   See CUT FLUSH; FLUSH BINDING; TRIMMING.

**Flutter**   In audio recording, inconsistent speed with variations over 15 Hz. See WOW.

**Flux** **(1)** In audio recording, lines of magnetic force or radiation. **(2)** In photography, the transfer rate of RADIANT ENERGY over a defined surface.

**Flyleaves** See FREE ENDPAPER.

**Foam** Aggregations of bubbles that can adversely affect photographic processing.

**Focal length** The distance between the FOCAL POINT and the lens when focused at infinity.

**Focal plane** The surface on which the transmitted image is at the sharpest FOCUS.

**Focal point** The point at which converging rays of light from a lens intersect.

**Focus** **(1)** The plane upon which an image being projected by a lens is at its sharpest. **(2)** To adjust a camera for a sharper image.

**Fog** Nonimage photographic DENSITY that can be caused by exposure to stray light during EXPOSURE, improperly compounded PROCESSING solutions, light leaks in CAMERA HEADs, or poorly stored or outdated photographic materials. (42:191) see also CHEMICAL FOG.

**Foil** See STAMPING FOIL.

**Fold endurance** See FOLDING ENDURANCE.

**Folder** See BONE FOLDER.

**Folder stock** A BOARD or BRISTOL used for the manufacture of folders for business filing.

**Folding endurance** The number of folds under specified conditions in a standard instrument that a paper will withstand before failure. (15:187) The tested specimen is repeatedly double-folded through a wide angle while under tension. A decline in folding endurance is the most sensitive indicator of AGING and deterioration of paper, and thus this is a very important indication of the DURABILITY of archival papers. (47:105)

**Foldings** A general term applied to printed sheets that have been folded to form SECTIONs. (47:106) See also LEAF; SECTION.

**Folding strength** See FOLDING ENDURANCE.

**Foldout** A map, table, diagram, etc., mounted at the end of a volume on a GUARD the full size of the LEAF of the book, so that when opened out, it may be consulted easily as the book is read. (47:264) Also called a throwout.

**Folio** A SHEET in its full size folded once, producing two leaves or four pages. See also LEAF.

**Foot** The bottom edge of a book or page. Also referred to as TAIL.

**Footcandle (fc)**   A common unit of light measurement. A footcandle is the density of light striking an object. One footcandle equals the ILLUMINA-TION produced when a light point source of one candle falls on a surface one foot away from the candle. It is the equivalent of about 11 LUX, or one LUMEN per square foot. Full sunlight with the sun in the zenith is approximately 10,000 footcandles on a horizontal surface. (31:8) See also CANDELA; LUMEN.

**Fore edge**   The front edge of a book; the side opposite the SPINE.

**Fore-edge painting**   A picture, painted on the fore edges of a book, that can be best seen when the pages are splayed out. "A double fore edge has two paintings, which can be seen singly by fanning the leaves first one way, and then the other. Gold is usually applied after the paintings have been done." (23:256)

**Formalin**   A solution of formaldehyde in water, 37 to 50 percent by volume. Should never be used as a FUNGICIDE on artifacts and is highly toxic.

**Format**   **(1)** Arrangement of images. **(2)** Medium in which a document exists, paper, film, etc.

**45 rpm audiodisc**   An ANALOG RECORDING, usually 7 inches (18 cm) in diameter, to be played at 45 revolutions per minute, and with a usual playing time of 5 1/3 minutes per side. (52:30)

**Forwarding**   "The processes or steps involved in BINDING a book. Variously defined as: (1) all of the binding processes following GATHERING, including covering; (2) the processes following sewing and up to covering; or (3) the processes following SEWING and including covering. In EDITION BINDING, the term SHEETWORK is usually used in lieu of forwarding." (47:108)

**Four-channel**   See QUADRAPHONIC; QUARTER-TRACK.

**Fourdrinier machine**   A papermaking machine invented by the Frenchman Nicholas Louis Robert in 1798, developed in England by Brian Donkin for Henry and Sealy Fourdrinier, but not placed into operation until 1804. The fourdrinier machine may have four sections: WET END, PRESS section, DRIER section, and CALENDER section (not all fourdriniers, however, have a calender section). "In the wet end the PULP or STOCK . . . flows from a HEADBOX through a SLICE onto a moving endless belt of wire cloth, called the FOURDRINIER WIRE or wire, of brass, bronze, stainless steel, or plastic. The wire runs over a BREAST ROLL under or adjacent to the headbox, over a series of tube or table rolls or more recently drainage blades which maintain the working surface of the wire in a plane and aid water removal. The tubes or rolls create a vacuum on the downstream side of the NIP. Similarly, the drainage blades create a vacuum on the downstream side where the wire leaves the blade surface, but also performs the function of a DOCTOR blade on the upstream side. The wire then passes over a series of SUCTION BOXes, over the bottom COUCH ROLL (or suction couch roll) which drives the wire and then down and back over various guide rolls and a stretch roll to the breast roll. The second section, the press section, usually consists of two or more presses, the function of which is to mechanically remove further excess water from the sheet and to equalize the surface characteristics of the FELT and WIRE SIDEs of the sheet. The wet WEB of paper, which is transferred from the wire to the felt at the couch roll, is carried through the presses on the felts, the texture and character of the felts varying according to the grade of paper being made. The third section, the drier section, consists of two or more tiers of driers. These driers are steam-heated cylinders, and the paper is held close to the driers by means of fabric drier felts. As the paper passes from one drier to the next, first the felt side and then the wire side comes in contact with the heated surface of the drier. As the paper enters the drier train approximately one-third dry, the bulk of the water is evaporated in this section. Moisture removal may be facilitated by blowing hot air on to the sheet between the driers in order to carry away the water vapor. Within the drier section and at a point at least 50 percent along the drying curve, a breaker stack is sometimes used for imparting FINISH and to facilitate drying. This equipment is usually comprised of a pair of chilled iron and/or rubber surfaced rolls. There may also be a SIZE press located within the drier section, or more properly, at a point where the paper moisture content is approximately five percent. The fourth section of the machine is known as the calender section. It consists of from one to three calender stacks with a reel device for winding the paper into a roll as it leaves the paper machine. The purpose of the calender stacks is to finish the paper, i.e., the paper is smoothed and the desired finish, thickness or gloss is imparted to the sheet. Water, STARCH or other solutions, wax emulsions, etc., may be applied for additional finish. The reel winds the finished paper into a roll, which for further finishing either can be taken to a rewinder or, as in the case of some machines, the rewinder on the machine produces finished rolls directly from the machine reel." (15:190)

**Fourdrinier wire** An endless belt woven of metal or synthetic wires that forms the molding unit of the fourdrinier papermaking machine, carries the PULP from the breast box to the COUCHING ROLLs, and FELTs it into a sheet, or WEB, of paper. The mesh of the wire varies from fifty to ninety wires per inch according to the quality of paper made. WARP wires are in the MACHINE DIRECTION, while shute wires are in the cross-machine direction. Also called machine wire or WIRE. (23:662)

**Four-track** See QUARTER-TRACK.

**Foxed** See FOXING.

**Foxing**   Small, usually brownish spots appearing on paper; often attributed to action of FUNGI on trace metal (iron) in paper under humid
conditions. (45:88) Many questions about the actual source and development of foxing stains still remain to be answered.

**Frame**   (1) A SEWING FRAME. (2) A single photographic EXPOSURE,
consisting of the IMAGE AREA, frame MARGIN, and frame line. (42:191)
Sometimes called a shot.

**Free endpaper**   "That portion of an ENDPAPER which is not pasted down
to the cover but adhered to the end section of a book. Also called fly-leaf."
(23:260) See also ENDPAPERS.

**Freesheet**   Wood-free or GROUNDWOOD-FREE. Paper free of ME-
CHANICAL WOOD PULP.

**French joint**   "A free-swinging JOINT produced by setting the BOARD a
slight distance (approximately 1/8 to 1/4 inch, depending on the size of
the book) away from the BACKING SHOULDER. This type of joint
allows thicker covering material to be used, while still allowing the
covers to open easily. The French joint is one of the notable characteristics
of LIBRARY BINDING. Also called 'open joint.'" (47:110) See also
CLOSED JOINT.

**Frequency range**   A measure of the difference between the lower and
upper limits of a frequency group other than a frequency band, such as
audible frequency range, usually given in HERTZ. (1:102)

**Frequency response**   The variation of sensitivity with varying signal
frequencies. Usually, the frequency response of a tape is given in
DECIBELs relative to that of a referenced frequency OUTPUT level from
a REFERENCE TAPE.

**Frilling**   Separation or puckering of a photographic EMULSION from its
support. (44:30) Can be caused by excessive temperature, improper
compounding of the baths, poor adhesion qualities of the material,
improper hardening of the GELATIN, or the use of very soft wash water.
(42:191)

**Front edge**   See FORE EDGE.

**Front matter**   "The pages that precede the body of a book. It includes some
or all of the following: half title, frontispiece, title page, copyright page,
dedication, acknowledgments, preface or foreword, table of contents,
list of illustrations, and introduction. When printed as a separate SIGNA-
TURE or signatures, pagination is in lower case roman numerals. Same
as preliminary matter." (1:102)

**Full binding**   "A binding in which the covering material covers the back
and sides. Usually applied to a leather bound book. A book so bound is
described as 'full bound' or 'whole bound.' " See also HALF LEATHER;
QUARTER BINDING; THREE-QUARTER BINDING. (23:263)

**Full-track**   The full width of a magnetic tape in a single recording CHAN-NEL is used for MONOPHONIC recording. Sometimes called one-track, single-track. See also EIGHT-TRACK; HALF-TRACK; QUARTER-TRACK. (52:31)

**Fumigation**   The process of exposing records, archives, and manuscripts, usually in a vacuum or other airtight chamber, to poisonous gas or vapor to destroy insects, MILDEW, or other forms of life that may endanger them. (16:423) Fumigation, while more or less effective, does not confer lasting protection; therefore it may be necessary to also fumigate the areas in which the materials are stored. See also FUNGI. (47:111)

**Fungal etching**   (1) The degradation or scarring of the BASE material in a disc or tape as a result of enzymes and acids excreted by FUNGI during attack on the additives in the COATING. (2) Surface etching on discs or tapes resulting from excretions of fungi growing on the packaging that is in contact with the recordings. (4:287)

**Fungi**   A major group of the lower plants including saprophytic and parasitic plants which lack chlorophyll. A large number of the spores of fungi are always present in the atmosphere, and while paper is not a particularly suitable medium to support the growth of MOLDs and fungi, under favorable conditions, such as relatively high temperature and high RELATIVE HUMIDITY, paper will support the growth of these microorganisms, some of which have a similar action on paper to that of dry rot fungus on wood. (47:111) See also FOXING; MILDEW.

**Fungicide**   "A substance that can kill or prevent the growth of FUNGI. Many fungicides are highly chlorinated substances and cannot be washed out if protection is to last. Considerable care must be exercised when they are used in or near paper. While stable enough for most normal uses, the typical fungicide may not be sufficiently stable when it is to remain in paper for decades, even centuries, as paper almost always contains impurities, e.g., iron, which may accelerate the normal slow breakdown of a fungicide. In the usual case, the product of this breakdown is hydrochloric acid (HCl), minute amounts of which are capable of de-stroying any normal paper; therefore, before using any chlorinated organic fungicide, it must be determined whether or not it is stable in the presence of traces of iron, copper, manganese, etc., and, at the same time sufficiently effective to be of practical value when used in low concentra-tions, e.g., 0.1 percent of the weight of the paper." (47:111–112) See also ORTHO-PHENYL PHENOL (OPP); THYMOL.

**Fungistat**   An agent or preparation inhibiting the growth of a fungus.

**Furnish**   The mixture of PULP, chemicals, and other materials such as SIZING, FILLERs, dyes, or other additives from which a particular paper is made.

# G

**amma ferric oxide (Fe$_2$O$_3$)**   See FERRIC OXIDE.

**Gampi**   One of the three plants that provide FIBERs for fine Japanese handmade papers. (Others are KOZO and MITSUMATA.) The paper is very durable, translucent, and nonabsorbent. It is frequently formed on a screen covered with silk cloth, and thus, does not have the CHAIN LINES distinguishable in other Japanese papers. (29:115) See also JAPANESE PAPER.

**Gas bells**   In photography, bubbles forcing the EMULSION to separate from the support; caused by strong chemical action and resulting in minute holes in the negative. (21:13) See also PINHOLE.

**Gas development**   Conversion of a LATENT IMAGE into a visible image in the presence of a gas vapor.

**Gathering**   **(1)** The process of collecting, and arranging in proper order for binding, the printed SHEETs or SECTIONs of a publication. **(2)** The group of leaves formed by folding and combining the one or more sheets or half sheets which make up a section (SIGNATURE). The sheet is the printer's unit, while the gathering is the binder's unit. (47:113–114)

**Gauffered; gauffering**   Decorations on the (usually) gilded edges of a book. Done by means of heated finishing tools or rolls which indent small repeating patterns. (47:114)

**Gelatin**   **(1)** A colorless, odorless albuminous material extracted from animal bones, hides, etc. It is used as a high-purity alternative for glue in paper COATING and SIZING. (15:196) **(2)** In photography, a COLLOIDAL protein is used as a medium to carry SILVER HALIDE crystals in suspension in EMULSIONs, as a protective layer over emulsions, as a carrier for dyes in filters, etc. (42:191)

**Gelatin emulsion**   A COATED, LIGHT-SENSITIVE layer on film, paper, or glass in which the medium is a natural protein COLLOID. (44:30) See also EMULSION.

**Gelatin print**   A COLLOTYPE.

**Gelatin process**   See COLLOTYPE.

**Generation**   One of the successive stages of photographic reproduction of an original or a MASTER. The first image of the document is called the first generation and is the CAMERA FILM. Copies made from the first are second generation, and copies made from the second are third generation, etc. (23:267)

**Generation loss** **(1)** In audio recording, any time an ANALOG RECORD-ING is re-recorded or copied, the degradation of signal from the first recording to the copy constitutes a generation loss. (4:287) **(2)** In photographic or xerographic reproduction, the loss of DENSITY and/or RESOLUTION with each succeeding generation.

**Generation, *n*th** "The number of photographic generations from the ORIGINAL or MASTER. For example, the second generation is a copy from a camera film or master." (21:13)

**Generation test** A method of testing the number of usable generations which can be produced. In microfilm, successive generations are produced until one is deemed not usable or legible.

**Ghost image** Unwanted multiple images due to reflections in the camera system or the FILM BASE.

**Gigahertz** One billion HERTZ.

**Glass support** A FILM BASE upon which POSITIVE or NEGATIVE EMULSIONs are coated. (44:30)

**Glassine** A translucent material often used to make ENVELOPEs and SLEEVEs for storing photographic NEGATIVEs for the short term. It is usually acidic and should not be used for archival storage purposes. (45:88)

**Gloss** COATED PAPER that has been SUPERCALENDERed (polished) for smoothness. Shiny in appearance. (9:14) Also, a typical characteristic of highly reflective photographic prints.

**Glossy print** A photographic PRINT with a hard, highly reflective surface created by drying on a FERROTYPE PLATE or similar hard surface. See also FERROTYPE. (1:106)

**Glue** Protein-based ADHESIVEs made from animal hides and bones. Hide and bone glues make up the two major types of ANIMAL GLUE. Hide glue, which is the superior of the two, yields a fairly NEUTRAL pH in solution, usually in the range of 6.5 to 7.4, although wider variations are possible. Bone glue is generally acidic, having pH values of 5.8 to 6.3. Glue is much too brittle for use in bookbinding; therefore PLASTICIZERs are added to improve elasticity and resilience. Glue is susceptible to MOLD; consequently preservatives, such as ORTHO-PHENYL PHE-NOL, are sometimes added to prevent mold and bacterial growth. The term "glue" is sometimes used loosely in a general sense as synonymous with adhesive. (47:118) See also ADHESIVE.

**Gouge** Commonly used defect term for AUDIODISC and CYLINDER recordings. It is used interchangeably with dig and needle dig. (4:287) See also CHIP.

**Goyu**  A Japanese handmade paper, white in color and made from 90 percent KOZO. It is ACID-FREE, has CHAIN LINES, and is used for printing, printmaking, and for HINGEs in the mounting of paper objects. See also JAPANESE PAPER.

**Gradation**  In photographic materials, the rate of DENSITY CHANGEs in the image.

**Grain**  **(1)** The direction in which most of the FIBERs in a piece of paper are oriented. Grain is usually found only in MACHINE-MADE PAPERs, although it is also present in some handmade oriental papers. (28:25) See also AGAINST THE GRAIN; MACHINE DIRECTION; WITH THE GRAIN. **(2)** Individual LIGHT-SENSITIVE SILVER HALIDE particles in a NEGATIVE that are changed into black metallic silver by development. The grain becomes more apparent in a print when the negative is enlarged. Generally, the more sensitive (i.e., faster) films have more grain (larger particles) than less sensitive (i.e., slower) films (smaller particles). (46:154)

**Grain size**  Measure of the size of individual silver particles in photographic material.

**Graininess**  A characteristic of processed photographic film or prints resulting from an uneven distribution of the grains that make up the image. The defect, most apparent in ENLARGEMENTs, may appear as a pattern of small dots or uneven color distribution. Graininess is a subjective property, as perceived by the viewer. An objective assessment of graininess is termed granularity. (1:107)

**Grammage**  Generally the metric equivalent BASIS WEIGHTs of paper or paperboard expressed in grams per square meter instead of pounds per REAM.

**Gramophone disc; Gramophone record(ing)**  See AUDIODISC.

**Gray scale**  A group of contiguous neutral density areas ranging in predetermined steps from black to white and used to expose film to establish its sensitometric curve. Synonymous with "gray wedge" and "step tablet." (21:14)

**Green tape**  In magnetic tape recording, an abrasive tape used to clean and lap heads that are unevenly worn, stained, scratched, etc. It should be used with caution and should not be used on ferrite heads. (49:155)

**Greying**  Commonly used defect term for AUDIODISC recordings. It indicates widespread needle wear which results in a discoloration or "greying" of a part or all of the playing area surface of the disc. It usually means that the disc has been extensively played, or that it has been played with too heavy a stylus tracking weight. Sometimes called steeling. (4:288)

**Grid area**   The main part of a MICROFICHE, defining the space in which images will be arranged, usually in a standardized array.

**Grid gauge**   A device to determine if images on a MICROFICHE are at their defined grid positions.

**Grid pattern**   The horizontal and vertical lines on a MICROFICHE, which divide the IMAGE AREA into a standard array.

**Grinder**   A rotating pulpstone against which logs are pressed and reduced to PULP. A method of producing MECHANICAL WOOD PULP or groundwood.

**Groove**   The spiral path cut or embossed by a STYLUS on a CYLINDER or ANALOG RECORDING. Also called a CUT. See also LATERAL CUT; VERTICAL CUT. (52:31)

**Gross density**   The DENSITY of the entire film structure, including all coated layers and the base.

**Groundwood**   See GROUNDWOOD PULP.

**Groundwood-free**   Paper containing less than 5 percent MECHANICAL WOOD PULP by microscopic staining techniques is considered groundwood-free. (15:204)

**Groundwood pulp**   "MECHANICAL WOOD PULP (stone groundwood, refiner mechanical pulp, thermomechanical pulp), having a yield of over 90 percent and thus containing a great deal of LIGNIN. By extension the term sometimes refers to chemi-mechanical and SEMI-CHEMICAL PULP, which have yields of 50–90 percent." (33:20) It is "produced by pressing a barked log against a pulpstone and reducing the wood to a mass of relatively short FIBERs." (15:205) The process produces short CELLULOSE fibers and does not eliminate noncellulose ingredients such as lignin, and retains all of the impurities of wood. Groundwood pulp paper is weak, impermanent, and acidic, and deteriorates quickly upon exposure to light and air. NEWSPRINT is the most common example of groundwood pulp paper. (45:88)

**Guard**   **(1)** "A strip of cloth or paper pasted around or into a SECTION of a book so as to reinforce the paper and prevent the sewing thread from tearing through. . . ." **(2)** "A strip of cloth or paper on which an illustration, map, etc., may be attached and sewn through with the section, thus allowing free flexing."(47:124)

**Guarding**   "The operation of attaching a GUARD for the purpose of providing a hinge for a map, illustration, etc., to strengthen the fold between two CONJUGATE LEAVES, or to assist in relieving the strain of the ENDPAPER caused by the opening of the book." (47:125)

**Guillotine**   A machine used for squarely cutting large numbers of sheets of paper and BOARD, and also in LIBRARY BINDING for TRIMMING the edges of books.

**Gum Arabic**   A water-soluble gum employed in bichromated COLLOID photographic processes to form a RELIEF IMAGE. (44:30)

**Gum Tragacanth**   A gum obtained from Asiatic and Eastern European plants. It consists of bassorin and tragacanthin, and forms a gel in water. Gum tragacanth has been used extensively in the prepartion of MAR-BLING size. (47:126)

**Gutta-percha binding**   See CAOUTCHOUC BINDING.

**Gutter**   The adjoining INNER MARGINS of two facing pages of a book or document; the margins at the sewn fold of a SECTION.

**H**air hygrometer   An instrument for measuring the water content of the atmosphere. A hair, or bundle of hair fibers, will lengthen as the relative humidity (RH) increases and shorten as the RH decreases. This change in the length of the hair is transmitted to a pointer on a dial or to a recorder pen. A hair hygrometer is not as accurate as a PSYCHROM-ETER and should be calibrated every month (or every time it is moved) against a reliable psychrometer. Hair hygrometers are most accurate between 30 and 80 percent RH. (29) Most must also be REHYDRATEd on a regular basis, at least annually. (30:79) See also HUMI-CHEK HY-GROMETER; HUMIDITY; HYGROMETER; PSYCHROMETER; SLING PSYCHROMETER.

**Hairline**   Any very fine lines (scratches) on processed photographic materials.

**Halation**   Uncontrolled reflection of light from the FILM BASE to the EMULSION, causing ghost images or FOG. The defect is usually avoided through the use of an ANTIHALATION undercoat in DYE-BACK film, such as AHU film. (1:108)

**Half binding**   A style of book cover in which the SPINE and the COR-NERS are traditionally of one material and the sides of another, e.g., HALF CLOTH, HALF LEATHER, etc. See also QUARTER BINDING.

**Half cloth**   A book with a cloth SPINE and sides usually of paper-covered BOARDs. Also called half LINEN.

**Half leather**   "A term used to describe a book with a leather SPINE and CORNERS, but with the rest of the sides covered in cloth." (23:279)

**Half linen**   See HALF CLOTH.

**Halfstuff**   PULP made by cooking, washing, defibering, and bleaching rags. After beating, it is called WHOLE STUFF or STUFF.

**Halftone**   A photomechanical process for reproducing CONTINUOUS-TONE photographs. The halftone process gives the appearance of blacks, whites, and grays by converting an image into a pattern of clearly defined dots of varying sizes. The process creates the illusion of tone GRADATION.

**Half-track**   The division of a magnetic tape along its length into two recording CHANNELs. Also called dual-track, two-track. See also EIGHT-TRACK; FULL-TRACK; QUARTER-TRACK. (52:31)

**Halide**   Any compound of chlorine, iodine, bromine, or fluorine and another element; known as halogens. The silver salts of these halogens are the LIGHT-SENSITIVE materials used in SILVER HALIDE EMULSIONs. (42:191)

**Halon**   A chemical gas compound used to extinguish fires by chemically suppressing the combustion process so long as an adequate concentration of the gas remains. Halon 1301, Bromotrifluoromethane ($CBrF_3$), is the least toxic of gaseous fire extinguishants, and the only one approved for spaces occupied by humans. It is the gas used in typical "Halon systems" and is nontoxic at usual working concentrations. Halon 1211, Bromochlorodifluoromethane ($CBrClF_2$), is a more toxic type of Halon used in hand-held fire extinguishers. Halon, commonly used as a generic term, is a trademark for fluorohalocarbons manufactured under license by Allied Chemical Company. The use of halon in fire suppression systems will eventually be phased out, however, because of its effect on the ozone layer. (30:78; 37:118)

**Hand-colored**   A local application of colored pigments or dyes to enhance a photographic POSITIVE, particularly portraits. (44:30) Also used as a technique to add color to black-and-white printed material, usually in limited editions.

**Handmade paper**   Paper made by hand MOLDs in single sheets, having rough or DECKLE edges on four sides. The mold is dipped into a VAT containing the STOCK and is lifted with a shaking movement, which causes the FIBERs to mix together and form the SHEET.

**Hand sewing**   SEWING by hand through the folds of SECTIONs of a book, using a SEWING FRAME. See also BENCH SEWING.

**Hand viewer**   Any number of small devices providing views of a photographic image, usually MICROFORMs or transparencies.

**Hardback**   A book published in stiff COVERs. Also called hard bound. The opposite of PAPERBACK.

**Hard bound**   See HARDBACK.

**Hard copy**   **(1)** A human-readable copy (usually on paper) produced from information that is not easily readable by human beings. **(2)** An enlarged copy of a microimage, usually EYE LEGIBLE.

**Hard cover**   See HARDBACK.

**Hardener**   Compounds used in film processing to harden the GELATIN of EMULSIONs and to raise its melting point. Hardeners make photographic material more resistant to scratches and prevent the emulsion from softening in warm processing baths. Commonly used compounds include aluminum potassium sulfate, chromium aluminum sulfate, and formaldehyde solution. (1:110)

**Hard water**   Water with concentrations of mineral salts. Not conducive for use in film processing systems without deionization.

**Hardwood**   "Wood obtained from a class of trees known as Angiosperms, such as birch, maple, oak, gum, eucalyptus, and poplar. These trees are characterized by broad leaves and are usually DECIDUOUS in the temperate zones." (15:213) See also DECIDUOUS.

**Harmonic distortion**   Distortion that occurs as a component of sound recording or reproducing equipment is saturated when a large signal is applied and new frequencies, which are some exact multiple of the frequency of the input signal, appear in the sound reproduction. Same as AMPLITUDE distortion. (1:110)

**Hazard**   This usually refers to a condition that may increase the chances for a LOSS. (54:51)

**Haze**   A photographic effect caused by scattered light from the FILM BASE or other source.

**HD³**   High-density digital data.

**Head**   **(1)** The top of a BOOK as it sits upright. (38:215) The top edge of a LEAF, BOARD, or bound volume, opposite from the surface on which the volume rests when it is shelved upright. (26:14) **(2)** The margin at the top of a PAGE. **(3)** The top of the SPINE of a book where the HEADBAND is placed. **(4)** In magnetic tape recording, see ERASE HEAD; RECORD HEAD; PLAYBACK HEAD. (4:288) See also FOOT.

**Head and tail**   The top and bottom edges of a BOOK.

**Headband**   An ornamental piece of colored silk or cloth attached to and projecting slightly above the head of the book at the SPINE. Originally, the headband consisted of a thong core, similar to the BANDS on which the book was sewn, around which the ends of the threads were twisted and then laced into the BOARDs of the book. In EDITION BINDING they are almost always manufactured separately and then attached, while in LIBRARY BINDING they have mostly been replaced by a length of cord around which the covering material is rolled at both HEAD and TAIL. (47:129)

**Headbox** "A large flow box on a FOURDRINIER papermaking machine. The FURNISH of dilute STOCK is pumped into the headbox and from there flows onto the WIRE where it is formed into the WEB of paper." (47:130)

**Headcap** "The leather covering at the HEAD and TAIL of the SPINE of a book, formed by turning the leather on the spine over the head and tail and shaping it." (47:130)

**Head contour** In a recording or playing device, the complex shape of the contacting surface of a head either as a result of manufacturer, head lapping, or wear. Usually refers to the wear pattern of the head over its useful life. (49:155)

**Header** See HEADING.

**Heading** Up to four lines of EYE LEGIBLE data placed at the top of MICROFICHE to identify its contents and place the fiche in a series of fiche. (42:191)

**Heads out** In magnetic tape recording, having the beginning of the program information (recorded content) at the head or outside of the REEL of tape or film ready for immediate playback or projection without the need to REWIND. (4:289)

**Head stick; sticktion; stick-slip** In magnetic tape recording, common words for a large increase in head-to-tape friction caused by (1) a sticky by-product exuded by the tape under certain conditions of tape age, temperature/humidity, and head-to-tape pressure, or (2) very smooth tapes coupled with large area heads. The medium usually vibrates against the head while the tape/disc is moving. (49:155)

**Head-to-tape contact** The degree to which the surface of the magnetic COATING of a tape approaches the surface of the record or reproduce heads during normal operation of a recorder. (49:155)

**Heartwood** The hard central portion of a tree root or branch, in which all cells have died although the tree is still living. It is usually darker colored than the surrounding sapwood. (15:214)

**Heat filter** Normally a glass filter used to eliminate heat without stopping the transmission of light rays. Used to reduce heat at the film plane in DUPLICATORs, some cameras, and READERs.

**Heat pump** "A reversible mechanical refrigeration device which can switch evaporator and condenser functions at will, allowing the device to do either heating or cooling." (30:78)

**Heat-set tissue** A lens tissue especially prepared for use in mending tears in paper, strengthening margins, and for laminating weak or badly torn leaves. The tissue is made of pure CELLULOSE consisting of more or less 100 percent RAG CONTENT, no COATING or additives, has a pH of 7.0, and is coated on one side with an acrylic resin. (47:130)

**Heat splice**   See SPLICE.

**Height (of a book)**   The longest dimension of a book as it sits upright on its TAIL. Synonymous with LENGTH.

**Heliotype**   See COLLOTYPE.

**Hemicelluloses**   CELLULOSE having a DP (degree of POLYMERIZA-TION) of 150 or less (i.e., smaller molecules with fewer "building blocks"). A collective term for beta and gamma cellulose, cellulose that is soluble in hot ALKALI. The contribution of hemicelluloses to development of initial strength in paper is well recognized. It is related to FIBRILLATION and bonding. But hemicellulose-rich pulps have a strong tendency to discolor during thermal aging. (33:20)

**HEPA**   High-efficiency particulate air filter.

**Hermetically sealed**   The airtight sealing of AUDIODISCs in protective envelopes or SLEEVEs, usually done in a controlled, dust-free environment. (4:289)

**Hertz (Hz)**   A unit of frequency equal to one cycle per second. Named for physicist Heinrich R. Hertz. See also GIGAHERTZ; KILOHERTZ.

**High contrast**   Photographic images in which light and dark areas are represented by extreme differences in DENSITY. (42:191)

**High fidelity**   "An imprecise term generally applied to recordings capable of reproducing a wide range of the original sounds with minimal distortion." (52:31)

**Highlights**   An area of a photographic image that is bright and which reproduces as a DENSE area on a NEGATIVE and as a light area on a POSITIVE. (44:30)

**High reduction**   REDUCTION RATIOs of 31x through 60x. See REDUC-TION RATIO.

**Hill-and-dale cut**   See VERTICAL CUT.

**Hinge**   **(1)** The part of the book identified by the groove along the front and back COVERs where they join the BACKSTRIP or SPINE, allowing the book to be opened easily. The hinge fits into the SHOULDERs after the TEXT BLOCK is rounded and BACKED. **(2)** The part of the SUPER that extends beyond the edges of the spine and is used to attach a book to its CASE. See also JOINT. **(3)** A paper STUB or GUARD attached to a loose PLATE, or the folded edge of a plate that allows it to be sewn into a binding along with the SECTIONs. **(4)** A flexible paper strip(s) used to attach an artwork to its MAT along one edge, allowing it to be lifted for inspection of its VERSO. **(5)** Material, usually gummed cloth tape, that joins the WINDOW BOARD to the BACKBOARD of a mat along one edge, thereby permitting the window board to be opened. (28:25; 38:215) See HINGE IN.

**Hinge in**   "To HINGE in a LEAF or group of leaves that are attached to one another, a paper or cloth strip is adhered along the BINDING EDGE of the leaf (or leaves) so that the strip extends beyond the binding edge. This assembly can then be hinged into a TEXT BLOCK by pasting up the part of the paper or cloth strip that extends beyond the leaf (or leaves), and adhering the strip to the binding edge of a leaf in the text block." (26:14) See HINGE.

**Hollander**   The original name given to the BEATER. (15:216) Invented in Holland about 1670, this machine pulps and refines rags or FIBERs for papermaking and replaced the stamping mill. The Hollander "consists of an oval VAT, partially divided in the middle. On one side, a cylinder fitted with blades rotates against a stationary base plate, also fitted with blades. The PULP is propelled around the vat, gradually being refined for the sheet forming process." (29:115) See also BEATER.

**Hollow**   **(1)** "The open space between the SPINE and the back of a hollow or loose-back book." (1:112) **(2)** The LINING attached to both the spine of the TEXT BLOCK and the inside of the spine of the covering material. The purpose of the hollow is to assist in the opening of the book and helping it to lie flat. (47:132–133)

**Hollow back (hollow back binding)**   "A binding in which there is a space between the SPINE of the TEXT BLOCK and the spine of the COVER, caused by the covering material being attached at the JOINTs and not glued to the spine of the text block. Sometimes a HOLLOW is glued to the text block and covering material; in LIBRARY BINDING, however, generally only an INLAY is glued to the covering material, while in EDITION BINDING there is usually no support of any kind. The advantages of the hollow back, which is used almost universally in library and edition binding, are: (1) the tooling or lettering on the spine will not flex or crack; (2) in hand binding, covering is less exacting; (3) in edition and library binding, the cover (CASE) can be made separately; (4) in hand binding, sewing is faster because it is on TAPES rather than CORDS; and (5) overall, it is a much more economical method than TIGHT BACK binding." (47:133)

**Hood**   Device on microfilm readers to reduce the amount of AMBIENT LIGHT striking the imaging area.

**Horizontal mode**   See COMIC MODE.

**Hosho**   A soft and lightweight Japanese handmade paper, white in color and made by the SULFITE process. Hosho is ACID-FREE, has narrow LAID LINES, and CHAIN LINES about one inch apart. It is used for printing and printmaking.

**Hosokawa Ohban**   A Japanese handmade sheet of 100 percent KOZO. Used as a backing or support sheet for maps, documents, etc., especially the larger pieces because it is slightly heavier than most Japanese papers.

**Hot-melt adhesives** "RESINOUS ADHESIVES which are liquid when hot and solid when cool. They are applied at temperatures between 350 to 400°F (175 to 205°C) and produce a bond almost immediately on contact with a cool surface such as the SPINE of a TEXT BLOCK. Hot-melts are used extensively for binding PAPERBACKs. They are not suitable for books that will be rounded and BACKED because the glue becomes stiff when cool. In addition to being relatively inflexible, hot-melt adhesives are not PERMANENT." (38:215) See also ADHESIVE BINDING.

**Hot spot** An area in a photographic PRINT with extraordinarily low DENSITY (high density on a NEGATIVE), usually the result of uneven illumination during creation of the image.

**hr** See HIGH REDUCTION.

**Hub** The cylindrical object at the center of a tape REEL, around which the tape is wound. NAB hub refers to a standard set by the National Association of Broadcasters for all 10 1/2 inch and 14 inch diameter reels of professional recording tape. (4:289)

**Humectant** A material like glycerine used with a retaining agent to absorb moisture. When added to a film structure, it helps eliminate film CURL and brittleness when the film is stored in arid conditions.

**Humi-Chek hygrometer and thermometer** An electronic HYGROM-ETER and thermometer sometimes used by archivists, librarians and museum curators. See also HYGROTHERMOGRAPH.

**Humidifier** A device to add moisture to rooms or materials.

**Humidistat** "A control 'thermostat' which senses relative humidity instead of temperature." (29:78)

**Humidity** The actual amount of water vapor present in the air. See ABSOLUTE HUMIDITY; RELATIVE HUMIDITY.

**HVAC** Heating, ventilating, and air conditioning system.

**Hydrogen-ion concentration** The concentration of hydrogen IONs ($H^+$) in an aqueous solution. It is a measure of active acidity or alkalinity, and is expressed as the number of moles (1.0078 gram) of $H^+$ per liter of solution. It may also be expressed in terms of pH. See also pH.

**Hydrolysis** A chemical action involving water; literally, "splitting apart with water." Hydrolysis is a reaction that takes place during deterioration of CELLULOSE, SIZING compounds, and other organic and inorganic materials. It is facilitated by heat, enzymes, catalysts, and low pH, and consists of the formation of new substances from parts of the original molecule when the OH from the water joins up with one part of the molecule and the H joins up with the other part. (33:20)

**Hydrolyze** Where a compound decomposes or splits into other compounds by taking up the elements of water.

**Hydrometer**   An instrument used for measuring the SPECIFIC GRAVITY of a liquid. Used to measure how accurately PROCESSING solutions have been mixed.

**Hydrophobic**   Having little or no affinity for water; inability to absorb water.

**Hygrometer**   An instrument used for measuring the RELATIVE HUMIDITY, or percentage of moisture saturation of the air. See also COBALT THIOCYANATE; HAIR HYGROMETER; HYGROTHERMOGRAPH; PSYCHROMETER; and SLING PSYCHROMETER.

**Hygroscopic**   Ability of a material to absorb or emit moisture in response to changes in the RELATIVE HUMIDITY.

**Hygrothermograph**   An instrument for continuously measuring and recording RELATIVE HUMIDITY (hygro-) and temperature (-thermo-) on a chart (-graph), usually using a HAIR HYGROMETER and bimetallic-strip thermometer, which cause ink pens to move on a paper chart. The chart is usually cylindrical or circular, rotating once each day, week, or month. Most human-hair hygrothermographs, which are the typical type of equipment used, must be rehydrated on a regular basis, at least annually. (30:78–79) See also HYGROMETER; PSYCHROMETER; SLING PSYCHROMETER.

**Hypo**   SODIUM or AMMONIUM THIOSULFATE used as FIXER in photographic PROCESSING. See FIXER. (46:154)

**Hypo clearing agent**   A sulfite BATH used to eliminate HYPO from film.

**Hypo test**   See DENSITOMETRIC METHOD (SILVER); METHYLENE BLUE; RESIDUAL HYPO TEST.

**Hz**   See HERTZ.

I dentification of permanent paper   "The standard for PERMANENT PAPER (*Permanence of Paper for Printed Library Materials* (uncoated) ANSI Z39.48—1984 (New York: American National Standards Institute, 1985.) suggests that a statement noting compliance with the American National Standard Z39.48—1984 appear on the VERSO of the title page of a book and in the masthead or copyright area for periodicals, with a logo consisting of a circle surrounding an infinity symbol." (5)

**Illuminance**   The measure of light available at a given point on a surface. See also LUMINANCE.

**Illumination**   Provision of RADIANT ENERGY for exposure purposes.

**Illumination level meter**   See LIGHT METER.

**Image**   Images created from radiation.

**Image area**   **(1)** The part of a recording area reserved for the images. **(2)** The area of a JACKET containing FILM CHANNELs for the storage of microfilm images. (42:192) **(3)** The area of an exposure bounded by the FRAME MARGIN.

**Image arrangement**   See IMAGE ORIENTATION.

**Image contrast**   See CONTRAST.

**Image color**   The predominant tone of an image of a monochrome ARTI-FACT. The colors range from cold blue-black to warm red-brown. (44:30)

**Image orientation**   The arrangement of images on microfilm with respect to the film edge. The orientation or mode is described as CINE or COMIC. See CINE MODE; COMIC MODE.

**Image Permanence Institute**   See IPI.

**Image reversing film**   A duplicating film which, with normal processing, reverses the POLARITY of the previous film GENERATION, i.e., a NEGATIVE is generated from a POSITIVE or a positive generated from a negative. See also DIRECT IMAGE FILM. (1:115)

**Image rotation**   The ability of microfilm readers to turn the projected images so that they can be read right side up.

**Image stability**   The ability of an image, color or black-and-white, recorded on a conventional photographic, magnetic, or electronic image recording medium, to maintain its originally captured characteristics, DENSITY, color fidelity, RESOLUTION, etc. (8:153)

**Impact strength**   A measure of the work required to break a test sample of tape or base film by subjecting it to a sudden stress. (49:155)

**Imposition**   A term which means "in position," and originated in letterpress printing. (47:137) Pages of type or images are arranged so that they will be in proper sequence for reading when the sheet is printed and folded. (1:115)

**Impregnated fabrics**   See BOOK CLOTH.

**Inches per second (ips)**   The measurement of the speed at which tape passes through a tape player. Tape speeds are all based on the early standard of 30 ips for coated tape. Successive improvements in tapes, heads, and other equipment have permitted reductions to 15 ips and 7 1/2 ips for professional tapes, and 3 3/4 ips and 1 7/8 ips for home use. (4:290)

**Incident light**   The light radiation which actually strikes an object. Distinct from the light reflected or absorbed by the object.

**Incunabula** "Books and all printing from moveable metal type which can be dated before the year 1501. The date limitation probably derives from the earliest known catalog of incunabula, an appendix to Johann Saubert's *Historia bibliothecae Noribergensis ... catalogus librorum proximis ab inventione annis usque ad a. Ch. 1500 editorum, 1643.* 'Incunabula' derives its name from the Latin *'cunae'* (cradle) and refers to books produced in the infancy of printing." (47:137) Sometimes called cradle books.

**Inert gas** Gas such as nitrogen, having few or no active properties.

**Information area** That part of a document page containing information or graphics exclusive of margins.

**Infrared light** The part of the red end of the spectrum that is invisible to the naked eye.

**Inherent vice** "The tendency of an object to deteriorate or destroy itself without external help; a peril usually excluded from property policies." (25:94)

**Inlay** A strip of stiff paper used to stiffen the SPINE area of the CASE of a LIBRARY BINDING. It is attached to the covering material between the COVER BOARDS and exactly corresponds to the width of the spine of the TEXT BLOCK. EDITION BINDINGs generally do not have inlays. (47:139)

**Inner margins** The inside, blank edges of book pages that are exposed when the book is opened. When the SECTIONs of a book are intact (UNTRIMMED), the inner margins are exposed to the fold, and the book, if bound properly, will lie open easily. A properly made ADHESIVE BINDING also exposes the entire inner margin without damage to the binding. When alternate methods of sewing, such as SIDE SEWING or OVERSEWING, intrude upon the inner margins, the book is hard to read, awkward to hold, and difficult to photocopy or to film without disbinding. The total inner margin on facing pages is sometimes called the GUTTER. See also OVERSEWING. (38:216)

**Inner sleeve** See SLEEVE.

**Insert** **(1)** Any matter slipped loose into a book, newspaper, or periodical that is not an integral part of the publication, such as an advertisement. Synonymous with loose insert and throw-in. (1:119) **(2)** Strips of cut microfilm to be placed in FILM CHANNELs of a JACKET.

**Inset** A SECTION placed within another section so that they may be sewn through the folds of both. The inset is usually four pages or multiples of four pages and may be placed in the center of the outer section, or on the outside, where it is wrapped around the main section. (47:140)

**Insurance** "The contractual relationship which exists when one party, for a consideration, agrees to reimburse another for loss caused by designated contingencies. The first party is called the insurer; the second, the insured; the contract, the insurance policy; the consideration, the PRE-MIUM; the property in question, the risk; the contingency in question, the HAZARD or peril." (54:46–47)

**Insurance agent** "Representative of the insurer in negotiating, servicing, or effecting insurance contracts; he or she may be an independent contractor or an employee." (54:47)

**Insurance broker** "An insurance broker ordinarily is a solicitor of insurance who does not represent insurance companies in a capacity as an agent but places orders for COVERAGE with companies designated by the insured or with companies of his or her own choosing. Broker is frequently incorrectly used to designate an agent of more than one insurance company." (54:47)

**Interblock gap** A section of tape separating blocks of information. (49:155)

**Interlayer transfer** Loose material, such as oxide, that is generated by tape wear or a HEAD STICK condition which is transferred from the oxide to the back of the tape or from the back side to the oxide when tape is wound on a REEL. (49:155)

**Interleaved** An extra leaf inserted between printed pages, or with GUARD plates.

**Intermediate negative** A DUPLICATE NEGATIVE prepared for production of additional negatives or POSITIVEs. Also called a PRINT or PRINTING MASTER. (42:192)

**Internal tearing resistance** The force in grams required to tear a single sheet of paper after the tear has been started. See ELMENDORF TEST.

**Internally sized** See BEATER-SIZED; ENGINE SIZING; VAT-SIZED.

**Internegative** Duplication of a PRINT in a two-step process. The initial copy is a NEGATIVE called an "internegative" and used to make a DUPLICATE NEGATIVE. (8:153)

**Interpositive** Duplication of a PRINT in a two-step process. The initial copy is a POSITIVE called an "interpositive" and used to make a DUPLICATE NEGATIVE. (8:153) The positive is made from a negative by CONTACT PRINTing or through an optical system (i.e., camera or enlarger). COPY NEGATIVEs can be made from the interpositive. See COPY NEGATIVE. (46:154)

**Interstitial space** "Literally the space between two other things, usually interstitial space in construction refers to the space between a dropped ceiling and the floor structure above." (30:78)

**Interval** In statistics, a level of measurement in which cases are assigned numbers according to the rules of both NOMINAL and ORDINAL levels of measurement. In addition, there is a unit of measurement; that is, the distance from 5 to 6 is the same as the distance from 8 to 9 in terms of the amount of the VARIABLE which is being measured. An arbitrary zero point also exists. Example: Individuals may be measured on the variable IQ scale. (7:109)

**Intrinsic flux**   In a uniformly magnetized sample of magnetic material, the product of the INTRINSIC FLUX DENSITY and the cross-sectional area. (49:157)

**Intrinsic flux density**   In a sample of magnetic material, for a given MAGNETIZING FIELD STRENGTH, the excess of the normal FLUX density over the flux density in vacuum. (49:157)

**Intrinsic value**   "Term used to define or describe the qualities of ARCHI-VAL materials. Records have varying degrees of intrinsic value based on such factors as uniqueness or value of informational content, age, physical format, artistic or aesthetic qualities, and scarcity. Determination of intrinsic value is closely linked to decisions regarding PRESERVATION and physical treatment [CONSERVATION]. Materials having high intrinsic value generally warrant preservation in their original format, while records designated as having little or no intrinsic value often can be copied [or converted to another medium] to preserve informational content." (45:88)

**Invisible joint**   A JOINT in which a cloth strip reinforcing the fold of the ENDPAPERS is glued next to the COVER BOARD and back of the book and is concealed by the PASTEDOWN endpaper.

**Ion**   An atom or molecule with an electrical charge.

**IPI**   Image Permanence Institute, located at the Rochester Institute of Technology, devoted to research on image preservation.

**ips**   Inches per second.

**Iron oxide**   See FERRIC OXIDE.

**ISBN**   International Standard Book Number. A four-part, ten-character code given a book (a nonserial literary publication) before publication as a means of identifying it concisely, uniquely, and unambiguously. The four parts of the ISBN are: group identifier (e.g., national, geographic, language, or other convenient group), publisher identifier, title identifier, and check digit. (42:192)

**ISSN**   International Standard Serial Number. A single eight-character code that identifies concisely, uniquely, and unambiguously a serial publication regardless of language or country of publication. It is always displayed as ISSN 1234-5678. The first seven digits are the title number and the eighth is a check digit.

**ISO**   The International Organization for Standardization. ISO is concerned with setting a variety of standards for library, information, and related fields.

J acket   A flat, transparent plastic carrier with single or multiple FILM CHANNELs designed to hold single or multiple microfilm images. (42:192) See also DUST JACKET; FILM JACKET; SLIPCASE.

**Jacket cover**   See DUST JACKET.

**Jacket loader**   A mechanical device for cutting microfilm and inserting the cut portions in FILM CHANNELs of a jacket.

**Jam**   "A defect in microfilm that appears as parts of documents followed by a dark streak on the film." (21:16)

**Jamming**   Disorganized and usually destructive wrinkling of film or paper caused by a defective film or paper transport system.

**Japanese paper**   A very thin, strong paper made in Japan from long-fibered stock, such as KOZO, the paper mulberry. It may be used for MENDING, for the overall lining of paper as reinforcement, for reinforcing the folds of SECTIONs, or for mending HINGEs. Known for its properties of flexibility, strength, and PERMANENCE. Papers used in CONSERVATION and bookbinding include GOYU, HOSHO, HOSOKAWA OHBAN, KAJI, KITAKATA, KIZUKISHI, MISU, OKAWARA, SEKISHU, SEKISHU KOZOGAMI MARE, SEKISHU KOZOGAMI TURU, SEKISHU TORINOKO GAMPI, TAKENAGA, and UDAGAMI. (38:216)

**Jig**   A pattern, template, or device used to maintain mechanically the correct positional relationship between a piece of work and a tool or between parts of work during assembly. In HAND SEWING, a jig is used to determine the placement of holes at the SEWING STATIONS. In microfilming, very simple tape jigs are used to position material for filming to ensure consistent placement within each FRAME.

**Jog**   The operation of producing a smooth-sided pile of SHEETs or SECTIONs by knocking or vibrating them against a smooth, flat surface, either by hand or by means of a mechanical device known as a jogger.

**Joint**   The grooves that run HEAD to TAIL on the outside of the CASE, front and back, adjacent to the SPINE, along which the boards HINGE when they open. See also FRENCH JOINT; HINGE.

**Jordan**   A PULP REFINER consisting of a conical plug rotating in a matching conical shell. The outside of the plug and the inside of the shell are fitted with cutting bars which macerate fibrous material in a water suspension that is passed between them.

# K

**aji**   An ACID-FREE handmade Japanese paper of 100 percent KOZO. It is lightweight and sturdy. Used for CONSERVATION, wood-cuts, and letterpress. See also JAPANESE PAPER.

**Kalvar**   See VESICULAR FILM.

**Kaolin**   "A whitish earthy material composed primarily of the clay min-eral kaolinite, a form of aluminum silicate. In refined form, kaolin is used in papermaking as a FILLER, COATING component and opacifying agent." (15:238) See also PAPER CLAY.

**Kerfs**   Shallow SAW-CUTS, about 1/32 inch deep, made between 1/4 and 1/2 inch from the HEAD and TAIL of the gathered SECTIONs of a TEXT BLOCK. The loops of the KETTLE STITCHes formed by the SEWING of the SECTION, or the CORDS, fit snugly into the kerfs and do not show as bumps under the leather of a TIGHT BACK BINDING.

**Kettle stitch**   The stitches closest to the HEAD AND TAIL of each SIGNA-TURE of a TEXT BLOCK; used to secure each SECTION or signature together. Kettle stitches lock the SEWING thread after each complete pass of the thread along the SPINE of the text block and link each signature to the one sewn on previously. (26:15) The term may be a corruption of "catch-up stitch," or "kettle stitch" (the stitch that forms a little chain). (47:146) See also LOCK STITCH.

**Key**   A binder's tool for securing the BANDS when SEWING.

**Key slot**   A milled opening in the flange of a film spool into which camera or reader rewind keys fit.

**kg**   Kilogram.

**kHz**   See KILOHERTZ.

**Kilohertz (kHz)**   1,000 HERTZ.

**Kinescope**   A motion picture produced from televised images.

**Kitakata**   An ACID-FREE paper handmade in Japan from MITSUMATA and SULFITE PULP. Buff in color and silky to the touch. Used for MENDING of older books and documents. See also JAPANESE PAPER.

**Kizukishi**   Japanese handmade paper, buff in color and silky to the touch, made from 100 percent KOZO, and ACID-FREE. Used for MENDING and bookbinding since its fibers are compact and can be torn into a strong web. See also JAPANESE PAPER.

**Kozo**   One of the three principal plants that yield FIBER for the production of Japanese paper. (Others are MITSUMATA and GAMPI.) The name is loosely applied to several plants of the mulberry family, which have fibers suitable for papermaking. In general, the long kozo fibers make it the strongest and most dimensionally stable of Japanese papers, and its absorbent surface makes it useful for printing and printmaking. (29:116) See also JAPANESE PAPER.

**Kraft paper**   A paper produced by a modified SULFATE process, using only WOOD PULP. The word KRAFT is derived from a German word meaning "strong." It is a relatively coarse paper known especially for its strength. Unbleached kraft paper is brown, but it can be produced in lighter shades of brown, cream tints, and white, by the use of semi-bleached or fully bleached SULFATE PULPs. (47:147) See SULFATE PULP.

**Kraft pulp**   See KRAFT PAPER and SULFATE PULP.

**Krylon™ No. 1301**   A crystal-clear ACRYLIC coating for strengthening worn and decayed leather. Sometimes used for consolidating the surface of powdery suede bindings because the water in the POTASSIUM LACTATE solution may darken and spot the suede. Leather bindings that are so powdery that the covering material cannot be restored by oiling alone can be sprayed with Krylon™. Also recommended for spraying bookplates to prevent acid transfer to the FLYLEAF. (24:24, 53) The spray propellant does not contain fluorocarbons or VINYL CHLORIDE.

**Krytox™**   An industrial lubricant made of fluorocarbons by Du Pont. Used in conjunction with other compounds to clean metallic media such as magnetic tapes.

**L**acing-in   "Attaching the boards to the TEXT BLOCK by passing the BANDS or CORDS on which the book is sewn through holes punched or cut into the boards. The bands are first frayed out and moistened with PASTE and then passed through the holes or slots. Lacing-in began to decline in the 19th century in favor of SPLIT BOARDS and the FRENCH JOINT." (47:148–149)

**Lacquer disc**   An ANALOG RECORDING disc usually made of metal (usually aluminum), glass, or fiber and coated with an acetate or CELLU-

LOSE NITRATE lacquer compound into which the grooves are cut. Intended for instantaneous recording. The lacquer MASTER was the original step in the record production procedure leading to final pressed recordings after the use of a wax master and until the use of direct metal mastering became prevalent. Sometimes referred to as an ACETATE DISC. (4:291)

**Laid lines**  Closely spaced parallel WATERMARK lines. Created by the LAID WIRES on a paper MOLD, which are perpendicular to and attached to the CHAIN LINES. Laid lines usually run parallel to the long side of a sheet of HANDMADE PAPER and across the GRAIN of MACHINE-MADE PAPER. (47:49) Laid lines are sometimes simulated on machine-made paper by the DANDY ROLL of the papermaking machine. (45:88) See also CHAIN LINES.

**Laid mold**  A MOLD in which the cover or sieve is made up of wires laid parallel to each other, in contradistinction to a woven mold formed of wire cloth. It is used in making handmade LAID PAPER. (15:244; 47:149)

**Laid paper**  "Paper which, when held up to the light, shows thick and thin lines at right angles. They are caused by the weave of the DANDY ROLL, or in hand-made paper by the MOLD having long thin wires placed very close together and fastened to thicker ones at intervals of about one inch." (23:350) See also WOVE PAPER.

**Laid wires**  The closely spaced wires of a paper MOLD or a laid DANDY ROLL. See LAID LINES.

**Laminate adhesion**  The sticking together of layers of a laminated recording achieved through the use of a BINDER. See also DELAMINATION. (4:291)

**Laminated disc**  A recording medium composed of several layers of material held together by a BINDER. LACQUER DISCs, for example, are laminated. (4:291)

**Lamination**  "A process of reinforcing fragile paper, usually with thin, translucent, or transparent sheets. Most forms of lamination are considered unacceptable as CONSERVATION methods because of potential damage from high heat and pressure during application, instability of the lamination materials, or difficulty in removing the lamination from the item, especially long after the treatment was performed." (22:15) See also SILKING.

**Lamphouse**  A protective cover over the illumination source in a reader, printer, or enlarger.

**Lantern slide**  A 3 inch x 4 inch glass (though occasionally plastic) POSITIVE transparency designed for projection.

**Lap marks**  Impressions along the length of a film created by defective rollers or incorrect tension during PROCESSING. (1:127)

**Laser disc**   Includes COMPACT DISC, VIDEODISC, and DIGITAL OPTI-CAL RECORDING. The content of these media is digitally encoded (except for video on a videodisc, which is in ANALOG form) and etched into a reflective layer on the disc in the form of holes or PITs (depressions). A laser light beam is focused on the disc as it revolves. Where there are no depressions, the light beam simply moves on. Where there are depressions, the light beam is reflected back into the playback apparatus, which "reads" the reflections and eventually converts them back into a digital signal (analog for videodisc) for playback. See also CD-ROM; COMPACT DISC; DIGITAL OPTICAL RECORDING; VIDEODISC. (4:292)

**LAST**   See LIQUID ARCHIVAL SOUND TREATMENT.

**Latent heat**   Heat associated with a change in moisture content of the air, in contrast to SENSIBLE HEAT. It is heat that is there thermodynamically but not measurable by a simple dry-bulb thermometer. (30:78)

**Latent image**   An image contained on film or paper which becomes visible through PROCESSING. Irradiated SILVER HALIDE grains become visible only when subjected to the development process. (46:154)

**Latent image fade**   As soon as a SENSITIZED EMULSION is irradiated the image begins to fade, at first rapidly and then slowing dramatically. The amount and rate of change depends on time, temperature, humidity, storage conditions, and type of emulsion. When SILVER HALIDE film is used in PRESERVATION work, reels are held four hours in order to allow the entire REEL to achieve the same relative degree of fade prior to processing. (42:192)

**Lateral cut**   "A type of incision in an ANALOG DISC GROOVE that is perpendicular to the motion of the recording medium and parallel to its surface and that requires side-to-side motion of the STYLUS during playback. This is the standard CUT for analog discs." (52:32) See also VERTICAL CUT.

**Lateral reversal**   An image reversed from right to left; a mirror image. Some DIRECT POSITIVE images (DAGUERREOTYPEs and tintypes) reverse images laterally. Camera negatives are usually laterally reversed and inverted. The printing process corrects the image orientation. (46:154–155)

**Latitude**   The degree of change in exposure time that can be tolerated without affecting image quality.

**Layer-to-layer adhesion**   The tendency for adjacent layers of tape or film in a roll to adhere to one another. See BLOCKING. (49:157)

**Layer-to-layer signal transfer**   See PRINT THROUGH.

**Leader**   (1) A blank strip of film at the beginning of a reel of motion-picture film, filmstrip, or microfilm for projector or reader threading and as protection of the first frames. (2) A non-magnetic blank section of tape spliced to the beginning and end of a reel of recorded magnetic tape and between segments to indicate visually when recorded material begins and ends. (4:292) Also protects the first few inches of the tape. See also TRAILER.

**Leaf**   A SHEET of paper folded once forms a SECTION of two leaves or four pages and is called a FOLIO; folded twice, it forms a section of four leaves or eight pages and is called a quarto. A leaf consists of two pages, one on each side, either of which may or may not be printed on. Usually the RECTO has an odd number, and the VERSO the subsequent number, but in reprints this may not be the case. (23:355)

**Leaf attachment**   "The means by which the leaves of a TEXT BLOCK are attached, one to another. Leaves are most often attached along their binding edges by means of thread, adhesive, or staples. The latter method of LEAF attachment does not comply with the LIBRARY BINDING INSTITUTE Standard." (26:15)

**Leafcasting**   A mechanical method of mending paper documents by filling in holes and damaged areas with compatible PAPER FIBERS. A leafcasting machine is used to deposit fiber evenly in a SLURRY of PAPER PULP. (38:216)

**Leaflet**   "A small sheet of printed paper folded once to make two to four pages following the same sequence as in a book, but not stitched or bound. Often used to indicate a small, thin PAMPHLET." (23:355)

**Leakage**   See CROSSTALK.

**Leather bound**   A book covered in leather. Because of the flexibility of leather, it can be glued directly to the SPINE of a TEXT BLOCK. This type of binding is known as TIGHT BACK as opposed to CASE-BOUND. (38:216)

**Leather dressings**   Substances applied to leather, including book bindings, to prevent or retard deterioration and preserve and, to a limited extent, restore flexibility to leather. A great number of different leather dressings of varying degrees of effectiveness have been used to impart "new life" to deteriorating leather. They have ranged from simple paste-washing and/or coating with varnish to more or less carefully formulated and tested preparations. Most of the latter contain an oil which may be of animal, vegetable, or mineral origin, in order of probable decreasing relative value as preservatives. While such dressings may preserve, and to some extent restore, the flexibility of the leather, they cannot prevent chemical decay, nor can they restore leather that has become decayed because of chemical influences. The use of hard waxes in leather dressings is very controversial and probably should be avoided until research provides reliable answers. There are a number of leather dressings on the market, but probably the best for use on leather book bindings is a mixture of 60 percent NEAT'S-FOOT OIL (20°C, cold test) and 40 percent anhydrous lanolin, or 60 percent lanolin and 40 percent neat's-foot oil, depending upon the temperature and RELATIVE HU-MIDITY in the area of use (see Carolyn Horton's manual (24:49) for complete instructions). This simple, economical, and widely used dressing offers some important advantages over many other preparations. It is (relatively) less expensive, easy to prepare and apply, nontoxic, nonflammable, and contains nothing, insofar as is known at this time, that could possibly damage the leather. (47:154–155) The oil can be purchased ready-mixed, or the materials can be bought at a chemical supply house and mixed as follows: Warm the lanolin in a double boiler until it is melted. Add the neat's-foot oil and stir until the mixture is uniformly blended. It will form a soft salve. This formula was developed by the New York Public Library and was tested by the U.S. Department of Agriculture. It is formula No. Six in Horton's manual. The Horton manual should be consulted for complete instructions on its application. (24:49) See also POTASSIUM LACTATE.

**Leaves**   See LEAF.

**Legible**   Capable of being read.

**Length (of a book)**   See HEIGHT (OF A BOOK).

**Lens**   One or more pieces of OPTICAL glass used to collect and FOCUS images for photographic purposes.

**Lens coating**   Normally thin, transparent layer or layers of material applied to the LENS or lens system to reduce light reflection and enhance light transmission.

**Lens opening**   That part of a LENS through which light can pass.

**Lens speed**   The capacity of a LENS to transmit light.

**Letter book**   "Used in ARCHIVES to describe three types of material. (1) A BOOK in which correspondence was copied by writing the original letter with copying ink, placing it against a dampened sheet of thin paper (leaves of which made up the book) and applying pressure; (2) a book of blank or lined pages on which are written letters, either drafts written by the author or fair copies made by the author or by a clerk; (3) a book comprising copies of loose letters which have been bound together, or one into which such copies are pasted onto GUARDs or pages." (42:192)

**Liability**   Any legally enforceable obligation. (37:118)

**Library bindery**   A commercial bindery that binds books using mass production methods. (38:216) See LIBRARY BINDING INSTITUTE (LBI).

**Library binding**   "Various styles and methods of binding performed for libraries utilizing machine or hand methods, or a combination of each, and executed to provide optimum permanence and/or durability. Included are the first-time hardcover binding of loose periodical issues, CASE binding of paperbound publications, the REBINDING or repair of older volumes, and the prebinding of new publications specifically for high-volume circulation by public libraries (see PREBOUND). To be distinguished from EDITION BINDING." (1:130)

**Library Binding Institute (LBI)**   A nonprofit trade organization, founded in 1935 to develop cooperation among library BINDERs and related industries. LBI promotes high standards of fair dealing between library binders and their customers and the development and acceptance of binding standards. Membership is open to commercial library binders capable of doing work meeting the LBI standard, suppliers to library book binders, and those interested in the PRESERVATION of books and periodicals.

**Library corner**   The cloth used to cover the CASE is turned in at the CORNERS of the boards so as to take up the excess in two diagonal folds, one under each TURN IN. The cloth is not cut and the corner is given additional strength. The standard corner used by library binders. Sometimes called ROUND CORNER. See also SQUARE CORNER. (47:158)

**Library edition**   A publisher's term for an edition of a book in an especially strong binding, though not the equivalent of LIBRARY BINDING. (1:131)

**Library prebound**   See PREBOUND.

**Light arms**   The part of a camera supporting the lamps used to illuminate material to be filmed.

**Light box**   A workstation device equipped with backlighting in order to inspect film. (42:192)

**Light Damage Slide Rule**   A set of scales designed by the Canadian Conservation Institute to measure the damage light may inflict on an ARTIFACT, particularly to its colors. The slide rule demonstrates the damage to colors that will result from a particular combination of *intensity* and *exposure* and illustrates the results if one or both factors are reduced. The Light Damage Slide Rule has two sides, serving two functions: (1) to calculate light damage to an artifact; and (2) to assist in selecting and using appropriate bulbs in displays.

**Lightfast**   Ability of a material to resist fading upon exposure to light. (45:88)

**Light fugitive**   A characteristic of certain pigments and dyes which are subject to fading by exposure to light. (8:153)

**Light meter**   An ILLUMINANCE (or LUMINANCE) measuring device.

**Light scatter**   DIFFUSION of light rays by environmental particles or irregularities.

**Light sensitive**   Materials that are changed by the impact of RADIANT ENERGY (light).

**Light struck**   Fogged film.

**Light tight**   Normally any enclosure capable of prohibiting the entry of RADIANT ENERGY. Raw film cassettes and camera film units are all designed to be light tight.

**Lightweight**   A loose term describing paper lighter than 45 lb. (26 x 38 basis) or 67 grams per square meter. Heavily opacified; used for reference books, dictionaries, Bibles, etc. Sometimes called Bible paper or thin paper. (9:14)

**Lignin**   A three-dimensional amorphous POLYMER with a variable structure so complex that a definitive formula for it has never been written. It makes up 17 to 32 percent of wood; it surrounds the CELLULOSE FIBERs and provides the stiffness that enables trees to stand upright. It is chemically stable in wood, but becomes unstable when the wood is broken down to make paper. It is removed in PULPING with the use of hot chemicals followed by bleaching. Fully bleached PULP contains practically no lignin. (33:20)

**Lignin-free**   See LIGNIN.

**Limp binding**   Bound in thin, flexible cloth, LEATHER, paper sides, or VELLUM without boards.

**Line copy**   Material containing only text and solids with no tones other than black and white.

**Line count method**   When viewing RESOLUTION patterns on a test chart, this method requires that the viewer be able to count all individual lines of a pattern in order to establish the resolution. Most frequently employed in Europe. See also PATTERN RECOGNITION METHOD.

**Line density**   The OPACITY of individual lines or letters in an IMAGE.

**Line pairs**   See RESOLVING POWER.

**Linen**   Linen FIBERs are the straw of the flax plant. In the paper industry it usually refers to the linen rags and cuttings received from the textile industry, for use in the manufacture of high quality cotton fiber content paper. The CELLULOSE content of linen fibers is between 70 and 80 percent. Chemical PULP derived from the FLAX plant is called flax pulp. (15:251; 47:160)

**Linen paper**   Paper made from rags; originally paper made from LINEN rags. (23:375)

**Liner**   See ALBUM; SLIPCASE; SLEEVE.

**Lining**   Cloth and/or paper attached to the SPINE of the TEXT BLOCK to help the book keep its shape when binding it. Also called BACK LINING. See also FIRST LINING; MULL; SECOND LINING, SPINE LINING; SUPER. (23:375)

**Lining paper**   See ENDPAPERS; PASTEDOWN.

**Lint** **(1)** Dust, or loose fibers, which separate from the raw material, e.g., rags, during papermaking. (23:376) **(2)** Environmental dust or fines which are attracted to static charged film surfaces.

**Linters** See COTTON LINTERS.

**Liquid Archival Sound Treatment (LAST)** A trademarked lubricant and preservative fluid that works by reacting with VINYL and SHELLAC to alter the nature of the groove walls on an AUDIODISC, thereby, it is claimed, reducing wear and eliminating distortion. (4:293)

**Liquified Gas Process** See WEI T'O.

**lm** Abbreviation for LUMEN. See LUMEN.

**Load cells** Devices used to measure weight.

**Loaded paper** See COATED PAPER.

**Loading** "The adding of clay, CALCIUM CARBONATE, chalk, etc., to STUFF when in the BEATER of a papermaking machine, or flowed into the STOCK as it goes through the sluice-gate of the FOURDRINIER MACHINE. It fills the spaces between FIBERs and so imparts solidity to the paper and provides a better printing surface." (23:379)

**Lock stitch** "Any method of SEWING with thread whereby the STITCH-ING at each operation is 'locked' and cannot unravel if cut on either side of the completed stitch. Lock stitches are the type made by household sewing machines, although the machines used by library binders are often larger. Stitches are formed by a primary thread that runs along the top surface of the TEXT BLOCK being sewn; and a bobbin thread that runs along the bottom surface, and locks with the thread at regular intervals." (26:15) See also KETTLE STITCH.

**Longitudinal curvature** Any deviation from straightness of a length of tape or film. (49:157)

**Longitudinal lines** SCRATCHes or defects in a reel of film that run parallel to the edges of the film.

**Longitudinal direction** Along the length of the tape or film. (49:157)

**Long-playing audiodisc (LP)** "**(1)** In popular usage, a 33 1/3 RPM AUDIODISC, usually 12 inches (30 cm.) in diameter. **(2)** An ANALOG DISC to be played at 16 2/3 rpm, 33 1/3 rpm, or 45 rpm. Since the introduction of the COMPACT DISC, LPs are sometimes called 'black discs.'" (52:32)

**Long-playing sound disc** See LONG-PLAYING AUDIODISC (LP).

**Long-term film** Microfilm which will retain its original information-bearing characteristics for at least 100 years, if stored under proper conditions and the film is processed to ARCHIVAL STANDARDS. ANSI IT9.5, *Imaging Media (Film)—Silver Gelatin Type—Specifications for Stability*, prescribes the standards required to meet the conditions for long-term film. ANSI PH4.8,

*Photography (Chemicals)—Residual Thiosulfate and Other Chemicals in Films, Plates, and Paper—Determination and Measurement,* prescribes long-term film processing requirements. ANSI PH1.43, *Photography (Film)—Processed Safety Film—Storage,* and ANSI IT9.2, *Photographic Processed Films, Plates, and Papers—Filing Enclosures and Storage Containers,* prescribe long-term archival storage conditions. (48:18–19) See also ARCHIVAL FILM; MEDIUM-TERM FILM; SHORT-TERM FILM.

**Loop cartridge**   See CARTRIDGE.

**Loose back**   See HOLLOW BACK.

**Loose debris**   Material very lightly bonded to the tape or head top surface, removable by tape motion. (49:157)

**Loose in binding**   A book or TEXT BLOCK separated from its CASE.

**Loose insert**   See INSERT.

**Loss**   The basis for a CLAIM for indemnity or damages under the terms of an insurance policy. (54:47)

**Loss control**   A program of measures taken to reduce the possibility of accident, injury, fire, or other loss producing events. (37:119)

**Loss prevention service**   Engineering and inspection work done by insurance companies or independent organizations for the purpose of changing or removing conditions which would be likely to cause LOSS. (54:47)

**Louvers**   A series of narrow openings framed with (usually) adjustable overlapping slats covering the opening of a duct or plenum. The duct or plenum usually leads to the outside for bringing air into, or discharging air from a building. (30:78)

**Low contrast**   An image with relatively small differences between high and low DENSITY. (42:192)

**Low reductions**   Reduction ratios below 16x. See REDUCTION RATIO.

**LP**   Abbreviation for LONG-PLAYING AUDIODISC.

**Lubricant**   See ADDITIVE.

**lr**   See LOW REDUCTION.

**Lumen (lm)**   The LUMINOUS FLUX available on one square foot contained in a one-foot-radius sphere (or on one square meter contained in a one-meter-radius sphere) from a point source with a uniform luminous intensity of one CANDELA. (31:7) Lumen output is the amount of VISIBLE LIGHT given off by a source.

**Lumen per square foot**   See FOOTCANDLE.

**Lumen per square meter**   See LUX.

**Luminance**   Light intensity per unit area as perceived by a viewer or camera. See also ILLUMINANCE.

**Luminous flux** The time rate of flow of RADIANT FLUX to produce VISIBLE LIGHT. The measure of luminous flux is the LUMEN. (31:7)

**Lux** The metric measure of light value, one LUMEN or FOOTCANDLE is equal to 10.76 lux. (23:386) One lux equals one lumen per square meter, or approximately 0.09 footcandle (fc). A measure of energy accounting for the spectral sensitivity of the human eye. (50:201)

**Lying press** "A small, portable PRESS, usually made of wood, with two steel or wooden screws operating through bronze chucks, in which books to be BACKED by hand, TRIMMED with the PLOW, lettered or decorated, etc., are clamped. The lower face of the block on the bookbinder's left has a groove in which the plow runs." (47:162)

# M

**Machine binding** A type of binding using power-operated equipment to perform operations, in contrast to hand or craft binding. Includes EDITION and LIBRARY BINDING.

**Machine coated** Paper that has been coated with clay or a similar substance during the actual making of the paper to give it a smooth printing surface.

**Machine curl** Any film CURL perpendicular to edges of the film or the direction in which the film ran during manufacture.

**Machine direction** (1) "The direction in which paper travels through a papermaking machine. Most of the FIBERs lie in this direction; therefore paper folds more easily along the machine direction (said to be 'WITH THE GRAIN'), and a sheet of paper when wetted expands mainly across this direction, with a corresponding shrinkage of the paper on drying." (23:387) The paper is stronger in the machine direction, and also experiences less dimensional variation in the machine direction due to changes in HUMIDITY. The direction at right angles is known as the CROSS DIRECTION. See also AGAINST THE GRAIN; GRAIN. (2) The direction film travels through a film making machine.

**Machine finish** "A 'natural' FINISH as paper comes off the paper machine with only a modest attempt at compacting the WEB at the machine CALENDER. Smooth to the touch." (9:14)

**Machine-made paper** The continuous WEB, or roll, of paper made on CYLINDER MACHINEs or FOURDRINIER MACHINEs.

**Machine-sewn sections**   A group of folded SECTIONs (GATHERINGs, SIGNATUREs) that are sewn together through the fold on a machine. One needle does not sew ALL ALONG the section like HAND SEWING; instead several equally spaced threaded needles pierce the folds of individual signatures to attach them together with KETTLE STITCHes. See also SMYTH SEWING. (38:216)

**Machine wire**   See FOURDRINIER WIRE.

**Macroscopic**   Of a size that allows discrimination of information by the unaided eye, e.g., HEADING or title information on MICROFICHE or EYE LEGIBLE TARGETs on microfilm. (42:192)

**Magazine**   Any light-tight device used to load raw film stock or exposed but undeveloped film into cameras, PROCESSORs, etc.

**Magnesium acetate**   See POSLIP METHOD.

**Magnesium bicarbonate (MgC$_4$)**   A bicarbonate (Mg(HCO$_3$)$_2$) used in DEACIDIFYING papers. The bicarbonate is produced by passing carbon dioxide (CO$_2$) through a solution of MAGNESIUM CARBONATE. The document to be deacidified is immersed in a bath or sprayed with a solution of about 10 grams of magnesium carbonate per liter of water that has been treated with CO$_2$. The advantage of this method is that it is simple and effective. (47:164) See also BARROW PROCESS; DEACIDIFICATION.

**Magnesium carbonate**   When used with club soda, it forms a suspension instead of a solution and results in surface deposits. See also BARROW PROCESS; DEACIDIFICATION.

**Magnetic flux density**   See MAXIMUM INTRINSIC FLUX DENSITY.

**Magnesium methoxide**   See WEI T'O.

**Magnetic disc**   See DISK.

**Magnetic instability**   The property of a magnetic material that causes variations in the RESIDUAL FLUX DENSITY of a tape to occur with temperature, time, and/or mechanical flexing. Magnetic instability is a function of PARTICLE SIZE, MAGNETIZING FIELD STRENGTH, and ANISOTROPY. (49:157)

**Magnetic tape**   A paper, acetate, steel or plastic based film coated with a layer of magnetic particles, usually gamma ferric oxide or CHROMIUM DIOXIDE; some newer tapes use actual metal particles. The particles are usually of ACICULAR shape, approach SINGLE DOMAIN size, and are held in a BINDER and lubricated. (49:157) Magnetic tape is stored on REELs, in CASSETTEs, and in CARTRIDGEs. Standard width is 1/4 inch, but compact cassette tape is 1/8 inch and videotape ranges from 1/2 inch to 3 inches. (4:293)

**Magnetic tape backing**   See BACKING.

**Magnetic tape binder**   See BINDER.

**Magnetic tape duplication master**   A magnetic tape copied from a MASTER TAPE, and used to reproduce the multiple copies of cartridges, cassettes, and/or audiotape reels issued to the public. (52:39)

**Magnetite**   See FERRIC OXIDE.

**Magnetizing field strength**   The instantaneous strength of the magnetic field applied to a sample of magnetic material. (49:157)

**Magnification**   Apparent enlargement.

**Magnification range**   The degree or range of magnification possible in an OPTICAL system.

**Magnification ratio**   A measure of the degree an object is enlarged. Normally expressed in terms of DIAMETERS or as 16x (16 times larger), etc. See also REDUCTION RATIO.

**Magnifier**   A lens system designed to enlarge object images.

**Makeup air**   "Air provided to a space or system to make up for air lost through exhaust or leakage." (30:79)

**Manuscript**   A document of any kind which is written by hand, or the text of a music or literary composition in handwritten or typescript form (including generated by a word processor) and which, in that form, has not been reproduced in multiple copies.

**MAPS**   The MicrogrAphic Preservation Service, Inc., formerly Mid-Atlantic Preservation Service, Inc.

**Marbled edges**   "The three edges of a book cut solid and stained to resemble marble." (23:393)

**Marbled paper**   "Surface-color paper used by bookbinders. MARBLING is done by floating white paper, or dipping the edges of a sewn book before inserting into the cover, in a bath of GUM TRAGACANTH, the surface of which has been sprinkled with various colors, and combed out to a desired pattern." (23:393)

**Marbling**   "The process of coloring the ENDPAPERS and/or edges of a book in imitation of marble." (23:393) See also MARBLED PAPER.

**Margin**   (1) The area of a page beyond the text or image carrying portion. (2) In a photographic FRAME, the background area between the image and its neighbor and/or the edge of the film.

**Mask**   Material used to protect sensitized material from exposure.

**Mass deacidification**   See DEACIDIFICATION.

**Master**   A source cylinder, disc, document, microform, tape, or other medium from which duplicates or intermediates are made.

**Master cylinder**   An original CYLINDER recorded on wax, and from which duplicates were made by transferring variations in its GROOVE dimension pantographically onto wax blanks revolving on adjacent mandrels or spindles. (52:32)

**Master disc**   "**(1)** In the manufacture of ANALOG DISCs, an original positive (grooved) recording cut directly on a blank disc (usually a LACQUER DISC) by a lathe, and used to make the matrices from which LPs are pressed in multiple copies. An LP master disc may be cut directly from a live or studio performance, as in a direct-to-disc LP, or it may be cut from an edited MASTER TAPE. **(2)** In the manufacture of COMPACT DISCs, an original positive recording with pits etched on a blank disc by a laser activated by a digitally recorded master tape, and used to make the matrices from which compact discs are produced in multiple copies." (52:32)

**Master film**   Any film, normally the CAMERA MASTER, used to produce duplicates, such as intermediates, PRINT MASTERs, distribution copies, or SERVICE COPIES. See also PRESERVATION MASTER NEGATIVE. (42:193)

**Master tape**   A magnetic tape containing the final production version of an AUDIODISC (after studio editing, special processing, etc.) and used to make a MASTER DISC for the manufacture of audiodiscs, or a MAGNETIC TAPE DUPLICATION MASTER for the manufacture of recordings in a tape format. (52:32)

**Mat**   "A protective housing for flat artworks, usually consisting of two boards hinged together along one edge. In general, one board is solid (for support) and the other has a window cut in it (for viewing)." (28:25)

**Matboard**   A layered PAPERBOARD traditionally made from all-rag FIBER and used in the framing of works of art or photographs. THICKNESS is measured in layers or "plies": 2-ply, 4-ply, 6-ply. Though used for many CONSERVATION purposes, not all matboard is ALKALINE. It is no longer exclusively composed of rag fibers. (38:216)

**Matte**   **(1)** A type of COATED PAPER carrying less SURFACE COAT weight than DULL. Has a nonreflective surface, neither as smooth nor as refined as dull coated. (9:14) See also COATED PAPER. **(2)** A photographic PRINT with minimal capacity to reflect light.

**Matrix**   "**(1)** A generic term for any of the electroformed nickel molds originating from a MASTER DISC, and used in the manufacture of AUDIODISCs. Several generations of positive and negative matrices generally are used in the production process. From the positive master disc (GROOVED if an ANALOG DISC recording, pitted if a COMPACT DISC) a negative matrix (a 'father,' 'master matrix,' or 'disc master') with raised surfaces instead of grooves or pits is formed through an electroplating process. (This negative matrix can be used for direct PRESSING of a limited number of audiodiscs, but generally is not because of its relative fragility.) From this negative 'father' a 'mother' is formed, and the mother in turn is used to make the negative metal matrices (STAMPERs) used in the final pressing of audiodiscs. **(2)** In its narrowest sense, the term refers only to the final generation of stamper(s) used for the actual pressing of audiodiscs." (52:33)

**Maximum density (Dmax)**   The maximum obtainable density of a piece of exposed film. See also BACKGROUND DENSITY; DENSITY; MINIMUM DENSITY (DMIN).

**Maximum flux**   See MAXIMUM INTRINSIC FLUX.

**Maximum flux density**   See MAXIMUM INTRINSIC FLUX DENSITY.

**Maximum intrinsic flux**   In a uniformly magnetized sample of magnetic material, the product of the MAXIMUM INTRINSIC FLUX DENSITY and the cross-sectional area. (49:157)

**Maximum intrinsic flux density**   The maximum value, positive or negative, of the INTRINSIC FLUX DENSITY in a sample of magnetic material that is in a symmetrically, cyclically magnetized condition. (49:157)

**Mean**   A measure of central tendency which yields one number for one group measured on one VARIABLE. The mean indicates the average value of the variable for a group of CASEs and should be calculated on data measured on at least the INTERVAL level. (7:110)

**Mechanical binding**   "A category of LEAF affixing in which single leaves and separate front and back COVERs are mechanically joined through patterns of holes or slots made in their edges. Most mechanical bindings will lie flat when open, but are not strong. They may be loose-leaf and allow the contents to be readily changed, or permanent, such as PLASTIC COMB BINDING, POST BINDING, SPIRAL BINDING, twin-wire binding, and VELO-BINDING." (1:142)

**Mechanical damage**   "Damage caused to a book by physical manipulation in storage, handling, or use. Includes internal movement caused by rapid fluctuations in HUMIDITY and temperature." (38:216)

**Mechanical recording**   See ACOUSTICAL RECORDING.

**Mechanical wood pulp**   "Any WOOD PULP manufactured wholly or in part by a mechanical process, including stone-ground wood, chemiground wood and chip mechanical pulp. Uses include NEWSPRINT printing papers, specialty papers, tissue, toweling, PAPERBOARD and wallboard." (15:267) See GROUNDWOOD PULP.

**Medium contrast**   An image with relatively average differences between high and low DENSITY. (42:193)

**Medium reduction**   REDUCTION RATIOs of 16x through 30x. See REDUCTION RATIO.

**Medium-term film**   Microfilm which will retain its original information-bearing characteristics for at least ten years, if stored under proper conditions and the film is processed to ARCHIVAL STANDARDS. ANSI PH1.43, *Photography (Film)—Processed Safety Film—Storage,* and ANSI IT9.2, *Photographic Processed Films, Plates, and Papers—Filing Enclosures and Storage Containers,* prescribe medium-term storage requirements. All types of microfilms can satisfy medium-term storage requirements. (48:25) See also ARCHIVAL FILM; LONG-TERM FILM; SHORT-TERM FILM.

**Megahertz (MHz)**   One million HERTZ.

**Melinex™**   A strong, tough, dimensionally stable clear POLYESTER film used for ENCAPSULATING papers and other flat objects. Manufactured by I.C.I. America, Inc. See also ENCAPSULATION; POLYESTER.

**Mending**   Minor rehabilitation of a book not involving the replacement of any material or the separation of book from cover. Not as extensive a process as REPAIRING. (1:143) See also REPAIRING.

**Metal alkyls**   A chemical compound linking a metal atom or atoms with a hydrocarbon radical of the form $C_nH_{2n+1}$; very active. (55:107)

**Metallic support**   A base support of metal which maintains a photographic image. (44:30)

**Methyl alcohol**   See ALCOHOL; ALCOHOL SPOT-TEST.

**Methyl cellulose**   CELLULOSE methyl ether, produced by treating cellulose from wood or cotton with an ALKALI, such as sodium hydroxide, followed by methyl chloride. Methyl cellulose is a white granular solid, soluble in cold water but insoluble in hot water. It is used as an additive in ADHESIVEs to increase film strength, flexibility, and adhesion. (47:169) See also ADHESIVE.

**Methylene blue**   A chemical dye formed during testing of archival permanence of processed MICROIMAGEs using the methylene-blue method. (42:193) It is used to test for residual HYPO. See also DENSITO-METRIC METHOD (SILVER); RESIDUAL HYPO TEST.

**Mezzotint**   **(1)** Copper or steel engraving process where the surface of the PLATE is slightly roughened. Then the drawing is traced and the plate smoothed in places by scraping, burnishing, etc., to produce the desired high and low tonal effect. **(2)** An engraving produced by the mezzotint process. (23:401)

**MHz**   See MEGAHERTZ.

**Microcard™**   **(1)** A trademark of the Microcard Corporation referring exclusively to 3 x 5 inch cards with MICROIMAGEs arranged in rows and COLUMNs on PHOTOGRAPHIC PAPER. **(2)** More generally, an OPAQUE card of various sizes carrying microimages reproduced photographically. Resembles MICROFICHE with EYE LEGIBLE data at the top of the card. Different from other MICROFORMs since the PRINTs are

POSITIVE and opaque, and not readily reproducible. A microcard is not readable (except for the heading) without special optical aids. (23:402)

**Microdensitometer**   See DENSITOMETER.

**Microenvironment**   Atmospheric conditions within a small, confined space such as a PHASE BOX or a microfilm can. A microenvironment can act as a buffer against external changes in temperature and humidity and can protect against most air pollutants. (38:217)

**Microfiche**   A sheet of photographic film 105 x 148 mm (about 4 x 6 inches) or 75 x 125 mm (about 3 x 5 inches), with an EYE LEGIBLE header at the top. Contains images of data, photographs, text, or other information in horizontal and vertical rows ranging from 60 to 420 images of letter-sized pages, depending on the REDUCTION RATIO. The most popular source-document format contains 7 rows and 14 columns on a 105 x 140 mm sheet for a total of 98 images reduced to 24x.   Microfiche can be any of several formats, a POSITIVE copy created from strips of MICROFILM, or from individual FRAMEs cut from microfilm (usually 35mm or 70mm film), or made directly with a STEP-AND-REPEAT CAMERA on 105mm film. The sheets may be stored vertically like catalog cards but require ENVELOPEs to protect them from damage. Also called "fiche." (23:402; 48:12) See also COMPUTER-OUTPUT MICROFORM; ULTRAFICHE.

**Microfiche frame**   One cell of the MICROFICHE grid where an image may be located.

**Microfilm**   (1) A FINE GRAIN, high-resolution film used to record micro-images. Refers to roll film sufficiently long to be placed on REELs, CARTRIDGEs, or CASSETTEs and retrieved by manual or automatic means. Images may be POSITIVE or NEGATIVE and rolls may be 8, 16, 35, 70, and 105mm wide and up to several thousand feet long. Rolls can be cut to produce MICROFICHE. (2) To film originals for the purpose of creating microimages. (1:145)

**Microfilm camera**   See PLANETARY CAMERA; ROTARY CAMERA; STEP-AND-REPEAT CAMERA.

**Microform**   Generically, any microreproduction on flat or roll film, paper, or other material, e.g., MICROCARD, MICROFILM, MICROFICHE.

**Micrographics**   The science and technology of MICROIMAGE photography; designing indexing, storage, and retrieval systems for microimages; or using microimages in micrographic systems. Generally considered a subfield of REPROGRAPHY. (42:193)

**Microgroove**   "The fine GROOVE of a LONG-PLAYING AUDIODISC (about 225 to 300 CUTS PER INCH, or 88 to 188 cuts per cm). Microgrooves permit approximately three times as much material to be recorded on a side as in an equivalent space on an ANALOG DISC with a STANDARD GROOVE." (52:33)

**Microimage** Photographic images too small to be read with the unaided eye.

**Micromire** See MIRE.

**Microopaque** A MICROIMAGE print on OPAQUE paper or card. May be made by photographic or printing processes. See also MICROCARD. (23:403)

**Microphotography** Photographs reducing the image to such an extent that a visual aid is required to discern the features of the resulting image; 16mm or 35mm film is used, and the final microform may be MICROCARD, MICROFICHE, or MICROFILM. (23:403)

**Microprint™** A trade name of a 6 inch x 9 inch photographic paper product with MICROIMAGEs arranged in rows and COLUMNs. (1:145)

**Micropublisher** One who issues new or reformatted material in a microimage FORMAT.

**Microreproduction** Making microcopies of documents, the resulting images smaller than EYE LEGIBLE, on either OPAQUE or transparent materials. (23:404)

**Microscopic blemish** See BLEMISH.

**Mil** Unit of THICKNESS equalling one thousandth (0.001) of an inch, usually used as a measurement of plastic sheeting. (22:15)

**Mildew** "A growth caused by micro-organisms, whose spores, in a moist, warm environment, become MOLDs. They derive their food from the substance on which they form, e.g., the materials of a book. During their growth they produce citric, gluconic, oxalic, or other organic ACIDs, that can damage paper, LEATHER, cloth, etc. They also at times produce color bodies, leading to staining which is difficult to remove." See also FUNGI; MOLD. (47:170)

**Milky** Cloudy appearance of microfilm images. Can be the result of poorly fixed film or of nearly spent fixer solutions.

**Mill** "The SPINEs of books cut away on a milling machine to prepare them for DOUBLE-FAN ADHESIVE BINDING or OVERSEWING. The machine clamps the TEXT BLOCK, spine down, and moves it over a series of rotating blades that cut away approximately 1/8 inch of the BINDING MARGIN, thus removing old adhesive, thread, staples, and/or the folds of SIGNATUREs. After milling, a text block is comprised of loose leaves." (26:15)

**Millboard** See BINDER'S BOARD.

**Mill cut** The cut edge produced by the machine slitter or by CUTTERs. The trimmer makes a cut which is smoother and more accurate. (15:272) See also TRIMMING.

**Minimum density (Dmin)** The minimum obtainable density of a piece of exposed film. See also DENSITY; MAXIMUM DENSITY (DMAX).

**Mire**   The French word for test charts used to establish the legibility of MICROIMAGEs against an accepted standard. Mire #1, developed by the International Standards Organization (ISO), is used internationally. A set of 10x ISO Mire #1 legibility test charts is termed a micromire. (1:147)

**Mirroring**   A film defect in which silver images have been oxidized and produce a mirror-like glaze. The effect is visible over a light box, but is not seen on a READER.

**Misu**   A paper handmade in Japan of 100 percent KOZO. It has narrow-spaced LAID LINES, and the CHAIN LINES are less than one inch apart, giving a beautiful formation to this limp, attractive paper. It is not SIZEd and is ACID-FREE. Used in CONSERVATION activities. See also JAPANESE PAPER.

**Mitsumata**   One of the three plants (the others are GAMPI and KOZO) that provide materials for JAPANESE PAPERs. The mitsumata FIBERs are soft and absorbent, and the finished paper has a slight orange color. (29:116)

**mm**   Millimeter.

**Mold**   **(1)** "A multi-cellular, microscopic vegetable plant which forms cobweb-like masses of branching threads from the surface of which tiny fertile threads project into the air bearing the part of the plant from which spores develop. Mold may be of brilliant colors or black and white, depending on the type. Molds can develop on leather, cloth, paper, etc., especially in the presence of relatively high heat and RELATIVE HUMIDITY. See also FUNGI; MILDEW." (47:171) **(2)** The basic tool of papermaking. A rectangular wooden frame over which brass wires or wire cloth is stretched to serve as a sieve in order to permit water to drain away from the PULP fibers to form a sheet of paper. A wooden frame called a DECKLE fits round the edges of the mold and forms a tray with raised edges; this keeps the required thickness of pulp fiber on the wires until the excess water has drained away.

**Mold-made paper**   A DECKLE edged paper resembling that made by hand but produced on a machine. It is made on a cylinder or cylindrical MOLD revolving in a VAT of PULP. (15:275)

**Moment of inertia**   A measure of the rotational force required to accelerate or decelerate a REEL of tape or film. (49:157)

**Monaural**   See MONOPHONIC.

**Monk's record cleaner**   An AUDIODISC-washing machine, in which the disc is washed with distilled water, or a solution of distilled water and ethyl ALCOHOL, and then the solution and dirt are removed by vacuum suction, which prevents dust from being redeposited or trapped within the grooves during the drying process. (4:295)

**Monobath**   A solution that combines the action of DEVELOPER and FIXER. An inhibitor precludes fixing prior to development. Not an appropriate strategy for developing films intended for ARCHIVAL functions.

**Monomer**   A simple molecule that can combine with identical or different molecules of low molecular weight to form a POLYMER.

**Monophonic (mono)**   Sound recorded and reproduced via one CHAN-NEL. Also called monaural, one-track, single-track. (52:33)

**Morpholine process**   Developed by the BARROW Laboratory for mass DEACIDIFICATION application. Morpholine is a colorless organic liquid ($Na \bullet (CH_2)_2 \bullet O \bullet (CH_2)_2$), which boils at 128°C. It has been used as a VAPOR-PHASE DEACIDIFYING agent. It is inexpensive, easily used, and deacidifies rapidly in suitable chambers. Morpholine neutralizes free ACIDs in paper by swelling and adhering to the CELLULOSE molecules. Morpholine leaves an ammonia-like and slightly fishy odor in books up to three months after treatment. The ALKALINE RESERVEs dissipate quickly, especially in a humid environment, leaving the paper to revert to an acid condition in the presence of high RELATIVE HUMID-ITY. (47:172) It is a toxic chemical and a suspected carcinogen.

**Mottle**   A film anomaly characterized by blotches and uneven densities. Can be caused by poor agitation of solutions in processing, poor environ-mental storage conditions, or problems with the EMULSION itself.

**Mounting**   Attaching graphics or other flat materials to cloth, cardboard, or other surfaces by using PASTE, GLUE, or through a dry-mounting process. In dry mounting, a heat-sensitive intermediary paper is used, and heat and pressure are applied to meld the materials to the surface. (1:149)

**Mounting plate**   In magnetic tape recording, a means of holding the head body and mounting it into the TAPE TRANSPORT. It is the reference surface for most mechanical measurements. (49:157)

**mr**   See MEDIUM REDUCTION.

**MRD**   A Kodak-produced microfilm camera. The workhorse of most preservation microfilming laboratories, though often modified to im-prove its performance. It is no longer produced by Kodak.

**MRG**   A Kodak microfilm camera, no longer in production, designed to film very large documents and drawings. It is sometimes equipped with a subsurface lighting to enhance the capture of blueprints and drawings on translucent materials.

**Mull**   The coarse, loosely woven cotton fabric used principally to line the SPINEs of EDITION BINDINGs. Also called CRASH or SUPER. See also SPINE LINING FABRIC. (47:173)

**Mullen** "A test used to measure the BURSTING STRENGTH of paper. It is named after the instrument used in conducting the test, invented by John W. Mullen, in 1887." (47:173) See also BURSTING STRENGTH; POINTS PER POUND.

**Multiple exposures** Two or more successive EXPOSUREs of the same object.

**Multiplex** A system for recording two or more rows of images across the width of the film.

**Multi-zone system** "An HVAC system in which each environmental control zone is served by its own duct from a common central air handling system, in which cool or warm air is provided in the appropriate duct to temper each zone." (30:79)

**Mylar™** A clear POLYESTER film plastic manufactured by the Du Pont Company used for ENCAPSULATING papers and other flat objects; it is also used as the BACKING in many types of magnetic recording tape. Type D Mylar is a super clear, bright, transparent, strong, tough, dimensionally stable polyester film with outstanding surface characteristics. It is recommended for use in ENCAPSULATION. (27:21–22) See also ENCAPSULATION; POLYESTER.

# N

**AB** National Association of Broadcasters (NAB). A national group of broadcasters who have voluntarily formed a regulatory body for television and radio. Three of its standards have become widespread in the recording field: the NAB standard equalization curve for tape record/playback equalization, the NAB hub, and the NAB reel (and reel adapter). See EQUALIZATION; HUB; REEL-TO-REEL TAPE.

**Named or specific perils contract** Insurance coverage specifying what HAZARDs or perils are being insured against. (54:51) See also ALL-RISK.

**National Institute of Standards and Technology** See NIST.

**Neat's-foot oil** A pale yellow, fatty oil produced by boiling the feet and shin bones of hoofed animals. "Cold-tested" neat's-foot oil has been held at the freezing point for a period of time and then filtered. Neat's-foot oil is used in the preparation of some LEATHER DRESSINGS and in the fat-liquoring of leather. (47:175)

**Needle** See STYLUS.

**Negative** Developed film containing a reversed-tone image of the ORIGINAL object in which printed characters appear clear and the surrounding areas are dark. Light image areas are represented by heavy or dark deposits of silver (high relative DENSITY), and dark areas are light or transparent (very low density). Negatives printed on paper or duplicating film yield positive images, in which tonal values are similar to the original object. (46:155)

**Neutral** Having a pH of 7.0; neither ACID nor ALKALINE. (22:15) See also NEUTRAL pH.

**Neutral-black** In photography, a dark gray image without visible tints such as blue-black or brown-black. (44:30)

**Neutralization and alkaline buffering** A CONSERVATION treatment that acts chemically to stabilize paper against ACID deterioration. Involves neutralizing ACIDs present in the paper and BUFFERing to leave an ALKALINE RESERVE to guard against future acid attack, especially from atmospheric pollutants. Common parameters of treated paper are a pH of 8.5 and an alkaline reserve of 2 to 3 percent. (38:217) See also ALKALINE RESERVE; BUFFER; DEACIDIFICATION.

**Neutral pH** Exhibiting neither ACID nor base (ALKALINE) qualities; 7.0 on the pH scale. See also pH.

**Neutral-sized paper** A paper that has been SIZEd with a synthetic sizing material that allows it to be manufactured at a pH of 7.0 or higher. (6:42)

**Newsprint** A generic term applied to the type of paper generally used in printing newspapers. Newsprint is produced from MECHANICAL WOOD PULP at very high machine speeds, causing the FIBERs of the sheet to be very directional. Since the majority of the fibers are oriented in one direction, it helps the paper take the strain of the high-speed press run, an advantage in newspaper printing. The high percentage of mechanical pulp in newsprint leads to its early disintegration. (47:175–176)

**Newton rings** Rings of colored light produced when two surfaces, at least one of which is glass, are in close contact. Seen occasionally on film READERS.

**Nip** The line of contact between two rolls in a folding machine, a rolling press, a CALENDER stack, etc. (47:176)

**Nipper (nipping machine)** A machine used in EDITION BINDING to compress the SPINE of a newly sewn book. It is used in LIBRARY BINDING to remove the original backing SHOULDERs of a book that is to be rebound, usually when it is to be resewn through the folds. (47:176)

**Nipping** (1) Reducing the SWELL caused by the SEWING of a book or (2) removing the backing SHOULDERs of a book to be rebound, by applying pressure to the book at the SPINE only. (47:176) See also NIPPER; SMASHING.

**NISO**   National Information Standards Organization (Z39). The body responsible for preparing standards in library, information, and related fields for the American National Standards Institute, Inc. (ANSI). NISO is located at NIST in Gaithersburg, Maryland. Its Z39 committee actually develops the standards. Some NISO standards of interest in preservation are:

Z39.32—1981 Information on Microfiche Headings

Z39.41—1979 Book Spine Formats (Currently being revised)

Z39.48—1984 Permanence of Paper for Printed Library Materials (Revision in progress)

Z39.66—(New) Durable Hard-Cover Binding for Books (Issued 9/89)

**NIST**   National Institute of Standards and Technology. Formerly the National Bureau of Standards. The Institute conducts research providing the groundwork for physical and technical measurement systems and scientific and technological services for industry and government.

**Nit**   A measure of LUMINANCE equal to one CANDELA per square meter.

**Nitrate film**   Photographic film with a FILM BASE mainly composed of CELLULOSE NITRATE. Because nitrate film is highly flammable, it has been replaced by acetate and POLYESTER-base films. (42:193)

**NMA**   National Micrographics Association, former name of the Association for Information and Image Management (AIIM).

**Noise**   In magnetic tape recording, any unwanted electrical disturbances in the transmission and reception of data over a communications CHANNEL.

**Nominal**   In statistics, a level of measurement in which an individual or a case is assigned to a category of a VARIABLE. No order is implied by the classification. Examples: Dewey Decimal system, sex, political party affiliation. The number assigned to a category of a variable is a "placeholder" only, and does not imply that any arithmetical operations can be meaningfully employed. For example, sex: 1 = male, 2 = female. If a person has a 1 on the variable sex, it indicates that the person is a male; it does not indicate order with respect to sex. (7:110).

**Nonaqueous deacidification**   A method of DEACIDIFYING paper which utilizes alcohol, or some other non-aqueous solvent, as the carrier for the deacidifying chemical. Essential for use with materials whose ink will run when wetted by water. (47:177) See also DEACIDIFICATION; VAPOR-PHASE DEACIDIFICATION; WEI T'O.

**Nonaqueous solvent**   Chemicals (other than water) used to dissolve other chemicals. Nonaqueous solvents used in DEACIDIFICATION techniques include methanol. (55:107)

**Nonbook materials**   See NONPRINT MATERIALS.

**Noncurl backing layer**   A GELATIN layer sometimes applied to the FILM BASE opposite the EMULSION side to help control CURL.

**Nonperforated film**   Roll film with no SPROCKET holes. PRESERVA-TION MICROFILM is nonperforated in order to minimize the amount of exposed film edge that may admit oxidizing or other destructive agents.

**Nonprint materials**   "Those library materials which do not come within the definition of a BOOK, periodical or PAMPHLET and which require special handling, e.g. audio-visual materials, vertical file materials, MICROFORMs or computer software." (23:435-436)

**Nonprocessed recording**   "A recording usually made directly on a disc or magnetic tape during performance, playable immediately afterward, and generally existing as a unique copy. Also called an instantaneous recording." (52:34) See also PROCESSED RECORDING.

**Nonreversing film**   See DIRECT IMAGE FILM.

**Notching**   A method of preparing a SPINE for ADHESIVE BINDING that involves cutting thin slits of variable width and depth into the BINDING EDGE of the PAGE, thereby increasing the surface area in contact with the ADHESIVE. Particularly useful in conjunction with the DOUBLE-FAN ADHESIVE BINDING method used by LIBRARY BINDERS. (38:217)

**Nova Sina Mik 3000**   See ELECTRONIC HYGROMETER.

**NO$_x$**   Oxides of nitrogen.

**NRMM**   National Register of Microform Masters.

**NUCMC**   National Union Catalog of Manuscript Collections.

# O

**bjective lens**   The lens in a camera system that forms the image to be filmed.

**Occurrence policy**   "A policy in which a belated CLAIM is covered if it refers to an incident that occurred while the policy was in force." (25:95)

**OCLC**   Online Computer Library Center, Inc.

**Odometer**   A measuring device to determine the distance traveled. Used in some microfilm systems to locate images or sections of a reel of film.

**Okawara**   A Japanese paper handmade from 100 percent KOZO. Strong, soft, and supple with LAID LINES. Good for CONSERVATION pur-poses. See also JAPANESE PAPER.

**Oleic acid**   "A colorless liquid ($C_{18}H_{34}O_2$), soluble in ALCOHOL and ether, but insoluble in water. It occurs naturally in greater quantities than any other fatty ACID, being present as glycerides in most fats and oils. It is used in determining the oil penetrability resistance of BOOK CLOTHs, especially BUCKRAM." (47:180)

**OMB**   U.S. Office of Management and Budget.

**One-shot method**   (1) "The trade name for a method of applying ADHE-SIVE in high-speed paperback binding, in which one application of a HOT-MELT ADHESIVE is applied to the SPINE of each book, in distinction to the application of both hot and COLD-SETTING ADHESIVES. (2) A colloquial term for the process of DEACIDIFYING paper through the use of one ALKALINE solution, as opposed to methods requiring the use of double treatments." (47:180) See also ADHESIVE BINDING; DEACIDIFI-CATION; HOT-MELT ADHESIVES; TWO-SHOT METHOD. (47:180)

**One-track**   See FULL-TRACK; MONOPHONIC.

**One up**   In microfilming, an arrangement in which there is only one page per FRAME.

**Onlay**   A decorative panel or piece of paper, leather, or other material, glued to the surface of a book cover. (1:156)

**Opacity**   (1) The ratio of ILLUMINANCE of a film sample to the light transmitted by a sample. (2) The degree to which a material prevents light from passing through it.

**Opaque**   Incapable of transmitting light. See also MICROOPAQUE.

**Opaque support**   A material impervious to light. (44:30)

**Openability**   "The ease with which a bound book allows the leaves to lie relatively flat when the book is open, with no weight or pressure applied (especially along the BINDING EDGE). Openability depends on the size of the book, the weight and thickness of the paper, the GRAIN direction in the book (which should be parallel to the spine), the method of sewing, and the overall quality and structure of the binding." (47:181)

**Open back**   See HOLLOW BACK.

**Open joint**   See FRENCH JOINT.

**Open reel**   See REEL-TO-REEL TAPE.

**O-phenyl phenol**   See ORTHO-PHENYL PHENOL.

**OPP**   See ORTHO-PHENYL PHENOL.

**Optical**   (1) Of, or relating to, or using lenses, mirrors, etc., as in optical viewfinder and optical printer; (2) relating to light, its behavior and control, as in optical properties, optical rotation. (42:193)

**Optical axis**   The OPTICAL center of a LENS or lens system.

**Optical center**   The point center of an image with respect to length and width.

**Optical density**   See DENSITY.

**Optical disc**   See DIGITAL OPTICAL RECORDING; VIDEODISC.

**Optimum exposure**   Correct intensity of radiation and duration in order to get the best possible image for reproductive purposes.

**Ordinal**   A level of measurement in which individuals or CASEs are assigned to a category of a VARIABLE, such that the categories are ordered. Example: An individual may rank-order ten books according to his preference of the books. In this example the ten books constitute ten cases, and the variable is order of preference. (7:111)

**Orientation**   See PARTICLE ORIENTATION.

**Orientation direction**   The direction in which PARTICLE ORIENTA-TION takes place. (49:158)

**Original**   (1) In photography, the object, person, scene, or document that is to be imaged. (2) The initial image, usually made in a camera. (3) In REPROGRAPHY, the source document or intermediate copy from which copies are produced; thus the original may be a POSITIVE or a NEGA-TIVE. (1:160)

**Original film**   See CAMERA MASTER.

**Original negative**   The camera negative from which subsequent ORIGI-NAL PRINTs or duplicates are made. See CAMERA MASTER. (46:155)

**Original print**   Print made from an ORIGINAL or camera negative and contemporary with the time the photograph was made. See also COPY PRINT. (46:155)

**Orthochromatic film**   A silver EMULSION film sensitive to yellow and green light as well as to blue and violet. The lack of sensitivity to red means that dark red is reproduced as black. See also PANCHROMATIC FILM. (1:160)

**Ortho-phenyl phenol (OPP)**   A phenolic chemical ($C_6H_5 \cdot C_6H_4 \cdot OH$) that has been used for nonresidual MOLD control on library materials. This chemical is not registered for mold control in libraries in the United States, but has been used in the past for extensive mold infestations brought about by flooding and fires. It is also used in STARCH-based ADHESIVEs to inhibit mold growth and prolong the shelf life of PASTE. It is a solid at room temperature and is usually mixed with ethanol for aqueous or spray application. (41:119)

**OSHA**   Occupational Safety and Health Administration.

**O$_3$**   Ozone.

**Outer joint**   "The grooves in the covering material at which the BOARDs open. Also called outer HINGE. The term JOINT is sometimes used to indicate the ridge or abutment formed by the BACKING operation to accommodate the boards; however, this ridge is more appropriately referred to as the SHOULDER(s) of the book. See also FRENCH JOINT." (47:182)

**Out of contact**   In CONTACT COPYing, contact failure between EMULSIONs. Loss of contact between the emulsions results in blurred or indistinct images and image spreading.

**Out of focus**   An image formed when the LENS, film plane, and the object being photographed are not in proper relative positions.

**Output**   The magnitude of the reproduced signal voltage, usually measured as the output of the reproduced amplifier. (49:158)

**Overcasting**   A method of hand binding in which one SECTION is sewn to another by passing the thread through the BACK EDGE and diagonally out through the back. (1:161)

**Overcoat**   In photography, a very thin layer applied over the GELATIN layer designed to provide protection to the recorded images during processing or to act as a filter.

**Overdevelopment**   Descriptive of film which has higher than normal densities, both $D$min and $D$max, caused by high temperature during development, excess development time, overly strong DEVELOPER solution, etc.

**Overexposure**   A film in which the $D$max exceeds normal, but the $D$min remains within normal tolerances. Caused by excessive EXPOSURE time, excessive ILLUMINATION, or setting the lens opening to admit too much RADIANT ENERGY.

**Overlap**   A REEL FILM anomaly in which one image overlaps another. Caused by a malfunctioning FILM ADVANCE mechanism.

**Oversewing**   A method of SEWING the leaves of a book by hand or by machine, almost always the latter in LIBRARY BINDING. The sewing thread passes through the edges of each SECTION, in consecutive order, using pre-punched holes through which the sewing needles pass. The oversewing process generally entails the removal of the original SPINE LINING CLOTH, GLUE, original sewing, and the folds of the sections, which is usually accomplished by planing, grinding, sawing, or cutting the SPINE of the book, removing an eighth of an inch or more of the binding margin. Sometimes the spine is first NIPped to remove the original backing SHOULDERs before the folds are removed. The book, having been reduced to individual leaves, is then jogged, and a very light coat of glue is applied along the BINDING EDGE to hold the leaves together temporarily. A number of leaves, or a "section," between 0.055 and 0.065 inch in thickness (depending upon the thickness of the paper) is then sewn, either by hand, or more commonly by the piercing action of multiple threaded needles in an oversewing machine. The thread passes through the section perpendicular to the plane of the paper or obliquely. The latter, or diagonal method, is employed in oversewing machines. Oversewing results in a very strong LEAF ATTACHMENT. Altogether, about $5/16$ or $6/16$ inch of the binding margin is consumed by the process. (47:182–183) Drawbacks to oversewing are intrusions on the INNER MARGINS, the destructive action of the needles perforating the pages, and a condition called "mousetrapping," where a book springs shut if it is not held open firmly. Oversewn volumes do not open flat for photocopying, and BRITTLE paper will break off at the point of sewing. (38:217)

**Oxidation**  A chemical reaction that converts an element into its oxide; to combine with oxygen. See REDOX BLEMISH.

**Oxide shed**  In magnetic tape recording, the loosening of particles of oxide from the tape COATING during use. (49:158)

# P

Abbreviation for phonogram (sound recording). See AUDIODISC.

(p)  "Copyright symbol for sound recordings ('phonograms'). On the published copies of a sound recording the symbol generally appears on the label together with the date of copyright and, usually, the name of the copyright owner. The symbol has been used since 15 February 1972 when federal copyright protection was extended to sound recordings. The symbol also protects foreign recordings for countries party to international copyright agreements." (52:34) See AUDIODISC.

**Pack**  Refers to the form taken by tape as it is wound on a REEL or around a HUB. A good tape pack will be smooth and free of ripples, buckling, CINCHING, etc. (4:297) See TAILS OUT.

**Packing density**  The amount of useful digital information that can be recorded along the length of a tape measured in BITs per inch. (49:158)

**Page**  One side of a LEAF.

**Pallet**  A low, portable platform, usually of wood, used in warehousing.

**Pam box**  See PAMPHLET FILE.

**Pamphlet**  In a bibliographical sense, a pamphlet has been variously defined as a non-periodical publication of at least five but not more than

48 pages, exclusive of the cover pages (General Conference of UNESCO, 1964), a publication of not more than 100 pages, one less than 80 pages, and as a publication consisting of one folded SECTION (SIGNATURE), regardless of the number of pages (but generally never more than 128). (47:187)

**Pamphlet binder**  A COVER of PASTEBOARD, with a gummed and stitched binding strip, used to hold one or more PAMPHLETs. Until recently, the quality of the BOARD generally used for this type of binder, which is used in many libraries as a permanent binding, has been such that sooner or later (and usually sooner) it becomes highly acidified, transferring its acidity to the first and last leaves of the publication and acidifying them, also. (47:187) Thus the binder actually harms the material it was designed to protect. The cloth adhesive strip forms a straight line or fracture plane on the original pamphlet COVER or endleaf. As the acidic ADHESIVE on the strip causes the CELLULOSE FIBERs of the cover to weaken, the cover will break along this fracture plane, resulting in the loss of information on the first and last pages of the pamphlet. Eventually, the acid in the boards of the pamphlet binder will cause further damage to the material housed within. An archivally sound pamphlet binder is now available based on a design developed at the University of California. The binder features a high-density ACRYLIC-coated grey board with a three percent CALCIUM CARBONATE BUFFER and a pH of 8.5. It uses ACRYLIC-coated C-1 cloth, 100 percent cotton CAMBRIC SPINE reinforcement, and a 0.002 acrylic adhesive flap. (3) This type of pamphlet binder should always be used in place of the old brown acidic board style.

**Pamphlet box**  See PAMPHLET FILE.

**Pamphlet file**  A BOX or frame for holding a number of PAMPHLETs, unbound numbers of periodicals, or other materials unbound or in paper covers. (1:162)

**Panchromatic film**  A silver EMULSION film sensitive to the complete visible color spectrum and to ULTRAVIOLET. In black-and-white film, all colors are represented as various shades of gray. See also ORTHOCHROMATIC FILM. (1:162)

**Paper**  A fibrous mat produced by a filtration process in which a dilute SLURRY of FIBERs in water is caused to flow across a screen, allowing the water to drain out. The SHEET is then removed from the screen, pressed, and dried. (29:117) Paper can be characterized in a number of ways: the source of the fiber (ESPARTO, rag, wood); the process for making the PULP from which the fibers are extracted (CHEMICAL WOOD, GROUNDWOOD, MECHANICAL WOOD); the way the sheet is made (HANDMADE, LAID, WOVE); or its intended use (art, bond, book, COVER, NEWSPRINT). Its qualities are determined by the purity,

length, and FIBRILLATION of the fibers used, its CHEMICAL STABIL-
ITY, and the finishes achieved. (1:163) Book papers are made from
mechanical wood pulp (used for the cheapest publications and newspapers), chemical wood pulp (for most books), and esparto or rags, used for
high-quality handmade papers (for fine books). (23:460) Paper derives
its name from PAPYRUS (which is not paper).

**Paperback**   A FLAT BACK book that has a flexible paper COVER and
usually is adhesive bound. The paper cover is usually of heavier stock
than that used for the leaves of the publication itself. Paperback books are
often made up of single leaves secured by a HOT-MELT ADHESIVE.
They usually have relatively narrow INNER MARGINs, are often printed
on paper of poor to very poor quality (frequently with a high proportion
of MECHANICAL WOOD PULP), and are generally CUT FLUSH.
(47:188) Paperbacks with sewn SECTIONs can be given hard covers
while still retaining their through-the-fold format. See also ADHESIVE
BINDING; HARD BOUND. (38:217)

**Paperboard**   "A general term applied to sheets of fibrous material of the
same general composition as paper which are 0.012 inch or more in
thickness and certain grades 0.006 inch or more in THICKNESS." (1:163)

**Paperbound**   See PAPERBACK.

**Paper brightness**   The ability of a paper to reflect light.

**Paper clay**   "A white or light-colored clay, very low in free silica. The term
usually refers to KAOLIN." See KAOLIN. (15:297)

**Paper durability**   See DURABILITY (OF PAPER).

**Paper fibers**   The CELLULOSE FIBERs that make up a sheet of paper or
the layers of bookboard or MATBOARD. (38:217)

**Papermaking machine**   See CYLINDER MACHINE; FOURDRINIER
MACHINE.

**Paper permanence**   Ability of paper to maintain any or all of its properties
over time. See PERMANENCE; PERMANENT PAPER.

**Paper pulp**   See PULP.

**Paper support**   A base layer of paper onto which a LIGHT-SENSITIVE
EMULSION is coated. Paper supports show the largest variety of types
of photographic ARTIFACTs. (44:30)

**Papyrus**   A tall sedge *(Cyperus papyrus)* native to the Nile region, the pith
of which was sliced into longitudinal strips and pressed into matted
sheets. Used for writing material by the ancient Egyptians, Greeks, and
Romans. Although it is not paper, papyrus is the forerunner of paper and
the origin of the word. (15:300)

**Parallax**   An apparent change in relative position or shape of an object
being photographed or viewed resulting from a change in viewing

angle. This is a problem in cameras where the viewfinder does not focus through the lens. (1:163)

**Parameter** In statistics, a quantitative characteristic of a POPULATION, the value of which would be obtained if all members of the population were measured on the VARIABLE. (7:111)

**Parchment** Usually, the split skin of a lamb, sheep, or occasionally goat or young calf, prepared by scraping and dressing with lime (but not tanned, i.e., converted to leather) and intended for use as a writing or binding material. Ideal storage conditions for parchment are temperatures between 0° and 20°C (32° and 68°F), with a RELATIVE HUMIDITY of 50 to 65 percent. (47:190–191) See also VELLUM, with which the term is now virtually interchangeable. The distinction favored by collectors of MANUSCRIPTs tends to be that vellum is a more refined form of skin, and usually made from calf, whereas parchment is a cruder form, usually made from sheep, and thicker, harsher, and less highly polished than vellum. (1:164)

**Particle orientation** In magnetic recording, the process by which ACICULAR particles are rotated so that their longest dimensions tend to lie parallel to one another. (49:158)

**Particle shape** The particles of GAMMA FERRIC OXIDE used in conventional magnetic tape are ACICULAR with a dimensional ratio of about 6 to 1. (49:158)

**Particle size** The physical dimensions of magnetic particles used in a magnetic tape. (49:158)

**Paste** A soft, plastic ADHESIVE composition with semisolid consistency, usually water dispersible. Pastes most commonly used in CONSERVATION work are cooked wheat or rice STARCH. (28:25) They are generally prepared by heating a mixture of starch and water and subsequently cooling the HYDROLYZEd product. Paste has been used for centuries to join porous, nongreasy materials. Ready-made paste is available today in which the proportions of the ingredients are scientifically blended. The use of paste is declining in favor of cold RESINOUS ADHESIVES, such as POLYVINYL ACETATE. It is still used, however, for covering, pasting down ENDPAPERS, CASING-IN, REPAIRING torn leaves, etc. In paper conservation, rice starch and wheat starch pastes are used for HINGING, LINING, and in long-FIBER repairs. (47:192)

**Pasteboard** "A general term applied to both PAPERBOARDs and cardboards made by the union of thin layers of paper PULP; popularly used to denote any stiff BOARD of medium THICKNESS." (1:165) See also BINDER'S BOARD.

**Pastedown** The plain, colored, fancy, or MARBLED PAPER attached to the inside of the BOARD of a book after it has been covered, or when it is CASEd-in. The pastedown serves several purposes: it hides the raw edges of the covering material where it is turned over the edges of the board; it forms the HINGE between the TEXT BLOCK and the board or case; and in EDITION and LIBRARY BINDING (particularly the former), the pastedown and hinge are frequently the only means by which the text block is secured to its case. The pastedown is frequently referred to as the "board paper." It is also sometimes called the ENDPAPER (singular) or LINING PAPER. (47:193)

**Pattern recognition method**  When RESOLUTION patterns are viewed on a test chart, this method requires that the viewer be able to identify the direction of the lines of a pattern but not count them. See also LINE COUNT METHOD.

**Pattern sensitivity**  "A recorder inability to reproduce certain data system combinations (patterns)." (49:158)

**Peak sensitivity**  The radiant WAVELENGTH providing the most efficient response from radiant SENSITIZED material.

**Peeling**  Commonly used term referring to the widespread separation of the COATING layer of a laminated recording from its base or CORE. It is used interchangeably with FLAKING, although the latter usually implies more limited or local deterioration. (4:298)

**PEL**  Permissible Exposure Level.

**Pellon™**  A variety of POLYESTER, nonwoven, long-fiber fabrics. Will not stick to most ADHESIVEs. Used for interleaving between newly mended or repaired materials so they will not stick together while adhesive or PASTE is drying. Used as a barrier between HEAT-SET TISSUE and the TACKING IRON. See POLYESTER WEB.

**Pentachlorphenol (PCP)**  A crystalline compound ($C_6Cl_5OH$) produced by the reaction of hexachlorobenzene with sodium hydroxide, or of chlorine with phenol, and used, in concentrations of 0.1 percent by weight of the paper, as a FUNGICIDE. It is applicable either as an aqueous or nonaqueous solution. Being a highly chlorinated substance, it must be used in the presence of sufficient ALKALI to compensate for the probable liberation of hydrochloric acid, or in such small quantities, i.e., less than 0.1 percent, so as not to endanger the paper severely even if it does decompose slightly. PCP is colorless and is not likely to produce an appreciable odor. (47:195) It is highly toxic through the skin or inhalation.

**Perfect binding**  A type of binding, sometimes called ADHESIVE BINDING, in which the SIGNATUREs have been converted to individual pages by cutting, milling, or SANDING off the folded edges while being held in a clamp. They are attached to a PAPERBOARD COVER with an ADHESIVE. (15:307; 38:217; 47:195) See also ADHESIVE BINDING; FAN ADHESIVE BINDING.

**Perforated film**  Roll film provided with SPROCKET holes to pull film through the camera. Since the holes provide increased edge length through which oxidants or other agents can attack the GELATIN layer, this type of film is not suitable for PRESERVATION purposes. See also NONPERFORATED FILM.

**Permanence**  The ability of a material to resist chemical deterioration, but not a quantifiable term.

**Permanent-durable paper**  See PERMANENT PAPER.

**Permanent elongation**  The percentage elongation remaining in a tape or length of BASE FILM after a given load applied for a given time has been removed. (49:158)

**Permanent paper**  The American National Standard for permanent, uncoated paper (currently under revision) is published as *Permanence of Paper for Printed Library Materials* (uncoated) ANSI Z39.48—1984, specifies that permanent paper should last at least several hundred years without significant deterioration under normal library use and storage conditions. Such paper should meet the following minimum requirements: ALKALINE pH of 7.5; ALKALINE RESERVE of 2 percent as a buffering agent; suggested values for TEAR RESISTANCE and FOLDING ENDURANCE to ensure DURABILITY; and PULP free of GROUNDWOOD. The National Information Standards Organization has established a committee to revise the 1984 standard for permanent paper to add specifications for COATED PAPER. Coated paper has a smooth surface essential to printing high-quality half-tone illustrations. Although the COATINGs used by papermakers are generally alkaline, the core paper can be alkaline, NEUTRAL, or acidic. (5) See also DURABILITY (OF PAPER); PERMANENCE.

**Permanent record film**  See ARCHIVAL FILM.

**Permeability**  The rate at which a fluid (in either gaseous or liquid form) penetrates into a material. (47:196)

**Permed**  Magnetized to a level that cannot be removed with a hand-held degausser. (49:158) See also BULK ERASER.

**pf**  Abbreviation for PORTFOLIO.

**pH**  In chemistry, an abbreviation for HYDROGEN-ION CONCENTRATION. The letters "pH" stand for the French words for "hydrogen power." pH is a measure of the concentration of hydrogen IONs in an aqueous solution and is a measure of active acidity or alkalinity. The pH scale runs from 0 to 14, and each number indicates a tenfold differential. At 25°C (77° F), a pH of 7.0 is NEUTRAL; numbers below 7.0 indicate increasing acidity, with 0.0 being the most ACID. Numbers above 7.0 indicate increasing ALKALINITY, with 14 being most alkaline. Paper with a pH below 5.0 is considered highly acidic. BUFFERed storage materials typically have a pH between 7.0 and 9.0. (22:15) See also ACID; ALKALINE; HYDROGEN-ION CONCENTRATION.

**Phase box**   See PHASED BOX.

**Phased box**   "A four flap BOX originally invented to meet the immediate short-term protection needs of an item within the PHASED CONSER-VATION policy established by the Library of Congress. This type of box is now widely used to permanently protect fragile volumes in libraries around the country. They are easy to construct or may be purchased in several standard sizes from archival and library suppliers." (45:43)

**Phased conservation**   A concept developed at the Library of Congress to meet the short-term needs of items that would eventually be given full CONSERVATION treatment. (38:217–218)

**Phonocut**   See VERTICAL CUT.

**Phonocylinder**   See CYLINDER.

**Phonodisc**   See AUDIODISC.

**Phonogram**   See AUDIODISC; ℗.

**Phonograph**   "Derived from two Greek words: phone = voice/sound; graphos = writer/written. Edison applied this word to his first record-ing/reproducing machine of 1877. In general American terms a phono-graph was and is any machine reproducing sounds from indented, incised or engraved CYLINDER or AUDIODISC records; in general European terms a machine reproducing sounds from such cylinder records only." (4:298)

**Phonograph disc**   See AUDIODISC.

**Phonograph needle**   See STYLUS.

**Phonograph record**   See AUDIODISC.

**Phonorecord**   See AUDIODISC.

**Phonowire**   See WIRE.

**Photocopy**   A term applied to copies produced directly on film or paper photographically. The copies may be larger or smaller, but not in the MICROIMAGE range. Synonymous with photoduplication, photographic reproduction, photoreproduction. (1:168) See also REPROGRAPHY.

**Photoduplication**   See PHOTOCOPY.

**Photoflood**   A lamp designed to provide brilliant diffuse light.

**Photogelatin process**   See COLLOTYPE.

**Photograph**   An image produced by the action of light or other RADIANT ENERGY, such as x-rays, gamma rays, etc., on a PHOTOSENSITIVE material. Usually, but not always, formed by an OPTICAL system using a LENS and other optical devices. (1:168)

**Photographic film**   See FILM.

**Photographic paper**   An OPAQUE paper base, coated on one side (SIMPLEX paper) or both sides (DUPLEX paper) with a LIGHT-SENSITIVE EMULSION on which images can be recorded by exposure to RADIANT ENERGY and subsequent processing. Processed photographic paper may have POSITIVE or NEGATIVE images, may be either black-and-white or color, and is supplied in a number of sizes and types, which include hard, negative, normal, projection, soft, and CONTRAST paper. (1:168)

**Photographic reproduction**   See PHOTOCOPY.

**Photolithography**   "Lithography using plates prepared by a photomechanical process, as opposed to plates or stone with the image drawn by hand." (1:168)

**Photomacrograph**   A magnified photographic image of a subject. Also an image that can be read without magnification.

**Photomechanical**   "Any one of the processes of making printing plates by exposing a film negative or positive on the photosensitized plate surface." (1:168)

**Photometer**   A device to measure light intensity or brightness, LUMINOUS FLUX, light distribution, color, etc., usually by comparing the light emitted by two sources, one source having certain specified standard characteristics. (43:1085)

**Photometry**   The measurement of light intensity or of relative illuminating power. (43:1085)

**Photomicrograph**   A photo image of a magnified object, such as a photograph of an image magnified initially by a microscope.

**Photosensitive**   Receptive to RADIANT ENERGY.

**Photostat**   **(1)** A trade name of a photographic reproduction device used to record images of documents on SENSITIZED PAPER. **(2)** A copy made by such a device; it is optical and right-reading. (23:477)

**pH scale**   See pH.

**pH value**   See pH.

**Physical recording density**   In magnetic tape recording, the number of recorded FLUX reversals per unit length of track. (49:158)

**Piano roll**   "A roll of perforated paper from which sounds can be produced by pneumatic action in a player-piano. Also called a player-piano roll. The perforations activate the keys by regulating the air flow from a bellows." (52:34)

**Pickup felt**   See FELT.

**Pigment print**   A photographic PRINT which is a COLLOID RELIEF IMAGE and resists FADING strongly. (44:30)

**Pinch roller**  On magnetic tape recording machines, a free-turning wheel with a rubber surface which presses the tape firmly against the CAPSTAN to ensure consistent tape motion. (4:298)

**Pinhole**  **(1)** Substitute for a camera lens. **(2)** A small aperture. **(3)** Very small, clear spots on a negative.

**Pirate recording**  An illegally copied and marketed recording. A pirated copy may originate from a live performance, a broadcast, or an unauthorized duplication of a legitimate recording. Also called a bootleg recording, unauthorized recording. (52:35)

**Pit**  **(1)** Commonly used defect term for sound recordings which is similar to "dig" and GOUGE, although it might be a visible depression in the surface of the recording that causes no break in the modulated groove and, hence, no sonic distortion. See also CHIP; GOUGE. **(2)** The term used to describe the depressions in the surface of a LASER DISC which contain the digitally encoded program material to be read by the tracking laser beam in playback. (4:298)

**Planetary camera**  Usually a MICROFILM camera in which material being photographed and the film remain in a stationary position during the exposure. The film and the document are on fixed but different planes during filming. After each exposure the document is changed and the film is advanced one FRAME automatically. Also known as a flatbed camera. See also ROTARY CAMERA and STEP-AND-REPEAT CAMERA. (42:193)

**Plastic comb binding**  A method of MECHANICAL BINDING in which the teeth of a tube-like plastic comb are inserted into slots near the BINDING EDGE of the leaves and curl back upon themselves around the SPINE of the comb. (1:171) See also SPIRAL BINDING.

**Plastic support**  A flexible, transparent support upon which a sensitized EMULSION is coated. (44:31)

**Plasticizer**  **(1)** A material, such as glycerin (glycerol), sorbitol, triethylene glycol, etc., incorporated into an ADHESIVE during manufacture to increase its flexibility, workability, or distensibility. **(2)** A material added to the STOCK in the manufacture of a paper such as GLASSINE, or used in the papermaking mixtures to impart softness and flexibility. (47:199)

**Plate**  **(1)** An illustration, often an engraving taken from a metal plate, printed separately from the text of the book with one side of the LEAF blank, and often on different paper. Plates may be bound into a book or they may be loose in a PORTFOLIO. They are not generally included in the pagination. See also LEAF. **(2)** A flat block of wood or metal, usually of copper, nickel, or zinc, on the surface of which there is a design or reproduction of a type form, to be used for printing, engraving, embossing, etc. The method of printing may be relief, intaglio, or planographic.

**(3)** A photographic material composed of a GLASS SUPPORT coated with a photographic EMULSION. (44:31)

**Platen** **(1)** The flat plates in a BUILDING-IN MACHINE that apply pressure to the TEXT BLOCK. **(2)** A device for holding film in the FOCAL PLANE during exposure.

**Playback head** A device on a magnetic tape recorder that senses previously recorded signals on a tape as it passes over. Coils in the head convert passing magnetic fields on the tape, sensed at the head gap, into electronic audio signals for playback or reproduction. (4:299)

**Player-piano roll** See PIANO ROLL.

**Plenum** "In HVAC, a space used to collect or distribute air among many different spaces or ducts, effectively a very large duct; often the INTERSTITIAL SPACE between a dropped ceiling and the floor structure above." (30:79)

**Plow** In hand binding, a device used for TRIMMING the leaves of a book. Two parallel blocks of wood about four inches wide and eight inches long are connected by two guide rods and one threaded rod, with a cutting blade attached to the lower edge of one of the blocks. The left-hand part of the plow fits into a slot-like runner on the left cheek of the LYING PRESS, while the other block is fitted with an adjustable knife. The knife is usually moved inward by the turn of a screw, cutting into the leaves of the book as the plow is moved back and forth. The plow is now used very little except in the best of fine leather binding. (47:200)

**Plumming** See BRONZING.

**Pneumatic controls** A method of controlling an HVAC system by using a network of air-pressurized small tubes. Modulates air pressures to control equipment. The pneumatic method is one of the oldest control systems in the industry. (30:79)

**POC detector** A sensing device that alarms in response to visible (smoke) or invisible products of combustion (POC). (37:119)

**Pocket** A wallet-like receptacle made from LINEN or stiff paper inside a cover of a book (usually the back cover) to hold loose music parts, diagrams, or maps.

**Point** A unit of THICKNESS of PAPER or BOARD; one thousandth (0.001) of an inch. For example, 0.060 inch equals 60 points. See also MIL; THICKNESS.

**Points per pound** A ratio derived by dividing the BASIS WEIGHT of a sheet of paper in pounds by its THICKNESS in MILs. It is used to describe the DENSITY of paper or BOARD. The term is most frequently applied to the BURSTING STRENGTH. See also APPARENT DENSITY. (47:201)

**Polarity**   The characteristic of being either a POSITIVE or NEGATIVE image. Some photographic materials reverse polarity of the object photographed (a camera negative changes a POSITIVE image to negative, regular printing paper changes a negative image to a positive). Others maintain polarity (SLIDEs produce a positive image from a positive, direct duplicating film normally is used to produce a negative from a negative but can also produce a positive from a positive). See NEGATIVE and POSITIVE. (46:155)

**Polycarbonate**   A class of resins that are THERMOPLASTIC, tough, transparent, and nontoxic. (37:119)

**Polyester**   **(1)** Flexible transparent plastic sheeting made of POLYETHYLENE terephthalate and used as a FILM BASE because of its dimensional stability, strength, resistance to tearing, and relative nonflammability. All archivally sound microfilm stock is constructed on polyester base. (42:193). Polyester is very useful in PRESERVATION because when formulated with no coatings or additives it is inert and CHEMICALLY STABLE. Sold under a variety of trade names, including MYLAR™ and MELINEX™. Used to ENCAPSULATE documents and as a film base to make storage sleeves for PRINTs and NEGATIVEs. Its THICKNESS is often measured in MILs. Because polyester film is manufactured for many special purposes, it is essential that ordering specifications clearly indicate that film appropriate for CONSERVATION uses is required. Films with surface coatings should be avoided because some of these are manufactured in packaging grades which consist of POLYVINYL CHLORIDE. Persons ordering and using polyester film for conservation procedures should keep abreast of any changes in the manufacturer's line or method of designation. Ordering instructions should include: "Polyester clear film containing no PLASTICIZERs, surface coatings, UV inhibitors, or absorbents. ARCHIVAL QUALITY. Must be guaranteed to be nonyellowing at ambient temperatures with natural aging, dimensionally stable, and resistant to most chemicals, moisture, and abrasion. Must match in quality Mylar™ Type A, D, S, or Melinex™ Type 516, or the equivalent, and meet government specifications L-P-00670B(2) and L-P-377B." (27:21) **(2)** A material commonly used as the base film for magnetic tape. It has a higher HUMIDITY and temperature STABILITY than most other film-base materials. It also has greater strength and fungus and MILDEW resistance. (4:299) See also BACKING; ENCAPSULATION; MELINEX™; MYLAR™.

**Polyester film**   See POLYESTER.

**Polyester web**   "A thin, nonwoven synthetic fabric made from filaments of POLYETHYLENE terephthalate. Used to support paper during aqueous treatments and also as a non-stick surface through which moisture will pass during MENDING, drying, etc." (45:89) See PELLON™.

**Polyethylene**   A chemically inert, stable, highly flexible, transparent or translucent THERMOPLASTIC material. It has a low melting point, and when made with no surface coatings or additives, is suitable for ENCLOSUREs for photographs. (46:155) It is also used in PRESERVA-TION as a protective liner or SLEEVE for discs and tapes. It furnishes a smooth fungi-resistant surface and is also a moisture barrier for both the disc or tape and the external packaging (jacket or box). (4:299)

**Polymer**   A naturally occurring or synthetic substance consisting of giant molecules derived either by the addition of many smaller similar molecules, as POLYETHYLENE, or by the condensation of many smaller molecules with the elimination of water, ALCOHOL, or the like, such as nylon.

**Polymerization**   The process of joining two or more like molecules into a more complex molecule whose molecular weight is a multiple of the original and whose physical properties are different. (55:107) In recordings, ADDITIVEs are chosen to alter certain physical properties for a desired effect through polymerization. Sometimes these additives can also create undesired effects. (4:299)

**Polypropylene**   A stiff, heat-resistant, CHEMICALLY STABLE plastic. Common uses in PRESERVATION: sleeves for 35mm SLIDEs or films, containers. (22:15)

**Polystyrene**   Another form of plastic used in the production of AUDIODISCs. It has chiefly been used in the manufacture of seven inch 45 rpm single records. (4:300)

**Polyvinyl acetate**   "A plastic usually abbreviated as PVA. A colorless transparent solid, it is usually used in ADHESIVEs, which are themselves also referred to as PVA or PVA adhesives. There are dozens of PVA adhesives, some are "internally PLASTICIZED" and are suitable for use in CONSERVATION because of their CHEMICAL STABILITY, among other qualities." (22:15) See POLYVINYL ACETATE (PVA) ADHESIVE.

**Polyvinyl acetate (PVA) adhesive**   An internally PLASTICIZED ADHE-SIVE that dries quickly and remains flexible over time. PVA is one of the clear, water-white, THERMOPLASTIC synthetic resins produced from its MONOMER by emulsion POLYMERIZATION. It is readily diluted with water, is easily applied, and is safe to use because it contains no flammable solvents. In addition, there is no need to use preservatives or FUNGICIDEs because it does not deteriorate quickly and is unaffected by MOLD or FUNGI. The emulsion does slowly HYDROLYZE, however, and should not be stored for more than one or two years before use. Freezing also destroys the emulsion; therefore, precautions must be taken to avoid exposing it to temperatures near or below the freezing point. PVA results in a very strong bond. After drying, however, the film of most

PVA-based adhesives is not reversible in water, and therefore it is not suitable for paper repairs. It may be used when a flexible fast-drying adhesive is desired and REVERSIBILITY is not particularly important, e.g., in PAMPHLET BINDERs, folders, WRAPPERs, etc. (38:218; 47:202)

**Polyvinyl chloride (polymerized vinyl chloride) (PVC)**   A plastic which has been manufactured in the United States since the 1930s. It is not as CHEMICALLY STABLE as some other plastics, since it can emit hydrochloric acid (which in turn can damage library materials) as it deteriorates. It therefore has limited application in the PRESERVATION of books and paper. Some plastics called VINYL may, in fact, be polyvinyl chloride. In the sound recording industry it is used in the manufacture of AUDIODISCs, magnetic tape BACKING, and magnetic tape BINDER. It was used as a binder in 78 rpm SHELLAC type discs, and is the primary ingredient in contemporary LP discs. (4:300)

**Population**   In statistics, the total number of CASEs of interest, the total number of cases about which a generalization may be made. A population may be countable in number or so large that it might be considered infinite and therefore, practically speaking, uncountable. (7:111)

**Porosity**   That property a material has of containing interstices (i.e, small or narrow spaces). It is defined as the ratio of the volume of the interstices to the volume of the mass of the material, and depends upon the number, shape and distribution of the voids, as well as their shape and orientation. It is usually expressed as a percentage. The term is sometimes used incorrectly to indicate PERMEABILITY. (47:202)

**Portfolio**   "An inclosure used to protect loose drawings, PLATEs, papers, and the like. It usually consists of two sheets of BOARD covered with paper or cloth, with a wide cloth or paper joint forming the SPINE. It has flaps to contain the enclosed material. Abbreviated pf." (47:203) See also PROTECTIVE ENCLOSURE.

**Position A**   See CINE MODE.

**Position B**   See COMIC MODE.

**Positive**   Having the same tonal values (either black-and-white or color) and image as the object photographed. Sometimes made from a NEGATIVE in which the image and the tones are reversed compared with the ORIGINAL. (23:488) See also NEGATIVE; POSITIVE COPY.

**Positive copy**   A copy having the same tonal values and image as the ORIGINAL. Also called a positive PRINT. Can be created from a NEGATIVE using duplicating (REVERSAL) FILM. (23:488) See also POSITIVE.

**Positive print**   See POSITIVE COPY.

**Poslip method**   Developed by W. H. Langwell in England, this procedure uses a tissue paper impregnated with POLYVINYL ACETATE and magnesium acetate (as a DEACIDIFIER) for LAMINATION. It uses salts, substituting a weaker ACID for a strong one, and does not leave an adequate ALKALINE RESERVE.

**Postamble**   In magnetic tape recording, a group of special signals recorded at the end of each block on the tape for the purpose of electronic synchronization. (49:159) See also PREAMBLE.

**Post binder**   "A form of loose-leaf mechanical binder. The typical binder has two posts, which may either be self-locking or locked by caps or knurled thumb screws." (47:203) See also MECHANICAL BINDING.

**Postconditioning**   Processes such as rehydration of paper after DEACIDI-FICATION treatment. (53:5)

**Post-echo**   See ECHO.

**Potassium lactate**   A potassium salt of lactic ACID ($KC_3H_5O_3 \bullet H_2O$), used to treat leather in order to counteract acid present in the leather due to manufacturing processes or because of air pollution (sulfur dioxide), or as a safeguard against the future incursion of acid or acid-forming materials. There is some controversy over the use of this salt as a leather/acid buffer. The major arguments against it seem to be that it may cause a whitish discoloration to appear on the surface of the leather (potassium sulfate discoloration) and, unless applied to both the flesh and grain sides of the leather, it is ineffectual. If the latter argument is correct, it would mean that leathers used for bookbinding could be treated only one time. Potassium lactate should not be applied to powdery (RED ROT) leathers, nor to suede leathers, as it will result in the blackening of both. (47:203) See also KRYLON™ NO. 1301; LEATHER DRESSINGS.

**Potassium permanganate**   A chemical compound ($KMnO_4$) used to remove impurities through oxidation. (30:79)

**Pounds per point**   "The ratio of the BASIS WEIGHT in pounds divided by the THICKNESS in MILs. It is used to describe the density." See APPARENT DENSITY, BASIS WEIGHT, and THICKNESS. (15:324)

**PQ developer**   See DEVELOPING.

**Preamble**   In magnetic tape recording, a group of special signals recorded at the beginning of each block on tape for the purpose of electronic synchronization. (49:159) See also POSTAMBLE.

**Prebound**   New books having COVERs imprinted with a design like that on the original publisher's binding which have been bound according to the *Library Binding Institute Standard for Library Prebound Books* (1986). This type of binding should not be confused with publisher's EDITION BINDING, LIBRARY EDITION, or REINFORCED BINDING or other bindings not in accordance with the standard. Also called pre-library bound.

**Precoat**   A thin COATING applied to the FILM BASE designed to improve adherence of the EMULSION to the base.

**Preconditioning**    Processes such as dehydration of paper before DE-ACIDIFICATION treatment. (53:5)

**Precoupling**    Damage caused by the premature development of diazo material. (21:21)

**Pre-echo**    See ECHO.

**Pre-library bound**    See PREBOUND.

**Preliminary matter**    See FRONT MATTER.

**Premium**    The amount paid for an insurance policy, usually in installments.

**Prepared paper support**    In photography, a paper support coated with a layer of inert material in a GELATIN solution upon which a SENSITIZED EMULSION is coated. (44:31)

**Prerinse**    An initial water BATH prior to development.

**Preselection**    In DEACIDIFICATION, screening to determine which books can be safely treated. See also INTRINSIC VALUE; TRIAGE.

**Preservation**    "The activities associated with maintaining library and ARCHIVAL materials for use, either in their original physical form or in some other usable way."(42:193) Preservation includes CONSERVATION, but is considered a broader term than conservation. See also CONSERVATION.

**Preservation administrator**    "A person trained in PRESERVATION who helps design and administer a library's or other repository's program for maintaining books and other documents for use." (1:175)

**Preservation Advisory Committee**    Established in 1985 by the Council on Library Resources to guide initial work on long-term PRESERVATION work at U.S. libraries.

**Preservation copy**    **(1)** A sound recording designated for archival preservation; such recordings are played only under exceptional circumstances. (4:300) **(2)** Also used to designate the CAMERA MASTER of a PRESERVATION MICROFORM.

**Preservation duplicate**    **(1)** A duplicate copy of a sound recording designated for archival preservation. (4:300) **(2)** A SECOND-GENERATION photographic copy of a PRESERVATION MASTER NEGATIVE (CAMERA MASTER), usually a COPY NEGATIVE. Also known as a duplicate archive master.

**Preservation master negative**    A first-generation negative or CAMERA MASTER produced according to archival standards and stored under archival conditions. It should only be used to produce PRINTing MASTERs. Also known as an archive master. (42:194)

**Preservation microfilming**    Reformatting ORIGINAL material, usually print on paper material, by MICROREPRODUCTION of the text. Requires adherence to national technical standards in text preparation (collating and EYE-LEGIBLE TARGETS), selection of film type, production, processing, and storage of the archive master negative. Bibliographic control of items preserved by microfilming is important in order to avoid duplication of preservation efforts. (38:218) See also LONG-TERM FILM.

**Preservation microform**   Any microform generation originally produced according to preservation standards.

**Preservation transfer copy**   A dubbing made for archival preservation of a recording which cannot be preserved due to ongoing deterioration; or a dubbing made to serve as a PRESERVATION duplicate of a PRESERVATION COPY of a recording. (4:300)

**Press**   (1) A machine used to smoothly and steadily apply pressure evenly. (2) In a papermaking machine a pair of rolls between which the paper WEB is passed for: (a) water removal at the WET PRESS, (b) smoothing and leveling of the sheet surface at the SMOOTHING PRESS, and (c) application of surface treatments to the sheet at the SIZE PRESS. (15:325) See FOURDRINIER MACHINE.

**Pressboard**   A stiff, slick cardboard or thick-coated BRISTOL made of tough, dense, highly glazed rag or CHEMICAL WOOD PULP BOARD. It is used where strength and stiffness are required of a relatively thin (e.g., 0.030 inch) sheet. Pressboard is almost as hard as a sheet of FIBER BOARD and is used for the covers of notebooks and tablets. (38:218; 47:204) See also FIBERBOARD; SOLID BOARD.

**Pressing**   (1) An AUDIODISC molded from a negative metal STAMPER or MATRIX. (2) The total number of discs pressed at one time from the same matrix. (52:35)

**Press section**   See FOURDRINIER MACHINE; PRESS.

**Pressure marks**   An anomaly of PROCESSED FILM that may show up as linear areas of reduced or increased DENSITY. Caused by pressure somewhere in the filming/processing procedures.

**Pressure-sensitive tape**   An ADHESIVE tape that attaches to a surface when pressure is applied. ACETATE tape, or transparent MENDING tape, which has a matte surface and appears colorless when in the roll, has a much higher degree of permanence and does not change color; however, it can be damaging to library and archival materials. Cellophane tape darkens with age, is difficult to remove, and stains the paper to which it adheres. Benzene or ether, both of which are toxic (especially the former), flammable, and therefore dangerous to use, are solvents capable of removing pressure-sensitive tapes. (47:205) In most cases, a paper CONSERVATOR should be consulted before attempting to remove pressure-sensitive tape.

**Preventive maintenance**   Regular procedures for checking, adjusting, and servicing equipment, including evaluation of performance, determination of wear, and identification of problem conditions requiring attention.

**Princeton file**   A free-standing, box-like container open at the top, back, and the lower half of the front. It is used to hold PAMPHLETs, periodical issues, single sheets, etc., usually for storage on bookshelves.

**Print**   (1) A photographic copy. (2) To make such a copy.

**Print film**   A FINE GRAIN, high-resolution film mainly used for CONTACT PRINTing.

**Printing-out-paper (POP)**   Paper coated with a LIGHT-SENSITIVE EMULSION producing an image directly when CONTACT PRINTed in daylight ILLUMINATION. (44:31)

**Print master**   A SECOND-GENERATION microfilm used to create a variety of end user FORMATs. In PRESERVATION applications, an "insurance" copy of an archive master to preclude use of the archive master for preparation of end-user formats.

**Print-out**   In photography, increases in minimum DENSITY that occur in the light. (8:154)

**Print through**   The unwanted transfer of a magnetic field (and the sound signal) from one layer to another within a roll of tape. The magnitude of this induced signal tends to increase with the storage time and temperature and decrease with the unwinding of the tape roll. It is the function of the MAGNETIC INSTABILITY of the magnetic oxide on the tape. It causes ECHO or repeated sound from one layer of tape while the next layer is passing over the PLAYBACK HEAD. See ECHO. (4:300)

**Process camera**   A CAMERA specially designed to produce images on an intermediate photographically sensitive material from which PRINTs can be made, as in PHOTOLITHOGRAPHY. (1:178)

**Process control system**   See DISTRIBUTIVE CONTROL SYSTEM.

**Processed film**   Exposed film treated to produce a fixed or stabilized visible image. (42:194)

**Processed recording**   "A recording produced in multiple copies." (52:35) See also NONPROCESSED RECORDING.

**Processing**   A process in which exposed photographic material is exposed to one or more treatments or BATHs (liquid or gas vapor) which make the LATENT IMAGE visible and ultimately usable, e.g., DEVELOPMENT, FIXING, WASHING, drying. (42:194)

**Processor**   Any machine designed to provide all necessary steps to process photographic material, e.g., DEVELOPMENT, FIXING, WASHING, etc. (42:194)

**Programming**   A prefilming task performed after COLLATION to establish the number of frames to be filmed on each REEL. Programming is a combination of calculating the maximum number of exposures per reel based on both the REDUCTION RATIO and the FRAME position and deciding where an appropriate bibliographic or chronological break should be made to the end of each reel. (42:194)

**Protective coating**  A layer applied to processed microfilm to help reduce the impact of SCRATCHes, fingerprints, and skin oils on the images.

**Protective enclosure**  "A custom-made ENCLOSURE, such as a BOX, ENVELOPE, folder, PORTFOLIO, PULL-OFF BOX, or a SLIPCASE, that protects an item from dust, light, MECHANICAL DAMAGE, and most air pollutants." (38:218) An enclosure can be considered a holding activity or "phased treatment" for materials that are to be retained in their original FORMAT, but for which other CONSERVATION treatment is not feasible in the near future. (2) See also PHASED BOX; PHASED CONSERVATION.

**Provenance**  A record or indication of previous ownership of a book or manuscript. This may be shown by a special binding, or by a bookplate or inscription inserted or affixed by previous owners, collectors, or librarians holding the item. (23:502)

**PSIG**  Pounds per square inch gauge; pressure measured relative to atmospheric pressure, which equals 14.7 pounds per square inch. (55:107)

**Psychrometer**  A HYGROMETER used for determining RELATIVE HUMIDITY, i.e., the amount of moisture in the air. It utilizes paired wet- and dry- bulb temperature readings which are compared with a chart showing the measure of dryness of the surrounding air. (47:206) See also HYGROMETER; SLING PSYCHROMETER.

**Publisher's binding**  See EDITION BINDING.

**Pulldown**  The distance between identical points on adjacent FRAMEs, for instance, the distance between the left edge of frame one and the left edge of frame two. Required to determine the number of frames that will fit on a reel and for some frame-centering equipment.

**Pulled**  In bookbinding, a book which has its cover removed and all the sheets separated. (23:508) See also TAKE DOWN.

**Pull-off box**  A book-shaped box designed to hold a book, but also used to contain PAMPHLETs, MANUSCRIPTs, etc. Occasionally it opens at the side or front, but it more often consists of two separate parts, one telescoping over the other. When properly constructed, it provides nearly airtight protection. Also called pull-off case, or pull-off cover, and frequently, though incorrectly, a SOLANDER BOX. (47:207)

**Pulp**  The mechanically and/or chemically prepared fibrous mixture used in the manufacture of PAPER and BOARD. Mechanical PULPING simply separates the FIBERs, while chemical pulping purifies them of LIGNINs and other undesirable agents. See also CHEMICAL WOOD PULP; HALFSTUFF; MECHANICAL WOOD PULP; STOCK.

**Pulp board**   "BOARD manufactured in one THICKNESS, or by bringing two or more thicknesses of board or paper together into a single structure on a multiple-wire machine, as distinct from boards made by laminations of paper pasted together and called PASTEBOARD." (23:508)

**Pulper**   "A machine designed to break up, defiber, and disperse dry pulps, mill process BROKE, commercial waste papers, or other fibrous materials into SLUSH form preparatory to further processing and conversion into PAPER or PAPERBOARD. It normally consists of a tank or chest with suitable agitation to accomplish the dispersion with a minimum consumption of power. It may also be used for blending various materials with PULP." (15:331) See SLUSH.

**Pulping**   "The operation of reducing a cellulosic raw material, such as PULPWOOD, rags, straw, reclaimed PAPER, etc., into a PULP suitable for further processing into paper or PAPERBOARD or for chemical conversion (into rayon, cellophane, etc.)." (15:331)

**Pulpwood**   Wood which is suitable for the manufacture of WOOD PULP. The wood may be in the form of freshly cut logs from the forest, shorter logs suitable for the chipper or the GRINDER, or chips produced from groundwood. Whole trees remote from the pulp mill are also referred to as pulpwood. (15:332)

**Pulse-code-modulation recording**   See DIGITAL SOUND RECORDING.

**PVA**   See POLYVINYL ACETATE (PVA).

**PVC**   See POLYVINYL CHLORIDE (PVC).

**Pyrogallic acid**   1:2:3 Trihydroxybenzene $C_6H_3(OH)_3$. White, needle-like, water-soluble crystals used as a DEVELOPING agent. Rapidly oxidizes in solution. Also known as pyro or pyrogallol. A developing agent preferred by some photographers. (8:154)

**Pyrophoric**   Any material that spontaneously ignites when exposed to oxygen. (55:107)

**Pyroxylin**   A compound consisting of lower-nitrated CELLULOSE NITRATE, usually containing less than 12.5 percent nitrogen. It is used in the manufacture of pyroxylin-coated and impregnated BOOK CLOTHs. (47:209) See also COLLODION EMULSION; PYROXYLIN-TREATED BOOK CLOTH.

**Pyroxylin-treated book cloth**   "A cotton fabric completely and (usually) heavily coated with the CELLULOSE NITRATE compound, PYROXYLIN; or, a fabric completely filled with the same compound. Coated fabric is usually called a 'pyroxylin-coated,' and filled fabric is called a 'pyroxylin-impregnated.' A proxylin coating or FINISH enables BOOK CLOTH to resist wear and tear and is commonly used in the LIBRARY BINDING industry. Because of pollution generated during manufacture, pyroxylin cloth is gradually being replaced by ACRYLIC-coated cloths." (38:218) See also BOOK CLOTH.

# Q

**I** See QUALITY INDEX. (42:194)

**Quad** Abbreviation for QUADRAPHONIC.

**Quadraphonic** System of recording and reproducing sound using four separate CHANNELs and four separate loudspeakers in an attempt to recreate a 360-degree sound field around the listener. (4:301)

**Quality assurance** See QUALITY CONTROL.

**Quality control** The processes, procedures, and tests used to ensure that the end product of any production system (including production of PRESERVATION MICROFILM) meets the standards and expectations of the client. Also known as quality assurance.

**Quality index** A relatively objective relationship between legibility of printed text (characterized by a "smallest 'e' measurement," i.e., the size of the smallest printed "e" in the original text) and the RESOLUTION pattern resolved in a microimage of a test pattern. Used to predetermine legibility in succeeding GENERATIONs. (42:194)

**Quarter binding** A binding in which the SPINE and a very small part of the sides are covered with a stronger material than the rest of the sides. (23:511) See also HALF BINDING.

**Quarter-track** A tape format in which there are four separate tracks on 1/4 inch tape. The tape runs from left to right and the top track is usually recorded first, and then the third. To record the other two tracks the tape is turned upside down and once again fed left to right. For stereo, the first and third tracks are recorded at the same time, using a stacked head (one with both gaps in line). Quarter-track recording has a SIGNAL-TO- NOISE RATIO which is poorer than that of half-track or full-track recording in proportion to the relative tape widths. FOUR-CHANNEL stereo uses all four tracks in the same direction. Quarter-track tape is primarily intended for the consumer market (home use). Also known as four track. (4:301) See also EIGHT-TRACK; FULL-TRACK; HALF-TRACK.

**Quire** One twentieth of a REAM. Twenty-five sheets in the case of a 500-sheet ream of FINE PAPERS, and 24 sheets in the case of a 480-sheet ream of coarse papers.

**R**adiant energy    Energy transmitted in wave motion, i.e., the electromagnetic spectrum, including VISIBLE LIGHT, ULTRAVIOLET, INFRARED, heat, and others.

**Radiant flux**    RADIANT ENERGY emitted or received by a surface in a unit of time. Measured in watts, normally expressed as microwatts. (31:7)

**Rag content**    "A term used interchangeably with cotton FIBER content which indicates that a paper contains a percentage of cotton fiber PULP. The cotton fiber content normally used may vary from 25 to 100 percent." (15:334)

**Rag paper**    "Paper made from rags, especially cotton rags." (23:513)

**Rag pulps**    "Papermaking FIBERS made from new or old cotton textile cuttings. The term may also apply to COTTON LINTERS, i.e., ledger, blueprint, map, currency papers, etc." (15:335)

**Raised bands**    "(1) BANDS that appear as ridges running across the SPINE of a book when they protrude from the back. (2) False bands, made to imitate real raised bands." (1:184) See also BANDS; SUNK BANDS.

**RAMP**    Records and Archives Management Program. A part of UNESCO's General Information Program and the publisher of a number of works on preservation.

**Random number**    A number whose digits are obtained by chance, using a process whereby each digit is equally likely to be any one of a specified set. A random number can be considered free from statistical bias. (1:184)

**Random sample**    A SAMPLE obtained as a result of selecting items from a POPULATION, with each item in the population having an equal chance of being selected.

**Range**    In statistics, a measure of the difference between the largest value and the smallest in a set of data.

**Rare book**    A desirable book, sufficiently difficult to find that it seldom, or at least only occasionally, appears in the antiquarian trade. Among rare books are traditionally included such categories as incunables, American imprints before 1800, first editions of important literary and other texts, books in fine bindings, unique copies, and books of interest for their associations. The degrees of rarity are as infinite as the needs of the antiquarian trade, and the term is decreasingly used in libraries and other repositories, many of which prefer the terms "special" or "research" collection to rare book collection. (1:185)

**Rate-of-rise**   A thermal detector sensitive to the rapid rise of temperature in a fire. (37:119)

**Rattle**   A noise produced when a sheet of paper is shaken. See STARCH.

**Raw stock**   Unexposed, unprocessed photographic film, paper, or other recording material, normally as it comes from the manufacturer. (42:194)

**Reader**   An electromechanical device for viewing MICROIMAGES.

**Read/write erase head**   A three-gap head (read, write, and erase gaps) on one body (sometimes the ERASE HEAD is bolted to the READ/WRITE HEAD). (49:159) See also ERASE HEAD; RECORD HEAD.

**Read/write head**   A two-gap head (read and write gap on one body). (49:159) See also RECORD HEAD.

**Realia**   Three-dimensional objects such as museum materials, dioramas, models, and samples. (23:516)

**Real image**   In optics, an image formed by converging light rays, which exists where it appears to be. See also VIRTUAL IMAGE. (1:186)

**Ream**   Depending on the grade, either 480 or 500 sheets of paper in a particular batch.

**Reback**   "To put a new BACKSTRIP on a book without doing any other REBINDING." (1:186)

**Rebinding**   Constructing a completely new binding for a book, including renewing or reattaching the PAGEs, new ENDSHEETS and SPINE LININGs, and a new COVER. In LIBRARY BINDING, rebinding often means TRIMMING the SECTIONs and OVERSEWING; in hand bookbinding it means REPAIRING the sections and SEWING through-thefold. (38:218)

**Recasing**   **(1)** "Reattaching a book to its original COVER without disturbing the SEWING or method of LEAF ATTACHMENT." **(2)** "Replacing the original cover with a new cover without disturbing the original leaf attachment." (38:218)

**Receiving reel**   A collection REEL for accumulating film after processing. Also known as a take-up spool.

**Record**   **(1)** "In archives, a document made or received and maintained by an organization or institution in pursuance of its legal obligations or in the transactions of its business." (1:186) **(2)** An AUDIODISC, i.e., a sound recording.

**Recorded book**   See TALKING BOOK.

**Record head**    A device on a tape recorder which converts audio signals from a sound source to magnetic fields that magnetize the oxide particles on magnetic tape, thus "recording" the sound onto the tape. (4:301) See also ERASE HEAD; READ/WRITE HEAD.

**Recording hygrothermograph**    A HYGROTHERMOGRAPH containing a device upon which 24 hour or seven day recording charts may be affixed. The charts may be divided into two fields, one for recording temperature and the other for RELATIVE HUMIDITY.

**Record margin**    The change in SIGNAL-TO-NOISE RATIO achieved by reducing the record level from optimum while maintaining the reproduce level constant to reach a specific BIT ERROR RATE. (49:159)

**Record series**    "In ARCHIVES, a group of RECORDs maintained as a unit because they relate to a particular subject or function, result from the same activity, have a particular form, or because of some other relationship arising out of their creation, receipt, or use, and intended to be kept together in a definite arrangement." (42:194)

**Records center container/carton**    A corrugated cardboard box designed to hold one cubic foot of RECORDs, either legal or letter size, and used chiefly in records centers.

**Recto**    The right-hand PAGE of an open book or MANUSCRIPT, usually bearing an odd page number. Distinct from the VERSO, which is the reverse side. See also VERSO. (23:518)

**Recycled fiber**    Usually old newspaper or wastepaper used with very little REFINING, often with groundwood or semi-bleached KRAFT. (15:338)

**Recycled paper**    "Paper made in a range of qualities from reclaimed or recovered wastepaper, mechanically disintegrated into PULP and variously processed to remove unwanted materials such as ink. Unless made from carefully selected, long-fibered STOCK, it is of poor color and strength." (1:187)

**Redox blemish**    A silver GELATIN film defect caused by OXIDATION from a number of sources, e.g., the surrounding environment, poor packaging materials, etc. Image silver reacts chemically with oxidizing agents, resulting in photographs developing discoloration, red spots ("measles"), and/or mirroring. (46:155) This process can also weaken developer when it is exposed to oxygen. See also BLEMISH.

**Red rot**    Deterioration of leather in the form of red powdering, found particularly in East India leathers prepared with tanning of the catechol group. (35:36) See also KRYLON™; LEATHER DRESSINGS.

**Red spot(s)**    See REDOX BLEMISH.

**Reducer**    In photographic DEVELOPING, a chemical agent for reducing the DENSITY of images on materials SENSITIZED with silver GELA-

TIN. Also any developing agent that reduces SILVER HALIDE to metallic silver in the development process. (1:188)

**Reduction ratio**   The relationship of the linear dimensions of an originally photographed item and its image on the CAMERA MASTER; reflective of the number of times the image has been reduced. For example, 18x means that the image is 18 times smaller than the linear dimensions of the ORIGINAL. Reduction ratios can be classed as LOW REDUCTION (up to and including 15x), MEDIUM REDUCTION (16x through 30x), HIGH REDUCTION (31x through 60x), VERY HIGH REDUCTION (61x through 90x), and ULTRAHIGH REDUCTION (above 90x).

**Reel**   **(1)** A flanged HUB, or spool, made of metal, glass, or plastic for holding recorded or processed audiotape, VIDEOTAPE, motion picture film, or MICROFILM. **(2)** The tape or film wound on such a spool. (1:188) **(3)** The untrimmed roll of paper of full machine width wound on a large shaft at the DRY END of the paper machine. **(4)** The shaft on which the paper is first wound when it leaves the DRIERs. **(5)** Reeling. The operation of winding paper onto a reel. (15:339)

**Reel flange**   The metal sides for a REEL of tape. Professional 10 1/2 inch and 14 inch tape reels have flanges mounted on NAB hubs. (4:301)

**Reel-to-reel**   The nature of the transport system on playback or projection devices in which the spooled material is moved from one REEL or spool to a separate take-up reel or spool. (23:519)

**Reel-to-reel tape**   Magnetic tape wound in spools or packs around a HUB and not enclosed in any shell. So called because a full REEL or spool unwinds onto an empty reel (hub with flanges or sides) during the recording and playback process. (4:302)

**Reference tape**   A tape used as a reference against which the performances of other tapes are compared. (49:159) See STANDARD REFERENCE TAPE.

**Refiner**   A machine used to rub, macerate, bruise, and cut fibrous material, usually CELLULOSE, in water suspension. The refiner converts the raw FIBER into a substance suitable for formation of PAPER products on a paper machine. Refiners differ in size and design features but most can be classified as either JORDANs or disk refiners. See JORDAN. (15:340)

**Refining**   The mechanical treatment of PULP in a water suspension to develop the papermaking properties of hydration and FIBRILLATION and to cut the FIBERs to the desired length distribution. (15:340) See REFINER.

**Reflectance**   A measure of light intensity (LUMINOUS FLUX) reflected from a surface, as compared with the light intensity of light received by the surface. Reflectance is a property of OPAQUE materials, such as paper. Reflectance is measured with a REFLECTANCE DENSITOMETER.

The values are compared with those on a REFLECTANCE TEST TAR-GET to arrive at a relative measure of reflectance. (1:189) See also REFLECTED LIGHT.

**Reflectance densitometer** A device for measuring REFLECTANCE in terms of density. See DENSITOMETER.

**Reflectance density** A method of expressing REFLECTANCE in terms of DENSITY. If reflectance is $R$ and reflectance density is $D$, then

$$D = \log_{10} (1/R)$$

**Reflectance test target** A standard target (test) for which the REFLEC-TANCE value is known. It is used to compare reflectance DENSITOM-ETER values from a reflective material (paper) with the test target's known values.

**Reflected light** Light bouncing from a surface; specifically not transmit-ted or absorbed light. (44:31) See also REFLECTANCE.

**Reformat** To record information originally in one medium to another, as in microfilming, where information contained on print on paper mate-rials are converted to film.

**Refrigerant** A chemical compound which is compressed and then al-lowed to expand in order to move heat from one place to another, usually a chlorofluorocarbon, such as one of the Freon compounds made by Du Pont. (30:79)

**Register** **(1)** In printing, a term used to indicate that the type area of the RECTO of the sheet coincides exactly with that of the VERSO; also the adjustment of color blocks so that colors are superimposed with exact accuracy. Register is of considerable importance in multicolored print-ing. **(2)** In folding, the exact alignment of images so that the print of one LEAF is exactly over that of the preceding and following leaves. (47:215) **(3)** In photography, to achieve exact superimposition of two identical images.

**Rehydrate** Adding moisture back into a hygroscopic material, such as the human hairs in a hygrothermograph. This usually involves sealing the equipment in a moist container for a day or so. Most human-hair hygrothermograph equipment, which is the typical type of equipment used, must be rehydrated on a regular basis, at least annually. (30:79)

**Reinforced binding** "A special publisher's EDITION BINDING in which cloth is pasted to the BACK EDGEs of the ENDPAPERS and, sometimes, the first and last SECTIONs. Other methods of strengthening bindings can be used, and portions of an edition may be specially handled and issued as a LIBRARY EDITION. These edition bindings do not match the standards established for PREBOUND books." (1:190)

**Relative humidity (RH)**    The ratio, expressed as a percent, of the amount of water vapor actually present in the air to the greatest amount of vapor the air could hold at that temperature.

$$RH = \frac{\text{Actual vapor pressure (at a given temperature)}}{\text{Saturated vapor pressure (at that same temperature)}} \times 100.$$

The term describes the wetness or dryness of air at a given temperature and pressure and is temperature dependent; as the temperature increases, the RH decreases, if no additional moisture were added to the air. RH significantly affects paper and paper-based materials. Any change in water content of a paper fiber immediately manifests itself as a change in its dimensions, especially in the cross-direction of paper. The fiber diameter swells considerably as the moisture content increases resulting in stretching of the paper. Other properties of the paper are also affected, but the most significant change affecting printing is the change in dimension. Photographic materials also respond to changes in humidity, especially those with gelatin layers; expanding in the presence of humidity and shrinking as the humidity declines. In environments in excess of 50 percent RH these changes become dramatic, allowing entry to the gelatin layer of oxidants and other film contaminants. For preservation purposes, film should not be exposed to humidity levels in excess of 50 percent RH and for archive and print masters at or below 35 percent RH. (32:3; 45:89; 47:215–216) See also ABSOLUTE HUMIDITY.

**Relief image**    An image which shows a three-dimensional quality between the SHADOWs and the HIGHLIGHTS, and which swells when spot-tested with water. (44:31) See also FLAT IMAGE.

**Remanence**    The magnetic FLUX density that remains in a magnetic circuit after removal of applied magnetomotive force. (49:159) See also RETENTIVITY.

**Repairing**    "The partial rehabilitation of a worn book, the amount of work done being less than the minimum involved in REBINDING and more than the maximum involved in MENDING. Includes such operations as restoring the COVER and reinforcing at JOINTs. Not to be confused with mending." (1:191) See also MENDING.

**Replacement cost**    The cost of replacing damaged property without a depreciation deduction. (25:95)

**Representative sample**    A SAMPLE that is judged, or claimed, to have the same characteristics as, or to represent accurately, the POPULATION from which it came; an informally used term that should not be confused with RANDOM SAMPLE. (1:192)

**Reprography**    A generic term encompassing virtually all processes for copying or reproduction of printed, typed, or handwritten material, etc., using light, heat, electrical radiation, or MICROREPRODUCTION.

**Residual flux**   In a uniformly magnetized sample of magnetic material, the product of the residual flux density and the cross-sectional area. (49:159) See also RETENTIVITY.

**Residual hypo**   See RESIDUAL THIOSULFATE ION.

**Residual hypo test**   A chemical test to determine the amount of HYPO (or thiosulfate) remaining on photographic film or paper after PROCESS-ING. Testing methods include METHYLENE BLUE and SILVER DEN-SITOMETRIC. (1:193) See also DENSITOMETRIC METHOD (SILVER); METHYLENE BLUE; RESIDUAL THIOSULFATE ION.

**Residual thiosulfate ion**   Ammonium or sodium thiosulfate (HYPO) IONs remaining in film or paper after processing. Synonymous with residual hypo. (42:194)

**Resinous adhesives**   ADHESIVEs whose principal constituent is a water emulsion of POLYVINYL ACETATE (PVA) resin. (47:217) See also ADHESIVE BINDING.

**Resolution**   (1) In audio recording, resolution (or DYNAMIC RANGE) is the average peak-to-peak signal amplitude at the maximum flux reversal divided by the average peak-to-peak signal amplitude at the minimum flux reversal at the desired recording method. (49:159) See also DY-NAMIC RANGE. (2) The ability of a photographic system to record fine detail. (42:194) Image SHARPNESS is normally measured in lines per millimeter. Acceptable resolution for microfilming can range up from 100 lines per mm. A more subjective description of resolution is termed DEFINITION. To test for resolution, images are compared with patterns on a RESOLUTION TEST CHART, such as an NIST test chart (National Institute of Standards and Technology). Synonymous with sharpness and RESOLVING POWER. (1:193) See also RESOLUTION TEST CHART.

**Resolution test chart**   A standardized chart containing sets of increas-ingly smaller RESOLUTION test patterns. The pattern consists of a set of horizontal and vertical lines of specific size and spacing. The NIST Microcopy Resolution Test Chart 1010A is generally used in MICRO-GRAPHICS and is filmed as part of each REEL of PRESERVATION MICROFILM. In some cases, the chart is filmed at the beginning and the end of the film in order to ensure that there has been no change in the photographic system during filming. (42:194)

**Resolve**   To discriminate between adjoining parts. Also to be able to distinguish individual lines in a test pattern. See RESOLUTION TEST CHART.

**Resolving power**   A numeric expression of a photographic system's ability to discriminate adjoining parts. It is calculated by multiplying the REDUCTION RATIO by the number of the smallest test pattern for which lines can be discriminated. See RESOLUTION; RESOLUTION TEST CHART.

**Restoration (paper)**   The process of returning an item to its original condition. Restoration encompasses the entire range of work—MENDING, REPAIRING, and reconstruction. It is generally accepted that everything possible should be done to retain as much as possible of the original material, and that any added materials should be functional, chemically safe, strong, durable, unobtrusive, and reversible—if possible. (47:217) See also CONSERVATION; REVERSIBILITY.

**Restoration (photographic)**   The chemical or physical treatment of the ORIGINAL photographic image to restore its original condition and appearance as closely as possible. (8:154) See also CONSERVATION.

**Restrainer**   A compound in photographic DEVELOPERs that controls the rate of development and helps control chemical fogging.

**Retake**   Refilming of previously filmed material to correct a quality defect. (42:195)

**Retake rate**   A percentage calculation of the number of RETAKE FRAMEs divided by the total number of frames filmed. Often used to evaluate the quality performance of individual camera operators.

**Retentivity**   Measure of a tape's ability to retain magnetization after the force field has been removed. It serves as an indication of the tape's sensitivity at high frequencies. Also called RESIDUAL FLUX. See also REMANENCE. (4:302)

**Reticulation**   Wrinkling of the EMULSION surface of photographic materials, usually due to sharp differences in the temperature or pH of PROCESSING solutions. Reticulation can vary from a coarse, net-like structure to an almost invisible pattern which becomes obvious when the image is enlarged. (8:154)

**Retouching**   Changing the tonal values of a PHOTOGRAPH or removing blemishes. (44:31)

**Return air**   In an HVAC system, air drawn from an air conditioned or heated space or zone and returned to the air-handling system, usually used as SUPPLY AIR after it is filtered, tempered, and mixed with fresh air. (30:80) See also SUPPLY AIR.

**Reversal film**   **(1)** A camera film, usually silver, used to produce a POSITIVE ORIGINAL by means of a reversal development process. Sometimes called "direct-reversal film." **(2)** Also, colloquially, duplicating film that is used to make positives from NEGATIVE images. (1:194)

**Reversal process**   A two-stage development process that results in a POSITIVE rather than a NEGATIVE image. The reversal process is used extensively in color photography. (23:531)

**Reversibility** "The ability to undo a process or treatment with no change to the object. Reversibility is an important goal of CONSERVATION treatment, but it must be balanced with other treatment goals and options." (22:15)

**Rewind** **(1)** Usually a geared device used in pairs to wind film from one reel to another. Used at inspection stations to visually inspect film. **(2)** The act of moving film from one winding device to another.

**RH** See RELATIVE HUMIDITY.

**Rice starch** See STARCH PASTE.

**Right side of paper** "The side of a paper from which the watermark is read correctly. It is the WIRE SIDE in HANDMADE PAPERs and the TOP or FELT side in MACHINE-MADE PAPERs." (15:346)

**Rill** The groove on an AUDIODISC linking the end of one band or selection with the beginning of the next. (4:302)

**Rim (of an audiodisc or cylinder)** On an AUDIODISC, the rim is the area between the edge and the playing area, which can be sloped, concave, convex, flat, raised, lowered, etc. On a CYLINDER recording, the starting rim is the same as on a disc. The run-off rim is the area following the playing area. (4:303)

**Rinse** In photographic PROCESSING, to immerse in water for the purpose of removing chemicals deposited in previous processing stages. Also called BATH.

**Risers** "Vertical distribution elements of a building system, such as a piping riser to feed water, or a duct riser to feed tempered air up through a building." (30:80)

**Risk management** "The practice that analyzes, evaluates and identifies risks whose exposure to financial LOSS should be insured and others that are too small or remote which can be self-insured." (54:47)

**Risk manager** The person in an organization who is responsible for protecting it from predictable LOSSes. Through INSURANCE and/or other strategies designed to recover from any losses sustained, the risk manager implements measures to control and reduce the possibility of loss.

**RLG** Research Libraries Group, Inc.

**RLIN** Research Libraries Information Network, the computerized bibliographic database owned and operated by the Research Libraries Group. (42:195)

**Roll** **(1)** "Generic term for a roll of perforated paper from which sounds can be produced by a mechanical musical instrument. Also called a phonoroll." (52:36) See also PIANO ROLL. **(2)** A REEL wound with a standard length of tape or film.

**Roll microfilm**   Strips of microfilm that are or can be put on a REEL, spool, or CORE. (42:195)

**Roll-to-card printer**   A device for making individual pieces of film, e.g., fiche, from a roll of film using a CONTACT PRINTing process.

**Roll-to-roll printer**   A reel film duplicator used to copy REELs of film onto raw film stock in reel format using a CONTACT PRINTing process.

**Rosin size**   A solution or dispersion obtained by treating rosin with a suitable ALKALI. When properly converted in the papermaking process, usually by the addition of ALUM, the SIZE precipitates and imparts water (ink) resistance to paper. (47:221) Rosin is the residue obtained after distilling off the volatile matter (turpentine) from the gum of the Southern pine (chiefly from long-leaf and slash species). (15:351) See also ALUM; SIZE.

**Rotary camera**   A MICROFILM camera that films documents while both the film and documents are moved during exposure at identical speeds to prevent any apparent movement between the two. In some cameras, both sides of the document can be filmed. See also PLANETARY CAMERA; STEP-AND-REPEAT CAMERA. (42:195)

**Rough edges**   The UNCUT, UNTRIMMED, and DECKLE EDGEs of paper. (1:196)

**Round back**   A book which has been ROUNDED during the binding process and given a round back. The opposite of FLAT BACK. See also FLAT BACK; ROUNDING. (23:538)

**Round corner**   In book covers, a BOARD which is rounded at the CORNER before being covered; usually only in leather bindings. Sometimes called a LIBRARY CORNER. (1:196)

**Rounded**   See ROUNDING.

**Rounding**   "The process of molding the SPINE of a TEXT BLOCK into an arc of approximately one-third of a circle, producing the characteristic concave FORE EDGE of the book. Rounding takes place after the spine has been given a light coat of ADHESIVE, and is accomplished in hand bookbinding by means of light hammering along the spine with a round-headed hammer. A rounding and BACKING machine is used for library or EDITION BINDING. Edition bindings are generally rounded after the SPINE LINING has been applied. Rounding usually precedes backing." (47:221–222) See also BACKING.

**rpm**   Abbreviation for revolutions per minute, the speed of rotation of an AUDIODISC or CYLINDER.

**Rub**   (1) In binding, taking an impression of the lettering, call number, lines, etc., on the SPINE and/or sides of a book by placing a piece of light paper or tissue against the part to be copied and rubbing with a lead pencil, crayon, etc. The resulting pattern is used by binders to match volumes in sets when rebinding. Also called "pattern" or "rubbing." (47:222) **(2)** Commonly used defect term for sound recordings that refers to a visible mark on the surface of the recording (usually caused by another item or material having come in contact with the surface), which may not actually cause any distortion in playback. It is used interchangeably with SCUFF. (4:303) See also SCUFF.

**Rubbing**   See RUB.

**Rumble**   Low-frequency NOISE caused by the mechanism of a turntable or TAPE TRANSPORT. Rumble sometimes can be heard from AUDIODISCs themselves, having been induced during the recording or cutting stages. (4:303)

**Runouts**   "Lateral or 'to point of use' distribution elements of a building system, such as piping runouts to feed water to the point of use, or duct runouts to feed air to diffusers." (30:80)

**S**addle   "The part of a sewing or stabbing machine on which SECTIONs are placed to be brought up under the sewing needles and loopers, or the stitcher head." (47:225)

**Saddle sewing**   "The process of SEWING a SECTION, e.g., a periodical issue or PAMPHLET, through the center fold by means of thread. The term SADDLE derives from the saddle of the machine. Saddle sewing affords full OPENABILITY of the section, i.e., to the GUTTER of the binding margin. Saddle sewing may be done by hand, usually employing a figure-eight stitch, but it is more often done by machine." (47:225) See also SADDLE STITCHING.

**Saddle stitching**   Binding a periodical or PAMPHLET through the center fold by means of wire staples. Saddle stitching, which is done by machine, is fast and more economical than SADDLE SEWING and allows the publication to open fully to the GUTTER of the binding margin, as does saddle sewing. (47:225) See also SIDE STITCHING.

**Saddle warp**   Occurs on an AUDIODISC if the paper GRAIN of both labels on the disc is not running in the same direction when the labels are affixed to the VINYL. The natural curl of the paper may put unequal stress on the disc's center surfaces and can result in disc warpage when the disc is first removed from the press. (4:303)

**Safelight**   A light used in DARKROOMs which provides minimal light but which has no perceptible effect on film being handled.

**Safety film**   A relatively nonflammable film support (base) that meets ANSI requirements for safety film. (42:195) See also ACETATE FILM.

**Sample**   In statistics, a subset of the total number of CASEs; a subset of a POPULATION of cases. (7:112)

**Sample size**   The number of CASEs or observations in a SAMPLE, usually designated as "n." (1:198)

**Sanding**   Using sandpaper or a sand-wheel machine to rub down the edges of a book so as to remove as small an amount of paper as possible. (23:543)

**Saw cuts**   Grooves sawn in the back of a book. CORDS are placed in the grooves and sewn around when sewing SECTIONs together. See also CORDS; SAWING-IN; TAPES.

**Saw-kerf binding**   A method of binding single sheets with both thread and ADHESIVE. KERFS (dovetailed grooves) are cut across the SPINE at an angle and filled with adhesive. SEWING thread is woven around the kerfs and the kerfs again filled with adhesive. The forerunner of SMYTH-CLEAT SEWING.

**Sawing-in**   "Sawing grooves in the back of a book for the reception of the CORD in SEWING." (23:545) See also SAW CUTS.

**Scrape**   Commonly used defect term for sound recordings which implies a visible marring of the surface of the recording that appears to be deeper or more serious than a SCUFF or RUB and may cause some degree of sonic distortion. (4:304)

**Scratch**   **(1)** Commonly used defect term for sound recordings which implies a visible marring of the surface of the recording in the form of a single, thin line or "scratch" which will cause momentary distortion (usually referred to as a tick) when the stylus tracks over it. It is markedly less severe than a CRACK. (4:304) **(2)** In magnetic tape recording, a long, narrow, straight defect in the top surface of a head track; also applies to tape. (49:159) **(3)** In photography, a linear (straight, jagged, or curved) mar or gouge on either the base or EMULSION SIDE of a film. If it penetrates to the emulsion, it can not be considered an ARCHIVAL FILM since even if there is no loss of recorded information, it will allow entry to the emulsion of oxidants, MOLDs, FUNGI, etc.

**Screw press**   **(1)** A press used by bookbinders to flatten paper or books during the process of binding, especially after pasting or gluing. The press is operated by turning a wheel or lever attached to the upper end of a large-diameter perpendicular screw. The lower end of the screw is attached to a heavy iron plate. The papers or books to be pressed are placed on the bed of the press and are forced flat by the iron plate as the screw is turned. **(2)** Used by microfilming agencies to flatten long folded newspapers in preparation for filming. See also PRESS. (23:553)

**Scrim**   Synonymous with MULL.

**Scroll**   **(1)** A roll of material, e.g., PARCHMENT, usually bearing writing and rolled onto rods, which were generally fitted with handles. The scroll, and early forms of the MANUSCRIPT, was called VOLUMEN (roll) by the Romans and is the word from which volume is derived. (47:227) See also VOLUMEN. **(2)** The controlled movement of microfilm on a READER such that images move out of sight as others move into sight on the projection screen.

**Scuff**   An abrasion on film, either the base or EMULSION SIDE; most often caused by careless handling. See RUB.

**Second-generation microfilm**   A DUPLICATE made from the camera film. (42:195) Synonymous with first reproduction microfilm. In preservation circles, called the PRINT MASTER regardless of POLARITY.

**Second-generation negative**   See INTERMEDIATE NEGATIVE; PRINT MASTER.

**Second lining**   After the FIRST LINING has been pasted or adhered to the back of a book, a strip of brown paper the full size of the back of a book is glued into place. (23:555) See also LINING.

**Second original**   When ORIGINAL PRINTs or NEGATIVEs are photographically duplicated, the duplicate is often called a second original by conservators, curators, etc. (8:154)

**Section**   The unit of paper that is printed and folded into sets of 4, 8, 16, 32, 64, or 128 printed PAGEs and which, together with other like units, PLATEs, and INSERTs, makes up a complete BOOK. A section is usually folded from one SHEET of paper, but it may consist of one and one-half or two sheets, or even one sheet and an additional LEAF or leaves. The outside folds (BOLT) are TRIMMED, leaving the center, or inside, fold intact. Consecutive sections are sewn through-the-fold to form the TEXT BLOCK. Each section of a book bears a different SIGNATURE identification. *Signature* originally referred to a letter or numeral placed at the bottom of the first page of each printed sheet of paper to assist in collating the book. (38:219) Today, however, little if any distinction is made between section and signature, and the term is sometimes used synonymously with QUIRE and GATHERING. See also FOLDINGS; GATHERING; MACHINE-SEWN SECTIONS; SIGNATURE; SIGNATURE MARK.

**Sekishu**   Japanese handmade paper, white or natural in color and made from 80 percent KOZO and 20 percent SULFITE PULP; it shows small fibers dispersed throughout. It is ACID-FREE and used for printing and conservation. See also SEKISHU KOZOGAMI MARE; SEKISHU KOZOGAMI TURU; SEKISHU TORINOKO GAMPI.

**Sekishu Kozogami Mare**   Japanese handmade paper, off-white in color and made from 100 percent KOZO. Very similar to SEKISHU KOZOGAMI TURU (which it is often called) except it has doubled CHAIN LINES. It is ACID-FREE and used for MENDING.

**Sekishu Kozogami Turu**   An ACID-FREE Japanese handmade paper, off-white in color, and made from 100 percent KOZO. It has great strength and is used for all types of MENDING. Sometimes called SEKISHU KOZOGAMI MARE.

**Sekishu Torinoko Gampi**   A Japanese handmade paper, its color is off-white and it is made from 100 percent GAMPI. It is ACID-FREE and very strong, soft and silky, and looks as though it is glazed. Gampi is used for conservation and repair of valuable artworks on paper.

**Self-erasure**   The process by which a piece of magnetized tape tends to demagnetize itself by virtue of the opposing fields created within it by its own magnetization. This effect becomes increasingly stronger at short wave lengths (high frequencies). It can be circumvented by avoiding the use of excessive EQUALIZATION boost at high frequencies, by avoiding extremes of temperature when storing tapes, and by using high-quality tapes. (4:304)

**Self-insurance**   "A plan for setting aside funds to meet probable losses." (25:95)

**Selvage (selvedge)**   "The finished outer edge of a woven fabric. The selvage runs parallel to the WARP threads (GRAIN direction) of the fabric." (38:219) It is meant to be cut off and discarded.

**Semi-chemical pulp**   "The product of an intermediate process between MECHANICAL WOOD PULP (merely groundwood without the addition of chemicals or heat) and CHEMICAL WOOD PULP, which is obtained by the action of chemicals on wood chips." (23:559)

**Semi-pulp**   "A term applied to the product of the grinding process in papermaking, the groundwood still containing impurities and large fragments of wood." (23:560)

**Sensible heat**   Heat that causes the air to change its temperature, as opposed to LATENT HEAT. Heat that can be "sensed" by a simple dry-bulb thermometer. (30:80) See also LATENT HEAT.

**Sensing mark**   In REPROGRAPHY, a mark on film or paper (in microfilm, usually an optically applied rectangular mark below the image area) which activates an electrical device to carry out automatically a function such as counting frames, cutting paper, or stopping moving film. Also known as a blip. (23:560)

**Sensitize**   To coat or treat a material (such as film) so as to make it sensitive to RADIANT ENERGY. Also to treat a previously sensitized material to increase its sensitivity. (1:203)

**Sensitized paper**   Paper used in document reproduction that is coated with an EMULSION sensitive to light or heat as used in a THERMO-GRAPHIC PROCESS. (23:560)

**Sensitometer**   A device to expose sequential segments of SENSITIZED material at controlled levels of RADIANT ENERGY for increasingly long periods of time. In microfilm processing, the resulting strips are used to evaluate the performance of the processing system. See CONTROL STRIP.

**Separation loss**   The loss in OUTPUT that occurs when the surface of the COATING of a magnetic tape fails to make perfect contact with the surface of either the RECORD or reproduce HEAD. (49:159)

**Separation negatives**   NEGATIVEs for each of the primary colors; used in color reproduction work. (23:560)

**Sequential camera**   See STEP-AND-REPEAT CAMERA.

**Service bureau**   An organization equipped to provide micrographic and related services and which makes those services generally available. (42:195)

**Service copy**   A microform DUPLICATE intended for end use. Synonymous with distribution copy. In PRESERVATION, normally a third-GENERATION duplicate. (42:195)

**Setpoints**   "The specific temperature or RELATIVE HUMIDITY settings in an HVAC control system." (30:80)

**78 rpm sound disc**   An ANALOG DISC, usually 10 or 12 inches (25 or 30 cm) in diameter, to be played at 78 revolutions per minute, and with a playing time of approximately four minutes per side. Superseded during the 1950s by the LONG-PLAYING AUDIODISC. (52:37) See also SHELLAC DISC.

**Sewing**   "In BINDING, a method of LEAF ATTACHMENT in which SECTIONs are fastened to each other by thread or wire passed through the center fold or the side near the BACK EDGE. The major kinds of sewing are sewing through the fold and SIDE SEWING, which includes OVERCASTING, OVERSEWING, and CLEAT SEWING." (1:205) See also STITCHING.

**Sewing frame**   A frame of two upright threaded posts and a crossbar. The crossbar rests on two nuts threaded onto the posts. CORDS or TAPES are attached to the base and the crossbar and stretched taut by raising or lowering the crossbar. SECTIONs of a book are sewn by hand around the cords or tapes.

**Sewing on sawn-in cords**   "SIGNATUREs can be hand sewn through the fold onto sawn-in CORDS. SAW CUTS are first made across the SPINE of the TEXT BLOCK, perpendicular to the binding edge. The saw cuts become the sewing holes through which the threaded needle passes on its way in and out of the fold of each signature. Cords are set into the saw cuts perpendicular to the spine, so that the sewing thread passes over the cords as it runs from KETTLE STITCH to kettle stitch. The cords link the signatures, one to another, together across the spine." (26:16) See also SEWING ON TAPES.

**Sewing on tapes** "SIGNATUREs can be hand sewn through the fold onto cloth TAPES. Holes are punched through the folds of each signature; or SAW CUTS can be made across the SPINE of the TEXT BLOCK, perpendicular to the BINDING EDGE, to create holes through which the sewing needle can pass." (26:16) Signatures are linked together by sewing them onto tapes in approximately the same manner as SEWING ON SAWN-IN CORDS. See SEWING ON SAWN-IN CORDS.

**Sewing stations** The holes along the folds of a SECTION through which thread passes during the SEWING process.

**Shadow** An area of relatively low DENSITY in NEGATIVE images and of relatively high density in POSITIVE images. (44:31)

**Sharpness** (1) A subjective visual evaluation of the crispness of the boundary between a light and a dark area. (2) The degree of (line/edge) clarity. (42:195)

**Shaved** A book TRIMMED so closely that the lines of print are grazed, though not actually cut into. (23:565) See also CROPPED.

**Shedding** The loss of oxide or other particles from the COATING or BACKING of a magnetic tape, usually causing CONTAMINATION of the TAPE TRANSPORT and, by redeposit, of the tape itself. (49:159)

**Sheet** (1) A single piece of PAPER, BOARD, paper PULP, CELLULOSE ACETATE film, etc. (2) The continuous WEB of paper as it is being manufactured by machine, or the single piece of paper as it is being made by hand. (3) To cut paper or board into sheets of desired size from a roll or web. (4) Paper printed so that it may be folded to form consecutive pages. (47:233) See also GATHERING; SIGNATURE.

**Sheet microfilm** A rectangular piece of microfilm, generally MICROFICHE. (1:205)

**Sheetwork** In EDITION BINDING, the binding operations of folding, TIPPING, GATHERING, endsheeting, SEWING, and SMASHING. See also FORWARDING. (47:233)

**Shelf life** The period of time during which a material, such as film, remains a useful product.

**Shellac disc** An ANALOG DISC, usually 78 rpm, made of shellac or vinylite in combination with neutral fillers such as lampblack. Shellac discs could be solid shellac stock or laminated onto a board, fiber, plastic, or paper CORE. The shellac disc was the most common type of

AUDIODISC prior to the introduction of the LONG-PLAYING AUDIODISC. (52:37) The term "shellac disc" is sometimes used interchangeably with 78 RPM SOUND DISC. See also ACETATE DISC; LACQUER DISC; VINYL DISC; WAX DISC.

**Shield front**   A magnetic shield close to the front (top) surface of the READ/WRITE HEAD to reduce "feed through," i.e., CROSSTALK. (49:159)

**Shirokawa**   The white inner bark of plants (usually KOZO, MITSUMATA, or GAMPI) once it has been removed from the outer bark and the intermediate green membrane. It is used to make the most highly regarded Japanese handmade papers. (29:118) See JAPANESE PAPER.

**Short-term film**   Photographic film with a life expectancy of less than ten years. See also ARCHIVAL FILM; LONG-TERM FILM; MEDIUM-TERM FILM.

**Shot**   See FRAME.

**Shoulder**   "The outer edge of the curved SPINE against which the BOARDs fit." (38:219) "The shoulder is formed when a TEXT BLOCK is BACKED. During this process the outermost leaves on each side of the text block are bent outward at a 45 degree angle along the BINDING EDGE, to accommodate the boards. The ridge that is thus formed on either side of the spine is the shoulder." (26:16) See also BACKING; HINGE; JOINT.

**Shrink-wrap**   A flexible cellophane-type film that, when exposed to heat, shrinks to the contour of the enclosed material, e.g., a book or a commercial LP AUDIODISC and its SLIPCASE. The plastic is stretched very snugly around the package and can contract under high temperature, causing disc warpage.

**Shute wire**   See FOURDRINIER WIRE.

**Shutter**   Any device controlling the amount of time light is allowed to irradiate SENSITIZED materials.

**Sides**   Refers to the "right" and "wrong" sides of the SHEET. The term may also refer to the TOP and undersides or the FELT and WIRE SIDEs. See FELT SIDE; RIGHT SIDE OF PAPER; TOP; WIRE SIDE.

**Side sewing**   A method of LEAF ATTACHMENT in which the book is built up by sewing successive SECTIONs to one another with thread near the BINDING EDGE. All the sections are sewn together through the entire thickness of the TEXT BLOCK at one time. A very strong form of leaf attachment, but affording very little OPENABILITY. Also called stab sewing. (47:235) Includes OVERCASTING and OVERSEWING.

**Side stitching**   A method of securing the leaves or SECTIONs of a book with wire staples, from front to back of the entire thickness of the TEXT BLOCK. Side stitching is one of the strongest forms of construction and is frequently used in binding textbooks. The stitching is done by means of a machine that cuts the wire, forms it into a staple, drives it through the paper, and clinches it from the other side. The disadvantage of a side stitching, like SIDE SEWING, is that it affords almost no OPENABILITY in the book. Also called stab stitching. (47:235) See also SIDE SEWING.

**Signal-to-noise ratio**    The ratio of the power output of the given signal to the power output with the absence of the signal in a given BAND-WIDTH. (49:159)

**Signature**    "A SECTION or GATHERING of a book, stacked and folded as a group. Technically, sets of 4, 8, 16, 32, 64, or 128 printed pages, when folded, constitute a 'section,' while a 'signature' is only the sequential mark of identification printed on the initial PAGE of the section; today, however, little if any distinction is made between the two expressions. The term is not altogether synonymous with SHEET, because a sheet as printed may contain more than one section and, in the case of a half sheet, may constitute a section of fewer pages than others in the same publication. Thus books consist of many sections but those sections may not consist of the same number of leaves." (15:372; 47:235) See also GATHERING; SECTION; SIGNATURE MARK.

**Signature mark**    The letter or numeral, or combination of letters and numerals, printed at the FOOT of the first PAGE, and sometimes on subsequent leaves of a SECTION, as a guide to the binder in arranging them in their correct order. Today, books are often collated by a diagonal solid line or set of numbers across the SPINE. (23:571) See also SECTION; SIGNATURE.

**Sign maintaining**    Any photographic material that retains the POLARITY of the material being filmed or duplicated. DIAZO FILM is a sign maintaining film.

**Sign reversing**    Any photographic material that reverses the POLARITY of the material being filmed or duplicated. Most CAMERA FILMs are sign reversing films.

**Silica gel**    A colloidal form of silica, available in the form of pale amber–colored, highly absorbent granules, and used as a dehumidifier, especially in MICROENVIRONMENTs. When saturated, it can be dried by heating. Sometimes color-coded particles are added which change color as the gel becomes saturated. (47:235–236)

**Silicone release paper**    A thin, white, translucent paper coated with silicone resin on one or both sides to render the surface slippery and resistant to sticking. It will withstand the application of heat without sticking to or otherwise damaging work. Used with HEAT-SET TISSUE.

**Silking**    "The process of applying a thin, transparent, finely meshed silk cloth to one or both sides of a LEAF as a means of REPAIRING or preserving it. A leaf so treated is said to have been "silked." The process is generally reversible. (47:236) See also LAMINATION."

**Silver densitometric method**  See DENSITOMETRIC METHOD (SILVER).

**Silver gelatin film**  See SILVER FILM; GELATIN.

**Silver film**  FILM sensitized with SILVER HALIDE, including nongelatin dry-silver film as well as silver GELATIN film. When developed, the image is formed by metallic silver. Silver gelatin film is the only film suitable for ARCHIVAL PERMANENCE, given its extraordinary longevity when properly processed, maintained, and stored. (42:195) See also LONG-TERM FILM.

**Silver halide**  A silver compound and one of the halogens, i.e., chlorine, bromine, iodine, or fluorine. (42:195)

**Silver halide film**  See SILVER FILM.

**Silver recovery system**  Any of several kinds of systems designed to recover metallic silver from FIXER solutions. With increasing attention to the content of liquid EFFLUENTs from industries, these systems play an important role in removing the hard metal, silver, from those effluents.

**Simplex**  An arrangement of MICROFORM images in which a single image is photographed across the entire usable width of the film. The orientation can be either COMIC or CINE. (1:208) See also DUPLEX.

**Simulated stereo**  See ELECTRONICALLY REPROCESSED STEREO.

**Singer sewing**  A method of side or fold sewing with thread, publications which ordinarily would be stitched. PAMPHLETs are generally singer sewn through the fold, while multi-SECTION journals and books up to 1 1/2 inches are sewn through the side. A high-speed drill is located in front of a single needle and both are lowered and raised simultaneously as the publication is moved forward the length of the stitch desired. The drill creates a hole in the BINDING EDGE of the SHEETs, the threaded needle enters the hole while the next hole is being drilled for the succeeding stitch, and so on. (47:236-237) See also SIDE SEWING; SIDE STITCHING.

**Single**  An AUDIODISC issued separately. In popular usage, a 45 rpm or 78 rpm audiodisc containing one popular selection on each side, both sides typically being recorded by the same performer(s). (52:37)

**Single-domain particle**  All ferromagnetic materials are composed of permanently magnetized regions in which the magnetic moments of the atoms are ordered. These domains have a size determined by energy considerations. When a particle is small enough, it cannot support more than one domain and is called a single domain particle. (49:159)

**Single-section**  "A BOOK, PAMPHLET, etc., consisting of one folded SECTION. Most periodical issues are single-section publications." (47:237) See SECTION.

**Single-track**   See FULL-TRACK; MONOPHONIC.

**Single-zone system**   An HVAC system in which each environmental control zone is served by its own air-handling system. Each zone is provided cool or warm air as needed by its own air handler. (30:80)

**Size**   An additive that makes the FIBER surfaces of paper HYDROPHOBIC and keeps the paper from acting like BLOTTING PAPER when written or printed upon. Early papermakers dipped their handmade sheets into vats of GELATIN to size them, but the productive capacity of the paper machine called for an internal size that could be added directly to the SLURRY. For 150 years, ROSIN was the only practical internal size available, and it had to be used with ALUM in order to coat the paper fibers, which made the paper short-lived. Today a growing variety of SIZING compounds and systems makes it possible to size paper at any pH from 4 to 10. (33:21) Printing and writing papers are moderately sized or "slack-sized." Paper cups and milk cartons are "hard-sized." Paper tissue and towels are not sized at all. See also ALUM; AQUAPEL; ROSIN SIZE; SIZING.

**Sized paper**   Paper which has been treated to make it less receptive to water. For example, BLOTTING PAPER is unsized, while writing paper is hard-sized. See also SIZE.

**Size press**   See TUB SIZE PRESS; SURFACE SIZE PRESS.

**Sizing**   The process of adding SIZE to a papermaking FURNISH or the application of size to the surface of a paper or BOARD to provide resistance to the penetration of liquids and other properties. (47:238) See also BEATER-SIZED; CALENDER SIZING; ENGINE SIZE; SIZE; SUR-FACE-SIZED; TUB-SIZED.

**Sizing agent**   See SIZE; SIZING.

**Skew**   In microfilming, a measure of a document image from exact verti-cal. Generally accepted practice in PRESERVATION filming requires that images be no more than 9° from vertical.

**Sleeve**   The inner paper, GLASSINE, or POLYETHYLENE protective ENVELOPE for an AUDIODISC within a cardboard/paper outer jacket (SLIPCASE). ACID-FREE sleeves are used for record protection in archival situations. (4:306) Sometimes called jacket, liner, record cover, record jacket, or SLIPCASE.

**Slice**   "That part of a FOURDRINIER MACHINE which regulates the flow of STOCK from the HEADBOX or flowbox onto the WIRE in a sheet of liquid of even thickness or volume." (15:379)

**Slide**   A transparent POSITIVE IMAGE (usually photographic) on film or glass, intended for projection. Actual image areas may vary from MICROIMAGEs to 3 1/4 x 4 inches (called a LANTERN SLIDE). Most slides other than 3 1/4 x 4 inches and 2 1/4 x 2 1/4 inches are mounted in a cardboard or plastic frame whose outside dimensions are 2 x 2 inches.

The most common slide is a TRANSPARENCY of 35mm COLOR FILM mounted in a 2 x 2 inch mount. (1:209)

**Slide mount**    A 2 x 2 inch cardboard or plastic frame used for storage and projection of slides. (1:209)

**Sling psychrometer**    A HYGROMETER. Two thermometers, one a dry bulb, the other a wet bulb, are attached to a handle so they can be swung around while taking a temperature reading. The wet bulb thermometer has a fabric sleeve or wick fitted over the mercury bulb. The wick must be kept wet with distilled water when a reading is being taken. After swinging the instrument for two or three minutes, readings are taken from both thermometers, recorded, and entered into a hygrometric table. The value for the RELATIVE HUMIDITY is read where the two readings cross on the scale.

**Slipcase**    **(1)** A BOX made to order for a specific book, or other ARCHIVAL material, and used for protection. The simplest form of the slipcase is a cloth- or paper-covered box with one open edge into which the book is slipped with its SPINE exposed. (47:239) Slipcases do not provide safe storage from a CONSERVATION standpoint. Volumes are abraded every time they are slipped in and out of the cases, and spines are left exposed and thus suffer from light damage. (45:43) **(2)** In phonorecording, the outer container for an AUDIODISC recording, usually made of paper/cardboard, and containing credits, pictorial information, titles, narrative information (sometimes referred to as liner notes), etc. It is usually open on one end only, for slipping the disc in and out of the container. (4:306) See also SLEEVE.

**Slippage**    Any movement between two film materials during duplication or printing, resulting in a loss of RESOLUTION, and in serious cases, complete loss of useful image.

**Slips**    The free ends of the CORDS, thongs, or TAPES on which a book has been sewn, which are used to attach the BOARDs (or CASE) to the TEXT BLOCK. In LIBRARY BINDING today, when tapes are used, the slips are glued to the overhanging SPINE LINING cloth and both are then glued to the insides of the boards of the case. (47:239)

**Sludge**    A wooly precipitate that forms in FILM PROCESSING tanks if the tanks are not properly maintained and cleaned.

**Slurry**    A suspension of CELLULOSE FIBERs in water from which paper is made. (45:89) The PULP from the BEATER is added to water in the VAT and mixed to achieve the proper suspension for the sheet-forming process. The THICKNESS of the sheets will depend on the proportion of pulp to water in the slurry. (29:118)

**Slush**    A suspension of paper PULP usually containing from 1 to 6 percent of dry STOCK. (15:382)

**Smashing**   Reducing the bulk of the entire TEXT BLOCK in order to consolidate it and make it of a uniform thickness. (47:239) See also NIPPING; SMASHING MACHINE.

**Smashing machine**   A PRESS used in binderies for compressing folded SIGNATUREs to render them more compact for BINDING by driving the air from between the pages. (23:577) See also SMASHING.

**Smoothing press**   A type of PRESS sometimes used in the press section of a paper machine usually located next to the DRIER section. It is used to increase the smoothness and density of the paper WEB before drying. (15:382)

**Smyth-Cleat sewing**   A method of machine SEWING or lacing which combines thread and ADHESIVE to secure the leaves of a book. In a separate operation, the back of the SECTIONs are planed off, leaving the SPINE as smooth as possible. The block of leaves is then placed spine down in the Smyth-Cleat machine where a circular saw cuts a number of cleats completely across the back from HEAD to TAIL (the number depending on the dimension of the book). The sawn leaves then move into the sewing position where a single hollow needle laces thread around the cleats in a figure-eight stitch. The sewn TEXT BLOCK is then ready for application of HOT-MELT or cold POLYVINYL ACETATE ADHESIVE to the spine. (47:240–241)

**Smyth sewing**   A method of machine sewing through the center folds of SECTIONs. David McConnell Smyth (1833-1907) was the inventor of the first practical through-the-fold book sewing machine. See also MA-CHINE-SEWN SECTIONS. (38:219)

**SO$_2$**   Sulfur dioxide.

**Softener**   See PLASTICIZER.

**Soda pulp**   A CHEMICAL WOOD PULP produced under high tempera-ture and pressure where wood FIBERs are digested in solution of caustic soda or sodium hydroxide solutions. The soda pulp method is used in making paper from aspen, poplar, birch, oak, and other DECIDUOUS trees which cannot be treated by the SULFITE process. "Papers contain-ing a high proportion of soda pulp are very white and soft, and possess high bulk and OPACITY but low strength. Soda pulp is frequently used to give a soft FINISH to a sulfite pulp base paper." (47:241–242)

**Sodium thiosulfate**   A FIXING solution salt which removes any remain-ing unexposed SILVER HALIDEs from the FILM after development.

**Solander box**   Invented by Dr. Daniel Charles Solander, a botanist, while at the British Museum (1773–1782). The Solander box, which is made of wood, is generally of a drop-back construction. When properly fabri-cated the Solander box is almost dustproof and waterproof. (47:243)

**Solid board**   "A paperboard made of the same material throughout. Distinct from a combination board where two or more types of fiber stock are used, in layers." (22:15) See also BOARD; FIBERBOARD; PRESSBOARD.

**Sound cartridge**   See CARTRIDGE.

**Sound cassette**   See CASSETTE.

**Sound channel**   See CHANNEL.

**Sound disc**   See AUDIODISC.

**Sound recording**   The use of a magnetic tape recorder and related audio equipment, such as mixers, amplifiers, and sound sources, to record sounds on tape or magnetic film (or in special cases on motion picture film). See also AUDIODISC.

**Spacing**   In microfilming, the distance between the leading edge of one IMAGE and the trailing edge of the next.

**Specific gravity**   A mathematical expression of the weight of an object to the weight of an equal volume of pure water at its maximum DENSITY, which is at 4°C (39°F). Calculated by dividing the object's weight by the weight of displaced water. Because paper, leather, cloth, etc., do not lend themselves well to measurements of specific gravity, DENSITY is used more often as the reference in describing these materials. (47:244) See also APPARENT DENSITY.

**Specific heat**   The heat required to raise the temperature of one gram of a substance one degree centigrade. (55:107–108)

**Spectral**   Pertaining to the electromagnetic spectrum. A quantity measured with respect to a narrow wavelength interval, as spectral transmittance or spectral reflectance. (21:25)

**Spectrophotometer**   A device to measure the relative intensity of TRANSMITTED or REFLECTED LIGHT in narrow bands of the spectrum. (1:212) See also DENSITY.

**Specular reflection**   Reflection from glossy surfaces or mirrors.

**Speed**   **(1)** In photography, the rate of receptiveness of SENSITIZED material to RADIANT ENERGY. Expressed in any one of several standardized numerical systems, e.g., DIN, ASA, etc. **(2)** The maximum APERTURE of a LENS. **(3)** The rate of action of a chemical process, as in film development.

**Spherical aberration**   An OPTICAL defect in a LENS which appears in the form of blurred images. It occurs when the light rays passing through the edge of a lens and those that pass through the center do not FOCUS at the same point. Therefore, the failure of a lens to form a point image from a point source. (1:212)

**Spine**   The part of a bound book connecting the front and back COVERs and covering the folds of the SECTIONs.

**Spine lining** (1) Reinforcement of the SPINE of a sewn book, after gluing-up, ROUNDING, and BACKING, and before covering or CASING-IN. The spine lining material (which is usually a fabric) does not generally extend closer than within 1/8 inch of the HEAD and TAIL of the TEXT BLOCK. In EDITION and LIBRARY BINDING, the lining material, or initial liner, if there is more than one, extends beyond the edges of the spine and is attached to the BOARDs of the CASE; any subsequent lining, however, stops at the SHOULDERs of the spine. The purpose of lining the spine is to support it and to impart a degree of rigidity, while still maintaining flexibility for proper opening. (2) A term used incorrectly with reference to the strengthening or stiffening of the area between the boards of the COVERING MATERIAL of case bindings. This lining is more appropriately called the INLAY. (47:245)

**Spine lining fabric** "The fabric used to line the SPINE of a book. It is generally made of cotton, napped on the side which goes against the spine, and of a weight that will help support the spine while not decreasing its flexibility." (47:245) See also CRASH; MULL; SUPER.

**Spine lining paper** "A relatively heavy paper, usually KRAFT, sometimes COATED, and with either a creped or flat FINISH. The paper, which is applied with the MACHINE DIRECTION running from HEAD to TAIL of the TEXT BLOCK, should be of a thickness appropriate to the size and weight of the book. It is generally applied over the initial cloth LINING of large and/or heavy hand- and LIBRARY-BOUND books. Spine lining paper is seldom used in EDITION BINDING." (47:245)

**Spine stamping pattern** A stamping pattern referring to the arrangement of letters, numbers, and punctuation on the SPINE of a CASE. The color of stamping foil is also part of the stamping pattern. (26:17)

**Spine strip** See SPINE LINING.

**Spine title** The title that appears on the SPINE of a volume.

**Spiral binding** A form of MECHANICAL BINDING in which the leaves are drilled or punched near the BINDING EDGE to take a spiral-twisted wire or plastic coil which is drawn through the holes. Often used for PAMPHLETs, art reproductions, commercial catalogues, and occasionally books. (47:245) See also PLASTIC COMB BINDING.

**Spiral laid** "A term applied to a special type of DANDY ROLL, where the LAID WIRES run around the circumference of the roll producing lines parallel WITH THE GRAIN of the paper. This laid mark is characterized by the absence of CHAIN LINES." (15:390)

**Spirex binding** See SPIRAL BINDING.

**Splice** (1) In magnetic tape recording, a joining of two pieces of magnetic tape by cementing, taping, or welding, using a SPLICER. Cemented splices that overlap are called lap splices. Splices made without overlapping, by welding with heat or with an adhesive SPLICING TAPE, are called butt splices. **(2)** In microfilming, a joint made by cementing or ULTRASONIC or heat welding two pieces of film together so they will function as a single piece when passing through a camera, processing machine, viewer, or other apparatus. Most welds are called butt splices, since the two pieces are butted together without any overlap. Only ultrasonic splices are acceptable in PRESERVATION MICROFILMING. (42:195)

**Splicer** A piece of equipment used to join strips of magnetic tape, photographic film, or paper. (42:195)

**Splicing block** In magnetic tape recording, a nonmagnetic metal block with a channel that holds magnetic tape in precise alignment during the act of SPLICING. Additional straight and diagonal grooves provide a path for a razor blade for cutting the tape precisely before splicing. Similar structures are used on film splicers. (4:306)

**Splicing tape** **(1)** In magnetic tape recording, a special pressure-sensitive, nonmagnetic tape used to join two pieces of recording tape. In order to prevent dirt buildup on the recording heads or tape guide, and to prevent adjacent layers of recording tape from sticking together, splicing tape uses a special adhesive. **(2)** In photographic film splicing, any of a number of adhesive products used to join pieces of film. At least one is specially formulated for use in film processors. (4:307)

**Split boards** "The BOARDs of a book that are made up of two or more piles of board glued together, except for a distance at the inner edge into which the SLIPs or TAPES are glued when the boards are being attached. If only two boards are used they are of different thicknesses, with the thinner adjacent to the TEXT BLOCK. Split boards are used today almost exclusively in hand binding for books sewn on TAPES." (47:245–246)

**Split system** A DX cooling system in which the COMPRESSOR and CONDENSER are usually located outside the building, and the REFRIGERANT cooling coil and fan are located inside. (30:80)

**Spoking** In magnetic tape recording, a form of BUCKLING in which the tape PACK is deformed into a shape that approximates a polygon. (49:160)

**Spool** See REEL.

**Spool gauge** A device for checking the distance between flanges of REELs or spools.

**Spot** A flaw in the printing master caused by lack of cleanliness or an EMULSION pinhole. The fault may appear on the final reproduction as either a white spot caused by dirt or a black spot caused by the pinhole. (21:26)

**Spot exposure meter** A device for measuring REFLECTED LIGHT from a small area. Frequently used on microfilm cameras rather than general field exposure meters.

**Spotting**   Removing small blemishes from photographic negatives or prints. (21:26)

**Spring back**   "A strong type of binding used on account books, characterized by a clamping action that causes the book to snap open and shut." (1:213)

**Springwood**   "The portion of an annual ring produced during the early part of the growing season (in the spring); the inner portion of the annual ring. It is usually lighter (less dense) than the SUMMERWOOD." (15:392)

**Sprocket**   A toothed wheel used to engage the holes in PERFORATED FILM and used to transport or guide the film.

**Squeegee**   A device to remove excess liquid from film surfaces. It may be a blade, a roller, or a stream of focused air.

**Square**   The part of a book's COVER or CASE that extends beyond the edges of the TEXT BLOCK to protect the pages. (38:219)

**Square back**   See FLAT BACK.

**Square corner**   "Folding the COVERING MATERIAL over the BOARDs in such a way that after cutting a wedge-shaped piece at the CORNER, one TURN IN may neatly overlap the other. See also LIBRARY CORNER." (23:585)

**Squares**   See SQUARE.

**Squeal**   See STICK-SLIP.

**Stability**   The capability of NEGATIVEs or PRINTs to resist change by environmental factors such as light, heat, or atmospheric gases. (42:195) See CHEMICAL STABILITY.

**Stabilizers**   **(1)** Substances added to the basic compound of a disc or magnetic tape recording to prevent deterioration or the loss of desired physical properties. (4:307) **(2)** Chemical agents used to render sensitive materials no longer sensitive, thus "stabilizing" reactions to radiation.

**Stab marks**   Punctures made in folded sheets of printed paper preparatory to sewing.

**Stab sewing**   See SIDE SEWING.

**Stab stitching**   See SIDE STITCHING.

**Stage**   The part of a MICROFICHE READER which holds the sheet of film and allows it to be moved under the LENS from FRAME to frame.

**Stain**   In photography, local or general discoloration of PRINTs or NEGATIVEs. (8:154)

**Stamp**   The use of heated type pressed onto colored foil to make an impression on COVER MATERIAL. See also STAMPING FOIL.

**Stamper**   **(1)** The stamper is an ancient method of reducing rags and other raw materials to PULP for the papermaking process. It consists of a mortar and pestle powered by water, wind, or an animal. (29:118) **(2)** An electroformed negative metal mold used in the THERMOPLASTIC industry to press AUDIODISCs for mass production. (52:38) See also MATRIX.

**Stamping foil**    Coated POLYESTER film that is placed between hot type and COVERING MATERIAL for stamping. The film is coated, or laminated, on one side with atomized metals such as gold or aluminum and comes in rolls of various widths. See STAMP.

**Standard amplitude reference tape**    A magnetic tape that has been selected for given properties as a standard for signal AMPLITUDE. (49:160)

**Standard groove**    "The relatively wide or coarse GROOVE of a 78 rpm AUDIODISC (about 100 to 120 CUTs per inch, or 38 to 48 cuts per cm)." (52:38) See also MICRO-GROOVE.

**Standard reference tape**    A magnetic tape intended for daily calibration of magnetic tape recorders, the performance of which has been calibrated to the STANDARD AMPLITUDE REFERENCE TAPE. (49:160) See also STANDARD AMPLITUDE REFERENCE TAPE.

**Standing press**    A large floor PRESS, at one time used in virtually all binderies for operations requiring the application of great pressure; it is used today almost exclusively in hand binding. The standing press is used not only for the final pressing of a book, but also during the operation of cleaning off the SPINE and to press the BACKING SHOULDERs out of the SECTIONs of a book pulled for REBINDING. (47:249)

**Standpipe riser**    A large-diameter pipe rising vertically through a building to supply water to fire hose connections on the upper floors. (37:120)

**Starch**    "Starch was the original material for SIZING paper and may have been the first ADHESIVE. It is now used in addition to other sizing agents as a LOADING agent in order to give a hard 'RATTLE' and an improved 'FINISH' to paper. The starches commonly used in papermaking are obtained from corn, potatoes, tapioca, and wheat, the last named being the principal source of starch for PASTE used in bookbinding." (47:250) See also PASTE; STARCH PASTE.

**Starch paste**    "An ADHESIVE made from wheat or rice STARCH mixed with water. It will last only two or three days without refrigeration or the addition of a MOLD inhibitor. PASTE used for bookbinding and conservation usually contains a substance to discourage insect infestation." (38:220) See also PASTE.

**Static**    The distortion created in AUDIODISC or magnetic tape playback when the recording has a buildup of ELECTROSTATIC CHARGE. Also refers to interference or distorted reception in a radio broadcast signal. (4:307)

**Static eliminator** **(1)** A chemical compound used to reduce STATIC on the surface of film. **(2)** An ionizing bar designed to discharge static from film before it reaches discharge levels.

**Static marks** In photography, black spots, streaks, or tree-like marks produced on LIGHT-SENSITIVE materials by discharges of STATIC electricity during handling, duplicating, or winding (especially at high speed) and made visible by DEVELOPING. (42:195)

**Steeling** See GREYING.

**Step-and-repeat camera** A special planetary microfilm camera that exposes a set of separate images on a piece of film (part of a roll or a precut sheet) following a predefined FORMAT, usually in orderly rows and COLUMNs. If the ORIGINAL film was in roll form, it is cut after PROCESSING to create MICROFICHE. See also PLANETARY CAMERA and ROTARY CAMERA. (42:195)

**Step test** A series of EXPOSUREs at gradually increasing exposure values. Used to determine the OPTIMUM EXPOSURE values for filming.

**Stereograph** A pair of OPAQUE or transparent images which produce three-dimensional effects when viewed with stereoscopic equipment. (1:217)

**Stereograph slide** See STEREOSCOPIC SLIDE.

**Stereophonic (stereo)** Sound recorded and reproduced via two CHANNELs. Also called binaural, which sometimes refers to the reproduction of sound via two mutually exclusive channels, as in stereophonic headphone listening. (52:38) See also MONOPHONIC; QUADRAPHONIC.

**Stereoscope** An optical device with two lenses, enabling each eye to see a separate image of essentially the same scene recreating approximately normal parallax. Useful in viewing STEREOGRAPHS. (1:217)

**Stereoscopic slide** A pair of POSITIVE photographic SLIDEs made from NEGATIVEs taken from two slightly different viewpoints, providing three-dimensional effects when viewed through a STEREOSCOPE. (23:593)

**Stick-slip** Generally a low-speed phenomenon, a relationship between tension, temperature, HUMIDITY, wrap angle, head material, binder material of magnetic tape, and the elastic properties of the tape. When detected audibly, it is described as "squeal." (49:160)

**Sticktion** A term loosely used to describe the phenomenon of magnetic tape adhering briefly to transport components such as heads or guides, causing the tape to vibrate in its path through the equipment. (49:160)

**Sticky rollers** A device using special mildly adhesive plastics to clean film of dust and grime.

**Stiff back**    See TIGHT BACK.

**Stiffness**    In magnetic recording, resistance to bending of the tape; a function of tape THICKNESS and modulus of elasticity. (49:161)

**Stitching**    "A method of LEAF ATTACHMENT in which the leaves of the entire book or PAMPHLET are fastened together as a single unit, often with wire, rather than as a sequence of SECTIONs sewn together. See SADDLE STITCHING; SIDE STITCHING." (1:218)

**Stock**    (1) "PULP which has been beaten and refined, treated with SIZING, color, FILLER, etc., and which after dilution is ready to be formed into a sheet of paper." (2) "Wet pulp of any type at any stage in the manufacturing process." (15:398)

**Stop**    (1) In SILVER HALIDE material development, the process of bathing the film or paper in a mildly acidic solution to neutralize the ALKALINE DEVELOPER from the DEVELOPING BATH and arrest development beyond a desired point. (1:218) (2) The LENS APERTURE controlling admittance of light to the camera.

**Stop bath**    See STOP.

**Streak**    In photography, a light or dark area through a number of images, parallel to the edges of the film. (21:26)

**Strengthening (of paper)**    "Restoring the mechanical stability of BRITTLE paper through chemical means." (22:5)

**Stress marks**    In photography, dark streaks or lines on negatives caused by mechanical contact or friction. (21:26)

**Stretch**    A film defect manifested by a longitudinal blur or lengthened image. Caused by poor synchronization of film and original in ROTARY CAMERAs or between the two film surfaces in continuous printing. (1:219)

**Strip-up**    A technique used to produce MICROFICHE using short lengths of roll film and attaching them in rows to a transparent support. The resulting fiche is not an acceptable PRESERVATION product. (42:195)

**Stub**    (1) The portion of the original LEAF that remains in the volume after most of it has been cut out. Can be used as a support for TIPPING IN a replacement leaf. (2) A narrow section or strip bound into a book for the purpose of attaching PLATEs, maps, etc. (47:253) See also GUARD.

**Stuff**    Wet PULP ready to be made into PAPER. See HALFSTUFF; PULP; STOCK.

**Stylus**    (1) A small pointed device that transmits vibrations from a grooved ANALOG DISC or CYLINDER to the sound reproduction mechanism of a PHONOGRAPH. The LONG-PLAYING AUDIODISC stylus is diamond tipped and has a much longer playing time (life expectancy) than the earlier metal or sapphire stylus used for 78 RPM SOUND DISCs or cylinders. Also called a needle, phonograph needle. **(2)** The sharp, chisel-shaped tool used to cut sound vibrations on the surface of a grooved MASTER DISC during the recording process. (52:38)

**Subbing** A clear pre-coating that facilitates adhesion between an EMULSION and a FILM BASE. (1:219)

**Sublimate** Water passing directly from the solid state into vapor without becoming liquid. (37:120)

**Substrate** The base material from which a CD-ROM is made, a strong and transparent POLYCARBONATE plastic. (20:51)

**Suction box** Equipment which removes water from a SHEET being formed on the WIRE of a FOURDRINIER paper machine or from the wet FELT of a CYLINDER MACHINE prior to pressing. It is usually a box with a perforated top over which the wire or felt passes. Water is removed from the STOCK or WEB by suction. (15:401)

**Sulfate paper** See KRAFT PAPER.

**Sulfate pulp** One of the two principal chemical methods of converting wood into PULP for papermaking, the other being the sulfite process. In the sulfate process, CHEMICAL WOOD PULP is prepared by cooking wood chips under pressure and high temperature in a mixture of sodium sulfide and sodium hydroxide. The resulting paper is strong, and is often used unbleached, but it can be bleached white. The terms "sulfate" and KRAFT are generally used interchangeably. (47:254) See also KRAFT; SULFITE PULP.

**Sulfite pulp** One of the two principal chemical methods of converting wood into PULP for papermaking, the other being the sulfate process. In the sulfite process, "papermaking FIBER is produced by an acid chemical process in which the cooking liquor contains an excess of $SO_2$. The sulfite liquor is a combination of a soluble base (such as ammonium, calcium, sodium, or magnesium) and sulfurous acid. Calcium was commonly used in the past but is not as widely used now because of chemical recovery and pollution abatement problems." (15:403) Bleached or unbleached sulfite pulp is used in the manufacture of nearly all classes of paper. Sulfite PULPING is superior in the amount of LIGNIN removed and produces papermaking fibers that are white in color and can be bleached to higher whiteness with fewer chemicals than required for the SULFATE process. Paper made from sulfite fibers is not as strong as that made from SULFATE PULP. (47:254) See also SULFATE PULP.

**Summerwood** "The part of an annual ring produced during the latter part of the growing season (in the summer); the outer portion of the annual ring. It is usually denser than SPRINGWOOD." (15:404)

**Sump** "A pit built into a basement floor to collect casual water." (37:120)

**Sump pump** A pump installed permanently in or above a SUMP and designed to act automatically to remove water from it. (37:120)

**Sunk bands**   "CORDS or BANDS (in old books, often of leather) which are placed in grooves sawn into the backs of SECTIONs of a book to give a smooth back or SPINE. The sewing of the sections passes round the bands. The opposite of RAISED BANDS. Also called 'sunk cords.'" (23:603)

**Super**   A woven cloth in EDITION bindings that is glued to the SPINE of the TEXT BLOCK. The excess that extends past the ends of the spine (usually 2–3 cm) is used to attach the book to its CASE. Also called MULL or CRASH. (38:220) See also CRASH; MULL; SPINE LINING FABRIC.

**Supercalender**   A machine, separate from the papermaking machines, which consists of a stack of from five to sixteen rolls. Paper is passed through the rolls under pressure and given a high-gloss finish; it is then known as supercalendered. (23:603)

**Supply air**   In an HVAC system, the treated and tempered air delivered (supplied) to a space or zone to control conditions within. (30:80) See also RETURN AIR.

**Support**   See BASE STOCK.

**Surface-coated**   A term applied to any PAPER or PAPERBOARD which has one or both sides COATED with a pigment or other suitable material. See also COATING. (15:405)

**Surface finish**   Surface finish is the quality of the surface of a sheet of paper. Paper can be rough or smooth, absorbent or repellent, shiny or DULL. (26:17)

**Surface imprint**   The transfer of material from the packaging containing a recording to the surface of the recording itself due to high contact stress (caused by high temperatures, wrinkled or uneven surfaces of the packaging material, or improper and uneven storage pressure). This can result in poor playback because the transferred material may interfere with stylus tracking. (4:308)

**Surface-sized**   "The addition of resin or other materials to the surface of a sheet of PAPER or BOARD to render it more resistant to liquids, especially writing ink. The paper surface is treated with a SIZING material applied to the dry or partially dried sheet either on the paper machine or as a separate operation. (15:406) See also CALENDER SIZING; SURFACE SIZE PRESS; TUB-SIZED; TUB SIZE PRESS."

**Surface size press**   A section of a paper machine designed for relatively light applications of surface sizing agents or other materials to PAPER or PAPERBOARD, usually located between two DRIER sections. (15:406) See also TUB SIZE PRESS.

**Surface treatment**   Any process by which the surface smoothness of the magnetic tape COATING is improved after it has been applied to the BASE FILM. (49:161)

**Swell** "The additional THICKNESS in the SPINE of a book caused by the sewing thread and/or extensive GUARDING. While excessive swell is undesirable, some swell is required for proper ROUNDING and BACK-ING." (47:257)

**Swelling of the emulsion** A condition in which EMULSION absorbs water, either from the surrounding environment or from direct contact with water, causing the emulsion to expand. See WATER SPOT-TEST. (44:31)

**Symmetrical lens** A LENS system in which the front and rear groups are identical.

**Synthetic size** Nonacidic chemicals used to impart SIZE to paper during the papermaking process. Synthetic sizes enable papermakers to change the paper WET END chemistry from acid pH levels of 4.5–5.0 to the NEUTRAL 7.0 and produce ALKALINE PAPER. See also AQUAPEL; SIZE.

**System noise** In magnetic tape recording, the total NOISE produced by the whole recording system including the tape. (49:157–158)

**t** Abbreviation for the track(s) on a magnetic tape.

**Tacking iron** A small, lightweight iron with an adjustable thermostatic control used to heat and melt dry mount or HEAT-SET TISSUE.

**Tail** The bottom of a book as it sits upright, the very edge of the COVERs and SPINE. (47:259)

**Tailband** A decorative band similar to a HEADBAND but placed at the TAIL of a book. See also HEADBAND; HEADCAP.

**Tails out** A magnetic tape recording that is stored after recording or playback without being rewound, i.e., with the tail end of the tape outermost on the REEL. Tails out storage is preferable because the tape PACK tends to be smoother, therefore safer, than if the tape had been rewound. (4:308) See also HEADS OUT; PACK.

**Take down** To take a book apart and reduce it to its original SECTIONs.

**Takenaga** Japanese handmade paper, ACID-FREE, and used for CON-SERVATION. See also JAPANESE PAPER.

**Take-up tension** The tension or pulling force which the take-up REEL applies to magnetic tape as it leaves the CAPSTAN/PINCH ROLLER area of a tape recorder. (4:309)

**Talking book**    Originally a sound recording of a book produced for blind and/or physically handicapped persons. Also called a recorded book. The playback speed of a talking book recorded on ANALOG DISCs is usually 8 or 16 rpm; AUDIOTAPE reels are played at $1\,7/8$ ips (4.75 cm/s); and audiocassettes at $15/16$ ips (2.375 cm/s). Talking books produced on audiocassettes are also known as cassette books. (52:39)

**Tanning**    The process of converting hides or skins into leather.

**Tape cartridge**    See CARTRIDGE.

**Tape cassette**    See CASSETTE.

**Tape drive**    See TAPE TRANSPORT.

**Tape duplication master**    A magnetic tape copied from a MASTER TAPE and used to reproduce the multiple copies of audio cartridges, cassettes, and/or tape reels issued to the public. (52:39) See also MASTER TAPE.

**Tape mark**    A special control block recorded on magnetic tape to serve as a separator between FILEs and file labels. (49:161)

**Tape pack**    See PACK.

**Tapes**    The strips of cloth (usually LINEN), VELLUM, nylon, etc., to which the SECTIONs of a book are sewn, and whose free ends, or SLIPS, are attached to the BOARDs or are glued between SPLIT BOARDS to impart additional strength to the binding structure. See also BANDS; CORDS. (47:260)

**Tape skew**    The deviation of a magnetic tape from following a linear path when transported across the HEADs. The terms "static" and "dynamic" are used to distinguish the physically fixed and fluctuating components of total tape skew. (49:161)

**Tape-to-head separation**    The separation between a magnetic head and the magnetic tape caused by (1) the foil-bearing effect; (2) improper HEAD CONTOUR, which generates standing waves in the tape; and (3) surface roughness of the tape surface. These conditions are interrelated and are greatly influenced by tape tension and tape compliancy. (49:161)

**Tape-to-head separation changes**    In magnetic recording caused by: (1) HEAD CONTAMINATION, i.e., debris attached to the head, which causes the tape to lift away from the head forming a tent-like deformation of the tape. This tent does not move or change shape until the contamination is removed. (2) Tape contamination, i.e., particles attached to the tape result in a "tent" formed by particles that move across the head with the tape. (49:161)

**Tape transport**    The HEAD assembly, motor(s), and control mechanisms in a tape recorder or computer which move the magnetic tape past the heads. The mechanism extracts tape from a storage device, moves it across magnetic heads at a controlled speed, and then feeds it into another storage device. Typical storage devices are tape loops, bins, REELs, and magazines (CASSETTEs and CARTRIDGEs). (49:161–162) Synonymous with tape drive.

**TAPPI**   Technical Association of the Pulp and Paper Industry.

**Target**   In MICROPHOTOGRAPHY: (1) any document or chart containing identification information, coding, or test charts. (2) An aid to technical or bibliographic control that is photographed on the film preceding and/or following the document. (42:196)

**Tarnish**   A discoloration of silver images by the formation of silver sulphide. The discoloration color ranges from blue-black to yellow-brown and will be seen most frequently in high-silver-content areas. (44:31)

**Tawing**   An ancient process of transforming prepared hide or skin (usually pigskin or goatskin) into a white leather-like substance. Aluminum salts and other materials such as egg yolk, flour, salt, etc., are used to produce the change. (47:260–261) Since the process does not produce a skin that is stable when wet, a tawed skin is not actually leather.

**Tear factor**   "The TEARING RESISTANCE in grams (per sheet) multiplied by 100 and divided by the BASIS WEIGHT in grams per square meter." (15:412) See ELMENDORF TEST.

**Tearing resistance**   The force required to tear a paper sample under standardized conditions. In ARCHIVAL work, the two most important measures of tearing resistance are: (1) internal (or continuing) tearing resistance, where the edge of the sheet is cut before the actual tear is made; and (2) edge tearing resistance, i.e., the resistance offered by the sheet to the onset of tearing at the edge, and which appears to be dependent on both the extensibility and the TENSILE STRENGTH of the paper. See DURABILITY (OF PAPER); ELMENDORF TEST.

**Tear ratio**   The relationship between the MACHINE DIRECTION and CROSS DIRECTION tearing resistance of paper, or the WARP and filling direction of a fabric. (15:412; 47:261) See TEARING RESISTANCE; DURABILITY (OF PAPER).

**Technical target**   A carefully produced set of RESOLUTION patterns, sometimes including scale and DENSITY reference areas that help identify the reduction and resolution of the PROCESSED FILM. See also TARGET.

**Tengujo**   See TOSA TENGUJO.

**Tensile strength**   The property of a material, such as paper, which enables it to resist breaking under tension. (47:262) Measuring the tensile strength of a paper is a way of measuring the relative bonding between the FIBERs. An instrument ascertains the strain required to break a strip of paper of a given length and width. The forces required to pull the fibers apart in the MACHINE DIRECTION and in the CROSS DIRECTION are measured in pounds. Since tensile strength is tested by a pulling action (instead of a tearing action or a bursting action), the results should be higher in the machine direction than in the cross direction. (29:48) See also BREAKING LENGTH; BURSTING STRENGTH; TEARING RESISTANCE.

**Tentelometer**   A gauge for measuring the tension forced on magnetic tape by the TAPE TRANSPORT as the tape is wound from one REEL to another.

**Terminal equipment**   "The part of an HVAC system which is used to serve a temperature control zone, including DIFFUSERS, boxes, CONVECTORS, radiators and FAN-COIL UNITs." (30:80)

**Terylene   (1)** A generic name for a synthetic thread which has the advantages of nylon thread, but does not have the undesirable high degree of elasticity. Because of its lower elasticity, it does not present the problem of thread retraction after cutting. **(2)** It is also used in sheet form in the repair of documents and the leaves of books. (47:262)

**Test tape**   See ALIGNMENT TAPE.

**Text block**   "The body of a BOOK, including the leaves, or SECTIONs, before it receives its COVER. It excludes all papers added by the bookbinder, including BOARD papers, ENDPAPERS, ornamental bindings, etc." (47:262)

**Thermographic copy**   A copy or duplicate made by a THERMOGRAPHIC PROCESS.

**Thermographic process**   A document-copying process involving the use of liquid chemicals. Copies are made on heat-sensitive paper. The information on the original must be in carbon or metallic inks.

**Thermoplastic**   The general basic ingredient in most contemporary disc recordings which are synthetic or partially synthetic. Thermoplastic materials will repeatedly soften when heated and harden when cooled (a thermoplastic gradually becomes softer as the temperature increases). (4:310)

**Thickness**   The depth or space between opposite surfaces; the smallest of the three dimensions of a single SHEET of paper or PAPERBOARD. Also called caliper. (15:417) See also POINT.

**Third generation duplicate**   See SERVICE COPY.

**33 1/3 rpm sound disc**   An ANALOG DISC, usually 12 inches (30 cm) in diameter, to be played at 33 1/3 revolutions per minute, and with a normal playing time of twenty to thirty minutes per side. (52:39)

**Three-knife trimmer**   "A cutting machine designed to trim all three edges of a book in two cuts but with only one handling of the book. The FORE EDGE knife makes the first cut, returns to its raised position, and the other two knives simultaneously cut the HEAD AND TAIL." (47:263) See also GUILLOTINE.

**Three-quarter binding**   A BINDING in which the material used to cover the SPINE extends up to half the width of the BOARDs. The COVERING MATERIAL is stronger than that on the rest of the sides. See also HALF BINDING; QUARTER BINDING.

**Three-up**   Three periodical issues imposed in a line, folded, SADDLE-STITCHED together, and then cut apart in the TRIMMING operation. (47:264)

**Throughput**   In microfilm production, the rate at which documents can be filmed.

**Throw-in**   See INSERT.

**Throw-out**   See FOLDOUT.

**Thymol (isopropyl meta cresol)**   A colorless, crystalline compound ($C_{10}H_{13} \bullet OH$) used as a preservative in PASTE and also as a FUNGICIDE. It can be applied as a solution in ALCOHOL or vaporized for use as a fungicide. (47:264) It is in crystalline form at room temperature, and sublimes to vapor when heated above 49°C (120°F). Thymol is toxic and can be absorbed through the skin; the major hazard is ingestion through inhalation. Thymol is not registered as a MOLD control chemical by the Environmental Protection Agency, is carcinogenic, and is not recommended for use in PRESERVATION procedures.

**Tight back**   A type of BINDING in which the COVER is adhered to the SPINE of the book, so that the spine does not become HOLLOW when open. The pages do not lie flat when the book is open unless the paper used is thin and not stiff. Also called stiff back. (23:617) See also FLEXIBLE BINDING; HOLLOW BACK (HOLLOW BACK BINDING).

**Tight joint**   See CLOSED JOINT.

**Tinted stock**   Film base stock that has a tint for ANTIHALATION purposes which is not removed in PROCESSING.

**Tip in**   A LEAF is attached to the INNER MARGIN of another leaf through the application of a thin line of ADHESIVE. (26:17)

**Tip on**   A LEAF that has been pasted onto the STUB of another leaf (e.g., a CANCEL) through the application of a thin line of ADHESIVE. (47:265) See also TIPPING.

**Tipping (tipping in)**   **(1)** Pasting the edges of a SECTION to adjacent sections. **(2)** Tipping on an INSET around or in a larger section. (47:265)

**Titration**   Chemical method for determining the strength or concentration of a given constituent present in a solution. (55:108) This is accomplished by adding a liquid reagent of known strength and measuring the volume necessary to convert the constituent to another form.

**Tonal range** **(1)** Number of precisely measured gradients of gray that photographic materials (PRINTs and NEGATIVEs) are capable of producing accurately. (46:155)

**Toning** **(1)** Changing the visual appearance of a silver image by converting some or all of the metallic Ag to a different species, such as $Ag_2S$ or $Ag_2Se$. **(2)** Diluted toning solutions, such as polysulfide, may be used to improve image STABILITY with very little or no change in the visual appearance of the image. (8:154) The IMAGE PERMANENCE INSTITUTE now recommends polysulfide toning for all PRESERVATION MICROFILM to inoculate it against oxidative attack regardless of the environment to which the FILM may ultimately be exposed. See ARCHIVAL PROCESSING; BLEMISH; OXIDATION.

**Top lighting** A filming method in which the ILLUMINATION is above the material to be filmed.

**Top side** See FELT SIDE.

**Top sizing** "SURFACE or TUB SIZING of paper which has already been internally SIZEd." (15:421) See SIZING; SURFACE SIZING; TUB SIZING.

**Torr** A unit of pressure equal to $1/760$ of atmospheric pressure, i.e., 1,333.22 millibars. (55:108)

**Tort** A violation of an obligation created by law, such as might cause injury to a person through the (alleged) negligence of another person.

**Tosa Tengujo** A Japanese paper consisting of 100 percent KOZO made by the SODA PULP process. Has long silky FIBERs and is lightweight. See also JAPANESE PAPER.

**Total thickness** Normally the sum of the thickness of the BASE FILM and the magnetic COATING as well as BACKCOATING when applied. The total thickness governs the length of magnetic tape that can be wound on a given REEL. (49:162)

**Track** **(1)** On a magnetic tape, a lengthwise magnetic division of specified width that is scanned by recording or playback HEADs, as in FULL-TRACK, HALF-TRACK, QUARTER-TRACK, and EIGHT-TRACK tapes. Each track normally stores the signal for one CHANNEL of sound. **(2)** Alternative term for a BAND on an ANALOG DISC or a GROOVE on an analog disc. **(3)** A section of a COMPACT DISC identifiable through coded information that indicates the beginning and end of the section, along with other information. Comparable to a band on an analog disc. (52:39)

**Trade binding** See EDITION BINDING.

**Trailer** **(1)** A blank segment of tape at the end of a REEL of motion-picture film, filmstrip, or microfilm for threading through the projector or other equipment and for the protection of the last FRAMEs. **(2)** A blank section at the end of a reel of magnetic tape or punched tape to protect the last few inches of the tape. (1:231) See also LEADER; MICROFICHE.

**Trailer microfiche**   In a related set of MICROFICHE, all fiche after the first in the series. See also MICROFICHE.

**Transcription disc**   A 33 1/3 rpm AUDIODISC, formerly 16 inches (41 cm) in diameter but more recently also 10 or 12 inches (25 or 30 cm) in diameter, recorded during a live performance or broadcast, and/or containing program material used in broadcasting. (52:39) See also NONPROCESSED RECORDING.

**Transfer**   See BLEED-THROUGH (PAPER); COATING TRANSFER (TAPE).

**Translucent paper support**   In photography, a PAPER SUPPORT which allows the passage of light because of the application of oils or waxes to the paper. (44:31)

**Transmission densitometer**   A device for measuring the DENSITY of a material using light passed through the material being measured. See also DENSITOMETER.

**Transmitted light**   Light which has passed through at least one material. (44:31)

**Transparency**   A photographic image that may be viewed by TRANS-MITTED LIGHT. (44:31)

**Triage**   The process of sorting materials, especially during or after a disaster, to determine priority or appropriate treatment. Also the determination of priorities for action in an emergency.

**Trimmed**   "Paper which has been trimmed on one or more sides to ensure exactness of corner angles and to reduce to the size required." (23:627)

**Trimming**   "The operation in which bound books and other printed materials are reduced to their final size before casing or attachment of the boards. Trimming a BOOK removes the folds at HEAD and FORE EDGE (bolts), thus freeing the leaves for turning; it also smoothes the edges, and divides TWO-UP or THREE-UP books or periodical issues into individual units, the latter operation usually being referred to as "splitting" or "cutting apart," even though it may be done as part of trimming. In EDITION and LIBRARY BINDING, trimming is done after SMASHING or NIPPING, while in hand binding it may come either before or after ROUNDING. In the manufacture of CUT FLUSH books, the book and COVERs are TRIMMED together. Most PAPERBACK books and periodical issues are produced this way. Trimming is, in such cases, the final step in binding. The LIBRARY BINDING INSTITUTE specifies that when volumes are trimmed, the trimming shall be as slight as possible." (47:268–269)

**Tub-sized**   SIZING paper by passing the WEB through a SIZE PRESS, or by hand dipping the WATERLEAF sheet into a tub of SIZE, or by carrying it through the size bath between two FELTs. (47:269) See also SIZING; SURFACE SIZING; TUB SIZE PRESS.

**Tub size press**   A unit of a papermaking machine, designed for relatively heavy applications of SIZING agents to PAPER or PAPERBOARD, usually located between two DRIER sections. (15:427)

**Turn in**   In a CASE, the COVERING MATERIAL turned over the outer edges of the BOARDs and INLAY, and onto their inner surfaces. (26:17)

**Two along**   A way of sewing by hand in which two SECTIONs are treated as one unit by alternately sewing each to CORDS or TAPES using a single thread from KETTLE STITCH to kettle stitch. Generally used to reduce the thickness in the back of a book comprised of many thin sections, by reducing the amount of thread added in sewing. (1:233; 47:270) Also called two-on. See also ALL ALONG.

**Two-shot method**   A method of applying ADHESIVE in high-speed PAPERBACK ADHESIVE BINDING. The adhesive binding machine applies a POLYVINYL (cold) adhesive as a primer followed by a HOT-MELT ADHESIVE. Slower than the ONE-SHOT METHOD, but it results in a stronger HINGE and good cover adhesion. (47:270) See also ADHESIVE BINDING; ONE-SHOT METHOD.

**Two-track**   See HALF-TRACK.

**Two-up**   (1) A method of imposing and processing two books (or periodical issues) as a single unit, all the way from printing through all of the binding processes. The two books or issues are separated at the TRIMMING station during binding. See also THREE-UP. (2) The process of printing two texts, or duplicate stereos made from the same form, side by side on the same sheet of paper. It is an economical way of printing short runs. (47:270) (3) In microfilming, filming two pages on a single FRAME.

**U**dagami   A JAPANESE PAPER made of 100 percent KOZO. Very lightweight with narrow LAID LINES, and CHAIN LINES about one inch apart. While looking very delicate and fragile, it is strong and opaque. Useful for mending art objects on paper. See also JAPANESE PAPER.

**uhr**   See ULTRAHIGH REDUCTION.

**μin**   Micro-inch (= $10^{-6}$ inch).

**UL**   Underwriters Laboratories, Northbrook, IL; a testing laboratory for equipment used in various areas including electrical devices, fire protection, security protection, and fire resistance. (37:120)

**Ultrafiche**   MICROFICHE filmed at a REDUCTION RATIO of 90x or more. (1:234) See also MICROFICHE.

**Ultrahigh reduction**   REDUCTION RATIOs above 90x. See REDUCTION RATIO.

**Ultramicrofiche**   See ULTRAFICHE.

**Ultrasonic**   A term which describes soundwaves of frequencies too high to be audible to humans. **(1)** Ultrasonic cleaning of AUDIODISCs is a system consisting of a tank, a cleaning solution, and an oscillator operating in the ultrasonic frequencies. **(2)** Ultrasonic SPLICEs are used to form very strong butt splices in POLYESTER-base reel films. Internal friction created by the sonic vibrations within the film helps create the splice. (4:311)

**Ultraviolet light (UV)**   Light waves beyond the violet portion of the visible spectrum, shorter than those of visible light. Its energy is much greater than VISIBLE LIGHT and can damage paper, photographs, and other materials if not shielded. See also UV FILTER.

**μm**   Micro-meter (= $10^{-6}$ meter); also referred to as a micron.

**Unauthorized recording**   See PIRATE RECORDING.

**Unbound**   The leaves or SECTIONs of a book or publication which have not been fastened together.

**Uncut**   A book whose edges have not been TRIMMED or cut by a GUILLOTINE. The folded edges (BOLTS) must be opened with a paper knife or BONE FOLDER. (23:639)

**Underdevelopment**   Light images resulting from too little development. Caused by weakened DEVELOPER solution, too short a time in the developer, or being developed at too low a temperature.

**Underexposure**   SENSITIZED material receiving too little RADIATION to create an acceptable image. Causes include too little radiation, too short an EXPOSURE time, too small an aperture, etc.

**Underwriter**   "An insurance professional trained in evaluating risks and determining rates and COVERAGE." (25:95)

**Uniformity**   In magnetic tape recording, the extent to which the OUTPUT remains free from variations in AMPLITUDE. Uniformity is usually specified in terms of the positive and negative deviations from the average output within a roll of tape. (49:162)

**Universal camera**   A specially designed camera capable of handling 16mm, 35mm, or 105mm film formats.

**Untrimmed**   The folded edges (BOLTs) of a book have not been cut, and must be separated by hand, and the uneven edges of the projecting leaves have not been pruned square by a cutting machine. Also called un-opened. (1:236) See also UNCUT.

**UV**   See ULTRAVIOLET LIGHT.

**UV filter**   A material used to filter the ULTRAVIOLET (UV) rays out of VISIBLE LIGHT. Usually UV filtering material is placed over windows or fluorescent light tubes or built into glass used in framing or exhibition cases. Certain ACRYLIC sheet materials have UV filtering and absorbing properties built in. Two examples are Plexiglas UF-1, which is practically colorless and does not interfere with color rendering, and Plexiglas UF-3, which is somewhat yellow but also a better UV absorber. See also UV MONITOR. (22:15)

**UV monitor**   "A device which measures the proportion of ULTRAVIO-LET radiation in the light as microwatts of UV radiation per LUMEN (lm) of visible light. If a light source emits more than about 75 μw/lm it requires a UV FILTER or absorbing material. The CRAWFORD UV MONITOR TYPE 760 is used by many museums and libraries to measure UV radiation." (51:21)

**μw**   Microwatt (= $10^{-6}$ watt).

**μw/lm**   Microwatts per LUMEN (UV content of light).

# V

**aluation clause**   "The clause that tells what the insured will be paid in the event of a CLAIM and how the amount of the claim will be calculated." (25:95)

**van der Waals' forces**   Weak, nonspecific forces between molecules.

**Vapor barrier**   A material, usually 6-mil POLYETHYLENE sheeting, used to prevent the flow of air and water vapor from reaching a cold surface where it might reach the DEW POINT and condense. (30:80)

**Vapor-phase deacidification**   PAPER in books is DEACIDIFIED by inter-leaving the pages with tissue paper impregnated with a dry volatile gaseous ALKALI. The compound vaporizes and penetrates the paper, neutralizing the ACID.

**Variable**   Any item, entity, or phenomenon to be analyzed. A variable is measured for each individual or CASE according to rules the researcher specifies. "Variable" indicates that the values vary from case to case. (7:114)

**Vat** **(1)** A term for HANDMADE PAPERs. **(2)** The tank containing beaten PULP from which handmade SHEETs are formed. **(3)** The oblong tank in which the cylinder of a CYLINDER MACHINE is mounted and which contains a STOCK suspension from which the sheet is formed. **(4)** The tank used for TUB-SIZED paper. (15:433)

**Vatman; vat person** The person who forms the SHEETs of paper by dipping the MOLD and shaking the SLURRY to distribute the FIBER. (29:118)

**Vat-sized** In papermaking, when the SIZE is added to the PULP before the pulp is used to form a SHEET. (23:650)

**VAV** Variable Air Volume system. Environmental control zones served by a common duct system providing cool air. Each zone is tempered by introducing a varied volume of cool air from the system. A "VAV box" is required for each zone. (30:80)

**Vellum** **(1)** Originally, a translucent or opaque material produced from calfskin. Today, however, vellum is generally defined as a material made from calfskin, sheepskin, or virtually any other skin obtained from a relatively small animal, e.g., antelope. Some authorities do not distinguish between vellum and PARCHMENT, although traditionally the former was made from an unsplit calfskin, and consequently had a grain pattern on one side (unless removed by scraping), while the latter was produced from the flesh split from a sheepskin, and consequently had no grain pattern. (47:277) **(2)** A strong, high-grade natural or cream-colored paper made to resemble vellum. **(3)** A term applied to a FINISH rather than a grade. Social and personal stationery are often called vellums. (15:435)

**Velo-binding** Projecting pins of a plastic strip are inserted through holes along the BINDING EDGE of the leaves and into matching holes in another plastic strip. The leaves are compressed by a machine which cuts the pins to the length, and fuses them to the strips. Velo-binding is fairly strong and permanent, but will not open flat. A form of MECHANICAL BINDING. (1:238)

**Vermin** Small, noxious, or disgusting animals or insects which are common and difficult to control. For example, roaches, fleas, lice, mice, rats, etc.

**Verso** The left-hand page of an open book or manuscript, usually bearing an even page number. The back side of a LEAF of paper. See also RECTO.

**Vertical cut** An early recording method whereby the sound signal was engraved in the bottom of the GROOVEs of an ANALOG DISC or CYLINDER instead of the sides, as in a LATERAL CUT recording. This technique produced an up-and-down motion of the STYLUS during recording and playback. Also called hill-and-dale cut, phonocut. (52:40) See also LATERAL CUT.

**Vertical mode**   See CINE MODE.

**Very high reduction**   REDUCTION RATIO of 61x through 90x. See RE-DUCTION RATIO.

**Vesicular film**   A SIGN-REVERSING duplicating film which uses heat energy to develop LATENT IMAGEs after EXPOSURE to ULTRAVIO-LET LIGHT. DIAZONIUM SALTS are suspended throughout a layer covering the plastic base. When exposed, the LIGHT-SENSITIVE element creates nitrogen bubbles in the layer which forms the latent image, which, in turn, becomes visible and permanent with the application of heat. (42:196) It is not generally an ARCHIVAL product. At one time the film was referred to as Kalvar, after the company that originally produced it. (1:239)

**vhr**   See VERY HIGH REDUCTION.

**VHS**   Abbreviation for video-home-system; $1/2$ inch VIDEOCASSETTE system originated by JVC and manufactured worldwide, aimed directly at the domestic market.

**Victrola record**   RCA trademark for a 78 rpm AUDIODISC.

**Videocassette**   A prepackaged VIDEOTAPE enclosed in a plastic unit containing magnetic tape (either prerecorded or blank) for video recording or playback, usually $1/2$ or $3/4$ inches in width. (4:312) The unit has two REELs, a supply reel and a take-up reel.

**Videodisc**   A flat, circular plastic platter on which both audio and video information can be stored for playback by means of a laser videodisc player. (4:312) See also LASER DISC.

**Videotape**   A MAGNETIC TAPE on which video and audio signals may be or are recorded for television use. The tape varies from $1/4$ to 2 inches in width and from 0.5 to 1.5 MILs in THICKNESS. The most common sizes for instructional and educational use are $1/2$, $3/4$, and 1 inch wide. (1:239)

**Videotape cassette**   See VIDEOCASSETTE.

**Vinyl**   **(1)** Short form of POLYVINYL CHLORIDE (PVC). The word is imprecisely used to refer to any of a number of plastics, many of which are not appropriate for use in preservation. For specific safe plastics, see ACRYLIC, POLYESTER, POLYETHYLENE, POLYPROPYLENE, POLYVINYL ACETATE. **(2)** A slang term for an AUDIODISC recording. (4:312) See VINYL DISC.

**Vinyl chloride**   See POLYVINYL CHLORIDE (PVC).

**Vinyl disc**   A microgroove long-playing (LP) 33 $1/3$ rpm AUDIODISC made of about 75 percent POLYVINYL CHLORIDE and 25 percent fillers, e.g., stabilizers, pigment, antistatic materials, etc. In common use since the 1950s. See LONG-PLAYING AUDIODISC.

**Virtual image**   In optics, an image formed by an extension of light rays, which does not exist where it appears to be, such as an image in a plane mirror. (1:240) See also REAL IMAGE.

**Visible light**   RADIANT ENERGY that can be see by the human eye.

**Visual range**   That portion of the light spectrum between the INFRARED and the ULTRAVIOLET which can be seen by the human eye. (1:240)

**VOCs**   Volatile organic compounds, including formaldehyde. Usually associated with discussions of off-gassing. (30:81)

**Void**   In magnetic tape recording, an area where material is missing on the surface of a head track; also applies to tape surface. (49:162)

**Volatization**   The process whereby a material is altered into a vapor (vaporization), caused by a reaction to other materials with which it is combined or to environmental conditions. It can be applied to the decomposition of certain materials contained in a SOUND RECORDING. (4:312)

**Volumen**   The PAPYRUS roll used in ancient Egypt, Greece, and Rome, written on one side only with a reed pen. The text was in columns, the lines running parallel the length of the roll. The final papyrus sheet of the volumen was rolled around a knobbed rod which served as a handle. "Volumen" is Latin for "a thing rolled up." (47:278) See also SCROLL.

**VPD**   See VAPOR PHASE DEACIDIFICATION.

# W   See WAVELENGTH.

**Warp**   **(1)** A bend or distortion caused by unequal pressure on one side of a material. Usually happens when paper or book cloth is moistened (expanded) and attached to only one side of a BOARD. Warp also occurs when a material such as leather or VELLUM shrinks in an overly dry environment. Warping can also occur when the GRAIN directions of attached materials are not parallel to one another. (38:220) **(2)** A series of parallel yarns extended lengthwise in a loom, thereby forming the lengthwise threads of a fabric. The warp direction of a cloth is the stronger of the two directions. (47:279) See also WEFT.

**Washboard**   "A defect in film that appears as alternate bands of greater and lesser DENSITY across the width of the film. This may be caused by fluctuating illumination or faulty document or film transport." (21:28)

**Washing**   When DEVELOPING photographic NEGATIVEs, or making PRINTs on SENSITIZED PAPER, the materials are thoroughly washed in clean running water after they have been in the FIXING solution so as to remove all traces of the developing or fixing solutions.

**Waste sheet**   A sheet of paper tipped to the outside over the permanent ENDPAPER to prevent it from becoming damaged or soiled during the binding of the book. (47:279)

**Waterflow alarm**   A device that sends a signal to a monitoring station when water moves through pipes in a sprinkler system. See also WATER SENSOR.

**Waterleaf**   **(1)** A completely unsized sheet of paper, having low water resistance. **(2)** HANDMADE PAPER in its initial stage of manufacture, consisting of paper FIBERs spread evenly over the surface of the hand MOLD; they are then removed and pressed between FELTs. As it is unsized, it is very absorbent and has low water resistance. (47:280)

**Watermark**   The image or symbol formed in a sheet of paper during its manufacture which is visible when the paper is held up to TRANSMIT-TED LIGHT. In HANDMADE PAPER, the watermark forms as less fibrous material settles over a raised area woven into the MOLD, resulting in a greater translucency of the sheet in that area. Watermarks are simulated in MACHINE-MADE PAPER by a raised area on the DANDY ROLL that impresses a design into the wet mat of fibers. (45:89)

**Water sensor**   A device that detects the presence of (and in some designs, the location) of free surface water. When water is detected an alarm is activated.

**Water source heat pump system**   An HVAC system in which the environ-mental control zones are served by a circulating loop of water. Each zone has its own HEAT PUMP (consisting of a COMPRESSOR, EVAPORA-TOR, CONDENSER, circulating fan, filter, and controls), which can heat or cool the zone by running the heat pump compressor to either cool the air and heat the water loop, or heat the air and cool the water loop. (30:81)

**Water spot**   "A defect in film that may be caused by (1) deformation of the GELATIN layer in an irregular spot pattern which is caused by water drops on the surface during drying, due to improper squeegeeing, or (2) residue from materials in the wash water." (21:28)

**Water spot-test**   A test to determine the presence or absence of an EMUL-SION on a FILM BASE. It involves the local application of water by means of a swab to a film surface. The SWELLING OF THE EMULSION by this solvent is a positive test. (44:31) See also ALCOHOL SPOT-TEST.

**Water tear**   A method of tearing JAPANESE PAPER or other paper into mending strips along a moistened line to produce a soft, feathered edge. (38:220)

**Wavelength**   The distance along the length of a sinusoidally recorded magnetic tape corresponding to one cycle. Abbreviated w. (49:162)

**Wavyness**   Nonflat HEAD top surface perpendicular to tape motion due to different wear rates in top surface materials in magnetic tape recording

**Wax cylinder**   A sound recording CYLINDER with a recording surface of wax; the earliest type except for the tinfoil cylinder, and more fragile than subsequent types. (52:40) See also AMBEROL CYLINDER; BLUE AMBEROL CYLINDER; CELLULOID CYLINDER.

**Wax disc**   The earliest type of ANALOG DISC, with a recording surface of a wax or soap compound. Prior to the advent of the LONG-PLAYING AUDIODISC in the 1950s, MASTER DISCs also were cut on blank wax discs. (52:40) See also ACETATE DISC; LACQUER DISC; SHELLAC DISC; VINYL DISC.

**Wear product**   Any material that is detached from magnetic tape during use. (49:162)

**Wear test**   See DURABILITY (OF MAGNETIC TAPE).

**Web**   The SHEET of PAPER coming from the papermaking machine in its full width. (47:281)

**Web press**   A printing machine on which the paper is fed from a continuous reel.

**Web sizing**   See SURFACE-SIZED; TUB-SIZED.

**Weft**   "The threads or yarns in a fabric that cross the WARP and extend from SELVAGE to selvage, i.e., the threads carried by the shuttle. The typical cloth is stronger, i.e., has a greater BREAKING STRENGTH, in the warp direction than in the weft. Also called filling." (47:282) See also BOOK CLOTH.

**Weft wire**   See FOURDRINIER WIRE.

**Wei T'o**   Richard D. Smith's registered trademark for a NONAQUEOUS book DEACIDIFICATION system. The name is the same as that of an ancient Chinese god that protects books against destruction from fire, worms, insects, and robbers, big and small.

**Wet-bulb temperature**   "The temperature read by a thermometer whose sensing bulb is covered with a wetted wick and exposed to the evaporative cooling effect of moving air. The reading, compared to an unwetted dry-bulb, indicates the amount of moisture in the air, since that affects how much water can evaporate from the wet-bulb." (30:81) See also DRY-BULB TEMPERATURE; SLING PSYCHROMETER.

**Wet end**   The part of the papermaking machine where the wet PULP is formed into a paper WEB, between the HEADBOX and the DRIER section. (47:448) See FOURDRINIER MACHINE; WEB.

**Wet press**   The dewatering unit used on a papermaking machine between the SHEET-forming equipment and the DRIER SECTION. It applies pressure, or a combination of pressure and suction to the sheet to remove as much water as practical from the sheet ahead of the driers. (15:449)

**Wet processing**   That set of photographic PROCESSING strategies that include the use of liquid chemistry and water.

**Wetting agent**   A compound used to reduce the surface tension of a liquid and increase the wettability of a solid surface. In papermaking, wetting agents are often used to improve absorbency and to improve pigment dispersion. (15:450) Water spots on photographic emulsions and/or negatives can often be alleviated through the use of a wetting agent. (1:241)

**Wheat starch**   See STARCH PASTE.

**Whip stitching**   The process of SEWING single sheets into "sections" (not to be confused with folded SECTIONs); the number of sheets sewn depends on the THICKNESS of the paper. The "sections" are then sewn on TAPES or CORDS in the usual manner of HAND SEWING. (47:283)

**White water**   Essentially spent and diluted chemicals from a PULP processing system, often desilvered and processed to remove pollutants prior to discharge from the plant.

**Whole stuff**   "The PULP used in making paper after it has been thoroughly beaten and bleached, and is ready for the VAT or the paper machine." (23:660) See also HALFSTUFF; STUFF.

**Width (of a book)**   The widest part of a book from the outside curve of the SPINE (or RAISED BANDS on the spine) to the front edge (FORE EDGE) of the COVER BOARDS. (38:220)

**Wind**   The way in which magnetic tape is wound onto a REEL. An "A-wind" is one in which the tape is wound so that the coated surface faces toward the HUB. (49:162)

**Winder/cleaner**   A device designed to WIND and clean magnetic tape to restore it to a quality that approaches the condition of a new tape providing the tape has not been physically damaged. (49:162)

**Window board**   "A piece of BOARD in a MAT in which an opening is cut to allow art work to be displayed." (28:26)

**Window opening**   "The aperture in the WINDOW BOARD." (28:26)

**Wire**   **(1)** The endless belt of woven metal or synthetic wires which forms the molding element of a papermaking machine, carrying the PULP from the HEADBOX to the COUCH ROLL, in the process felting it into a SHEET. See FOURDRINIER WIRE. **(2)** A magnetizable wire on which sound has been recorded. Also called an audiowire, phonowire, or wire recording. Wire was a popular recording medium in the U.S. during the

1940s and early 1950s, but magnetic tape generally had replaced wire by the mid-1950s. (52:40)

**Wire recording**  See WIRE.

**Wire side**  The side of a SHEET of paper formed in contact with the wire of the MOLD in handmade paper, or the FOURDRINIER WIRE of the papermaking machine. (47:283) See also FELT SIDE.

**With the grain**  Paper which has been folded or cut parallel to the GRAIN.

**White light**  Radiation having a SPECTRAL energy distribution that produces the same color sensitivity to the average human eye as average noon sunlight. (21:29)

**Wood fiber**  See FIBER.

**Wood pulp**  FIBER produced by the chemical or mechanical treatment of wood, or both, for use in making PAPER, PAPERBOARD, rayon, plastics, etc. (15:455) See PULP.

**Woof**  See WEFT.

**Working copy**  See SERVICE COPY.

**Worm hole**  A hole or series of holes bored into, or through, a book by a BOOK WORM.

**Wove**  A wire mark on a sheet of paper. See WOVE PAPER.

**Wove paper**  The wires on the framed papermaking MOLD are fine and woven like cloth, with the wires interlacing one another closely and evenly. The effect is produced in MACHINE-MADE PAPERs by the weave of the DANDY ROLL, and in HANDMADE PAPERs by the wires of the MOLD. Wove paper does not have CHAIN or LAID lines. (47:284)

**Wow**  **(1)** In AUDIODISC usage, a term used to describe changes in signal OUTPUT frequencies below 15 Hz caused by turntable problems. **(2)** Term used to describe changes in magnetic tape speed variations occurring at relatively low rates; however, the term "wow" is no longer used but is incorporated into the measurement of FLUTTER. See also FLUTTER.

**Wrapper**  The original paper COVER of a BOOK or PAMPHLET, to which it is attached as an integral part of the volume.

**Wrapper board**  "A solid covering board that is HINGEd to the MAT over the WINDOW BOARD to protect the art work beneath, and which may be swung back for viewing." (28:26)

**Wrapping band**  A strip of material, usually paper, placed around a REEL of PROCESSED FILM to protect it and retain it in its wound state. In PRESERVATION MICROFILMING, these bands are ACID-FREE.

**Write feedthrough**  See CROSS TALK.

**X**erography    A dry method of making POSITIVE copies on ordinary paper by the use of light and an electrostatically charged plate or drum. The process depends on static electricity to attract particles of black powder to unexposed areas of the image. A selenium-coated surface is given a positive electrostatic charge and the image is then exposed to it through a camera. Where light is reflected, the charge will be dissipated, leaving a positive charge in the image areas. When a negatively charged black resinous powder (toner) is cascaded over the selenium, it is attracted to the charged area. Paper which is then placed over the selenium and charged positively will have the powder image transferred to it, and the image is fused permanently to the paper by the application of heat.

**Y**ankee machine    "A machine on which machine-glazed papers are made. Its chief characteristic is one large steam-heated cylinder with a highly polished surface in place of the usual drying rolls. Machine-glazed papers are glazed on only one (the under) side, the other being in the (rough) condition in which it comes from the WET END of the machine." (23:669)

**Z**one, Environmental control    See ENVIRONMENTAL CONTROL ZONE.

**Z39**    Committee designation for the National Information Standards Organization (Z39). The committee is organized under the procedures of the American National Standards Institute, Inc. (ANSI) and develops national standards in library science, information science, and related publishing fields. See NISO.

# S ources

1. *ALA Glossary of Library and Information Science.* Edited by Heartsill Young. Chicago: American Library Ascociation, 1983.

2. ALA, RTSD, and the Library of Congress National Preservation Program Office. *Library Preservation: Fundamental Techniques. An institute held at Stanford University, Stanford, CA, August 26–30, 1985.*

3. *Archival Products Pamphlet Binders.* Des Moines, IA: Archival Products, 1988.

4. Association for Recorded Sound Collections. Associated Audio Archives Committee. *Audio Preservation: A Planning Study: Final Performance Report.* 2 vols. Prepared by the Associated Audio Archives Committee for the National Endowment for the Humanities. Silver Spring, MD: The Committee, Association for Recorded Sound Collection, 1988– .

5. Association of Research Libraries. "Terminology." *Paper Preservation in Library Collections: Basic Information.* Washington, DC: Association of Research Libraries, November 1988.

6. Aubey, Rolland. "Specifications and Test Methods Associated with Papers for Permanent Books, Records, and Documents." In *TAPPI Proceedings: 1988 Paper Preservation Symposium.* Atlanta, GA: Technical Association of the Pulp and Paper Industry Press, 1988.

7. Carpenter, Ray L., and Ellen Storey Vasu. *Statistical Methods for Librarians.* Chicago: American Library Association, 1978.

8. *Conservation of Photographs.* Rochester, NY: Eastman Kodak Co., 1985.

9. Council on Library Resources. Committee on Production *Guidelines for Book Longevity.* Washington, DC: Council on Library Resources, 1982.

10. Cunha, George Martin. "Mass Deacidification for Libraries." *Library Technology Reports* 23 (May/June 1987): 362–472.

11. Cunha, George Martin, and Dorothy Grant Cunha. *Conservation of Library Materials; A Manual and Bibliography on the Care, Repair, and*

*Restoration of Library Materials.* 2nd ed. Vol. 1. Metuchen, NJ: Scarecrow Press, 1971.

12. Darling, Pamela W. "To the Editor:" *Conservation Administration News* 22 (July 1985): 3, 20.

13. Davids, Lewis E. *Dictionary of Insurance.* 7th rev. ed. Savage, MD: Littlefield, Adams Quality Paperbacks, 1990.

14. DeCandido, Robert. "Out of the Question." *Conservation Administration News* 38 (July 1989): 24.

15. *Dictionary of Paper; A Compendium of Terms Commonly Used in the U.S. Pulp, Paper and Allied Industries.* 4th ed. New York: American Paper Institute, Inc., 1980.

16. Evans, Frank B., Donald F. Harrison, and Edwin A. Thompson. "A Basic Glossary for Archivists, Manuscript Curators, and Records Managers." *The American Archivist* 37 (July 1974): 415–433.

17. Folcarelli, Ralph J., Arthur C. Tannenbaum, and Ralph C. Ferragamo. *The Microform Connection; A Basic Guide for Libraries.* NY: R.R. Bowker Co., 1982.

18. Geller, Sidney B. *Computer Science and Technology: Care and Handling of Computer Magnetic Storage Media.* U.S. Department of Commerce, National Bureau of Standards, Institute for Computer Sciences and Technology. NBS Special Publication 500–101. Washington, DC: U.S. Government Printing Office, June 1983.

19. "Glossary." *Alkaline Paper Advocate.* 1 (March 1988): 9.

20. "Glossary; CD-ROM Buzzwords You Should Know." *CD-ROM Review; The Magazine of Compact-Disc Data Storage.* Premiere issue [1] (1986): 51.

21. *Glossary of Micrographics.* Association for Information and Image Management. Technical Report TR2-1980. Rev. ed. Silver Spring, MD: Association for Information and Image Management, 1980.

22. "Glossary of Selected Preservation Terms." *ALCTS Newsletter* 1:2 (1990): 14–15.

23. *Harrod's Librarians' Glossary of Terms Used in Librarianship, Documentation and the Book Crafts; And Reference Book.* 7th ed. Compiled by Ray Prytherch. Aldershot, Hants, England: Gower Publishing Company, Ltd., 1990.

24. Horton, Carolyn. *Cleaning and Preserving Bindings and Related Materials.* 2nd ed., rev. LTP Publication No. 16. Conservation of Library Materials, Pamphlet 1. Chicago: American Library Association, 1969.

25. *Insurance and Risk Management for Museums and Historical Societies.* Hamilton, NY: Gallery Association of New York State, 1985.

26. *Library Binding Institute Standard for Library Binding.* Edited by Paul A. Parisi and Jan Merrill-Oldham. 8th ed. Rochester, NY: Library Binding Institute, 1986.

27. Library of Congress. Preservation Office. *Polyester Film Encapsulation.*

Washington, DC: U.S. Government Printing Office, 1980.

28. Library of Congress. Preservation Office. Research Services. *Matting and Hinging of Works of Art on Paper.* Compiled by Merrily A. Smith. Washington, DC: Library of Congress, 1981.

29. Luebbers, Leslie Laird, "Glossary," *Paper—Art & Technology.* Edited by Paulette Long. San Francisco: World Print Council, 1979.

30. Lull, William P. *Conservation Environment Guidelines for Libraries and Archives.* The New York State Program for the Conservation and Preservation of Library Research Materials. Albany, NY: New York State Library, New York State Education Department, 1990.

31. Macleod, K. J. *Museum Lighting.* Technical Bulletin 2. Ottawa: Canadian Conservation Institute, April 1975, reprinted May 1978.

32. Macleod, K. J. *Relative Humidity: Its Importance, Measurement and Control in Museums.* Technical Bulletin 1. Ottawa: Canadian Conservation Institute, April 1975, reprinted May 1978.

33. McGrady, Ellen. "A Glossary for the March Issue." *The Alkaline Paper Advocate* 3 (May 1990): 19–21.

34. *Microforms in Libraries; A Manual for Evaluation and Management.* Edited by Francis Spreitzer for the Committees for the Reproduction of Library Materials Section and Resources Section of the Resources and Technical Services Division of the American Library Association. Chicago: American Library Association, 1985.

35. Middleton, Bernard C. *The Restoration of Leather Bindings.* Rev. ed. LTP Publication No. 20. Chicago: American Library Association, 1984.

36. Milevski, Robert J. Preservation Librarian at Princeton University.

37. Morris, John. *The Library Disaster Preparedness Handbook.* Chicago: American Library Association, 1986.

38. Morrow, Carolyn Clark, and Carole Dyal. *Conservation Treatment Procedures; A Manual of Step-by-Step Procedures for the Maintenance and Repair of Library Materials.* 2nd ed. Littleton, CO: Libraries Unlimited, Inc., 1986.

39. Morton, Bernard W. *Humidification Handbook; What, Why & How.* Hopkins, MN: Dri-Steem Humidifier Co., 1986.

40. Nyberg, Sandra. *The Invasion of the Giant Spore.* SOLINET Preservation Program Leaflet Number 5. Atlanta: Southeastern Library Network, 1 November 1987.

41. Parker, Thomas A. "Integrated Pest Management for Libraries." In *Preservation of Library Materials.* IFLA Publications 40/41. Vol. 2. Edited by Merrily Smith. Munich: K. G. Saur Verlag, 1987.

42. *Preservation Microfilming; A Guide for Librarians and Archivists.* Edited by Nancy E. Gwinn for the Association of Research Libraries. Chicago: American Library Association, 1987.

43. *Random House Dictionary of the English Language.* Unabridged ed. Edited by Jess Stein. NY: Random House, 1981.

44.  Rempel, Siegfried. *The Care of Black and White Photographic Collections: Identification of Processes.* Technical Bulletin 6. Ottawa: Canadian Conservation Institute, 1979.

45.  Ritzenthaler, Mary Lynn. *Archives & Manuscripts: Conservation. A Manual on Physical Care and Management.* Chicago: Society of American Archivists, 1983.

46.  Ritzenthaler, Mary Lynn, Gerald J. Munoff, and Margery S. Long. *Archives & Manuscripts: Administration of Photographic Collections.* SAA Basic Manual Series, Chicago: Society of American Archivists, 1984.

47.  Roberts, Matt T., and Don Etherington. *Bookbinding and the Conservation of Books; A Dictionary of Descriptive Terminology.* Washington, DC: Library of Congress, 1982.

48.  Saffady, William. "Stability, Care and Handling of Microforms, Magnetic Media and Optical Disks." *Library Technology Reports* 27 (January/February 1991): 5–116.

49.  Schwartz, Herbert M., Joe Pomian, and Sanford Platter. *Magnetic Tape Recording for the Eighties.* Edited by Ford Kalil. NASA reference publication 1075. Washington, DC: U. S. Government Printing Office, April 1982.

50.  Staniforth, Sarah. "Environmental Conservation." Chapter 26 in *Manual of Curatorship; A Guide to Museum Practice.* London: Butterworths, 1984.

51.  Thomson, Garry. *The Museum Environment.* 2nd ed. London: Butterworths, 1986.

52.  Thorin, Suzanne E. *The Acquisition and Cataloging of Music and Sound Recordings.* MLA Technical Report No. 11. Madison, WI: Music Library Association, 1984.

53.  Turko, Karen. *Mass Deacidification Systems: Planning and Managerial Decision Making.* Washington, DC: Association of Research Libraries, 1990, pp. 4–5.

54.  Ungarelli, Donald L. "Insurance, Protection, and Prevention." *Library & Archival Security* 9:1–2 (1989): 51; 47.

55.  U.S. Congress, Office of Technology Assessment. *Book Preservation Technologies.* OTA-O-375. Washington, DC: U.S. Government Printing Office, May 1988.